Macroeconomic Fluctuations and Individual Behaviour

The implications of real and nominal inertia

HANS VAN EES

Department of Economics
University of Groningen
The Netherlands

Avebury

Aldershot · Brookfield USA · Hong Kong · Singapore · Sydney

Published by
Avebury
Academic Publishing Group
Gower House
Croft Road
Aldershot
Hants GU11 3HR
England

Gower Publishing Company
Old Post Road
Brookfield
Vermont 05036
USA

A CIP catalogue record for this book
is available from the British Library.

ISBN 1 85628 229 5

Printed and Bound in Great Britain by
Athenaeum Press Ltd., Newcastle upon Tyne.

Contents

Foreword

This research has been carried out at the Department of Economics of the University of Groningen. I am indebted to the Netherlands Organization for the Advancement of Research (NWO) for providing the financial support for this research project. Furthermore, I benefitted from the comments and suggestions of my colleagues at the Department. In particular, I would like to express my gratitude to Simon Kuipers, Günther Knieps, Jan Pen, Ad Pikkemaat, Jan Snippe, Harry Garretsen, Siep Kronenberg and Nanno Mulder. Mrs J.Z. Tijman-Logtenberg provided many textual suggestions. Finally, I owe special thanks to Anneke Nieuwenhuis.

Groningen, 1991.

1 On the theory of the economy as a whole: purpose and outline of this study

1.1 Introduction

In decentralized economies, the economic behaviour of agents is regulated by a system of markets. To develop a truly general economic theory, all the implications of the market process should be considered, both with respect to individual behaviour as well as with respect to the performance of the economy as a whole. The degree of complexity of such a theory, however, is enormous, and, given the current state of the art, beyond the limits of economic theorizing. A more realistic approach may be the careful application of the *ceteris paribus* clause. This does not imply a permit for 'anything goes,' but rather the use of a methodological device that helps to keep the analysis manageable. An outstanding example of such a research strategy is the familiar distinction between macroeconomic and microeconomic theory. In this respect, microeconomic theory is the analysis of economic behaviour of the individual decision unit. Macroeconomic theory analyzes the performance of the economy as a whole by means of the developments in and between aggregates or a small number of sectors. However, the analysis of the behaviour of the economy as a whole is also an object of research of general equilibrium theory, which is mostly thought to belong to the domain of microeconomics. This resemblance raises two related observations. The first observation concerns the relationship between general equilibrium theory and macroeconomic theory. This observation lies at the heart of the microfoundations debate. The second and more fundamental observation considers the usefulness of the distinction between microeconomic and macroeconomic theory as such.

General equilibrium theory is above all the analysis of the allocation of a *given* level of output, *given* that the Walrasian auctioneer coordinates individual activities successfully. In the best developed general equilibrium model, the Arrow–Debreu–McKenzie model (ADM model), a unique equilibrium price vector exists for each set of endowments, preference orderings and technology that 'reconciles the potentially conflicting choices of all the economic agents' (Weintraub,1977, p. 9). Given endowments, preference orderings and production technologies determine a natural level of output. The actual level of output always coincides with this natural level of output since the equilibrium price vector guarantees the full utilization of resources in the economy. The determination of the level of output as a whole is hardly considered an interesting question in this context. On the other hand, the object of research of macroeconomic theory has been the study of the consequences of the failure of the market system to coordinate activities in order to achieve the best possible outcome for the economy as a whole in terms of the levels of employment, output, and welfare. The choice of a *macro*economic framework to analyze these consequences is only of secondary importance. The micro–macro distinction is not considered to be very relevant in this respect. More fundamental is the recognition that market economies can become stuck at low and suboptimal levels of output for prolonged periods.

Consequently, an alternative distinction between economic theories is suggested, a distinction which takes account of different objects of research and discriminates by alternative application of the *ceteris paribus* clause. On the one hand, we propose to classify micro and macro theories of the economy as a whole into theories that assume perfect coordination and into theories that do not take this assumption for granted. To the first category we reckon, for instance, the Walrasian equilibrium theory and new classical macroeconomics. As examples of the second category, we can think of Keynes' *General Theory* and the new Keynesian theory of coordination failures. On the other hand, we distinguish economic theories of the economy as a whole from those theories that focus on particular *characteristics* of individual behaviour (e.g. consumer behaviour, theory of the firm) and of markets (asymmetric information, customer markets). The latter two subcategories are referred to as partial economics. Inasmuch as these theories analyze the implications of these characteristics for the performance of the economy as a whole they belong to the category of theories that assume perfect coordination.

Being a theory that assumes perfect coordination it is no surprise that in the context of the general equilibrium model deviations from the natural level of economic activity can only result from exogenous shifts in the technological structure of the economy (e.g. technology shocks, preference shocks or input shocks), on the one hand, or from the *ad hoc* introduction of restrictions (wage and price rigidities) in the exchange process, on the other. This general equilibrium approach has served as a benchmark in the development of the economics profession in the explanation of low levels of economic activity. Since the publication of Hicks' 'Mr Keynes and the Classics,' the general equilibrium framework of IS/LM has dominated the analysis of deviations from the natural level of economic activity. Patinkin (1956) showed in the context of a general equilibrium model, that as a result of demand discrepancies, unemployment depended, finally, on the assumption of price or wage rigidities. His analysis marked the starting point of the microfoundations debate. The quest for microfoundations started from the argument that the behaviour of individuals in a situation of non–market clearing is different from this behaviour in situations of market clearing. As a result, the Walrasian equilibrium is not the natural focal point for the analysis of non-market clearing situations, which has always been a basic assumption of the neoclassical synthesis. These insights have been elaborated further in the context of the fixprice non-Walrasian equilibrium models. New classical economists, on the other hand, have criticized the *ad hocery* of the fixprice assumption. Instead, they have emphasized the existence of imperfect information. The assumption of perfect coordination has neither been challenged in the general equilibrium analysis nor in new classical macroeconomics. The coordination issue has been sidestepped through the introduction of a fictitious auctioneer and a representative subject, Robinson Crusoe. However, the recent new Keynesian reaction to the new classical criticism began a renewed interest in the restrictive implications of this fundamental proposition. This line of work focuses on the microfoundation of price rigidities and on the possibility of macroeconomic coordination failures. The latter implies that economies 'can get stuck at an inefficient equilibrium with a low level of "economic activity," even though a better equilibrium exists' (Cooper and John, 1988, p. 448). Hence, in some of these new Keynesian theories, the assumption of perfect coordination has been abandoned, whereas the assumption of market clearing and the optimizing framework of the individual agent have been maintained. Coordination is only less than perfect to the extent that multiple equilibria are allowed. The establishment of these equilibria and the degree of coordination to achieve this still fall beyond the scope of the analysis.

The intention of this introduction is to present the highlights of the debate sketched above. In section 2 the most important features of Keynes' economics are discussed. Section 3 deals with the neoclassical synthesis, whereas in section 4 the major aspects of the microfoundations debate are presented. Section 5 discusses new classical macroeconomics and the subsequent new Keynesian reaction. Finally, in section 6, we present the purpose and outline of this study in the context of the material discussed in the preceding sections. In this chapter, we touch only upon a number of important issues. Subsequent chapters provide more detail and information in this respect. Throughout, the analytical distinction developed earlier will be applied. We believe that this approach may illuminate our opinion: that the recent revival of the microfoundations debate emphasizes particularly the implications of peculiar and perhaps more institutional characteristics of markets (partial economics). Although this debate has improved our understanding of these implications, it cannot yet be claimed that considerable progress has been made since the 1930s regarding the understanding of the workings of a market economy as a whole (the issue of coordination).

1.2 Keynes' economics and general equilibrium theory

Since Keynes' theory gave rise to the development of modern macroeconomics and initiated the theoretical debate that still dominates the developments in a large part of the economics profession, it is reasonable to begin a discussion of this debate with a brief consideration of some elements of J.M. Keynes' *General Theory of Employment, Interest and Money* (Keynes 1936, hereafter GT). In the GT, Keynes attempts to show that classical theory is ill-suited for the analysis of the economy as a whole. Keynes' criticism is directed at the classical analysis of the determination of aggregate output and aggregate employment. In classical theory, the real wage and the level of employment are determined by the demand for and the supply of labour. The natural level of output corresponds to this level of employment. The rate of interest equilibrates savings and investment. In this context, consumption and investment represent competitive claims on a given quantity of output. Aggregate demand does not have any persistent impact on the level of aggregate output if prices are fully flexible. Expectations are only of minor importance, and the Quantity Theory of Money holds in a dichotomised economy. If prices are fully flexible, relative prices clear all markets. In classical analysis, unemployment is caused by wage or price rigidity.

Keynes' main criticism of classical theory centers around two related issues, the assumption of perfect coordination and the importance of expectations. Both issues imply that indeterminacy is an essential feature for the economy as a whole. The latter issue is connected with the role of money and, above all, of uncertainty in Keynes' theory. The former issue originates from the fact that classical economists analyzed economy-wide phenomena with the theory of the behaviour of the individual unit, assuming the perfect coordination of individual activities. The endogeneity in the GT of the level of output is a consequence of Keynes' rejection of the classical assumption of the 'invisible hand.' In the absence of a coordinating device like the 'invisible hand' (or of corresponding metaphors like the Walrasian auctioneer and Robinson Crusoe), economic agents need to make their own decisions with respect to the various prices at which trade takes place. In such a world, it is by no means clear why the resulting level of aggregate output should correspond with the natural level of output. The well-known examples of the Paradox of Thrift and the Fallacy of Composition in the labour market illustrate Keynes' criticism of the related classical assumptions of perfect coordination and of a given level of output for the economy as a whole.

> Though an individual whose transactions are small in relation to the market can safely neglect the fact that demand is not a one-sided transaction, it makes no sense to neglect it when we come to aggregate demand. This is the vital difference between the theory of the economic behaviour of the aggregate and the theory of the behaviour of the individual unit, in which we assume that changes in the individual's own demand do not affect his income (Keynes, 1936, p. 85).

In Keynes' conception, as opposed to classical theory, an increase in the propensity to save and a decrease in the propensity to consume do not lead to a corresponding increase in investment, but to a corresponding decrease in investment. The different components of aggregate demand are complements rather than substitutes, which represents an important departure from classical theory concerning the explanation of the level of output for the economy as a whole. This dependence of aggregate output upon aggregate demand reflects a fundamental, conceptual difference between Keynes' theory and classical theory. In classical theory, it is *assumed* that the price mechanism coordinates the decisions of the individual agents by referring to Adam Smith's invisible hand. In Keynes' GT, agents must form expectations about the behaviour of other agents and the issue at stake is precisely whether an individual may neglect the fact that demand is not a one-sided transaction. In a decentralized economy, the crucial question is how the price mechanism may establish a degree of coordination that ensures full employment. Keynes concludes that the price mechanism may not do the job. The coordination problem is a consequence of the individual lack of knowledge about the behaviour of other agents in the economy. Agents can neglect the impact of their activities on the behaviour of other agents neither in the present nor in the future. There is a temporary and an intertemporal coordination problem. Supply and demand schedules in the various markets are determined not only by relative prices as in classical theory but by expectations as well. To quote Heller, agents 'condition their expectations of demand (or supply) on some non-price variable of the economic system' (Heller, 1986 p. 158).

1.3 The neoclassical synthesis

Immediately after the publication of the GT Hicks (1937) incorporated Keynes' GT into a general equilibrium framework. This led to the original formulation of the well-known IS/LM model. In the 1950s and 1960s the IS/LM model virtually became Keynesian macroeconomics. It was left to Patinkin (1956) to show that in the static, general equilibrium model of *Money, Interest and Prices*, Keynes' unemployment equilibrium eventually rests on the assumption of price or wage rigidity. In IS/LM models, problems of coordination are not considered so that this issue more or less disappeared as a separate problem. Patinkin's aim was to show that the incorporation of the real balance effect in a Walrasian general equilibrium model, on the one hand, destroys the classical dichotomy but , on the other hand, renders the mutual existence of involuntary unemployment, and wage and price flexibility impossible in the long run. Patinkin's version of the IS/LM model, combined with a labour market characterized by sticky real wage rates constitutes the core of the neoclassical synthesis. The fundamental characteristics of the classical model remain intact even if the 'Keynesian innovations' (the theory of effective demand and the theory of liquidity preference) are incorporated into the classical model. Because of low adjustmentspeeds it can be argued that Keynesian and classical theories do not exclude one another, but focus on different situations (the short run and the long run, respectively). During the 1950s and 1960s economic research was directed toward the elaboration of the basic model, e.g. the microfoundation of the demand for money (Baumol, 1952 and Tobin, 1956) and the development of modern portfolio analysis (Tobin, 1958 and Markowitz, 1959). Theoretical research focused upon the impact of (monetary) policy on the level of nominal aggregate income, on the one hand, and the decomposition of the latter variable into real and purely nominal changes, on the other. The latter issue initiated the well-known debate about the Phillips curve. However, the debate between Keynesians and monetarists was above all an empirical debate. The theoretical framework as such remained undisputed (B. Friedman, 1978 and Laidler, 1982). Involuntary unemployment in a Walrasian general equilibrium model became a special case and was explained by referring to the liquidity trap (Hicks, 1937), price or wage rigidities (Patinkin, 1956), money illusion, or interest inelastic investment.

Blanchard (1987) illustrates the position of the neoclassical synthesis with the following simplified model (in logs):

$$Y = \delta_1(M-P) \qquad \delta_1 > 0 \qquad [1.1]$$
$$Y = \delta_2(W-P) \qquad \delta_2 < 0 \qquad [1.2]$$
$$W = W^* \qquad [1.3]$$

Y = aggregate demand
M = aggregate money balances
P = general price level
W = nominal wage level

[1.1] represents aggregate demand that is a reduced form of IS/LM. Equation [1.2] is a reduced form of aggregate supply on the assumption that aggregate demand equals aggregate supply. Equation [1.3] gives the level of nominal wages. Nominal wages are exogenously fixed, either by assumption (the wage–rigidity case) or by reference to the existence of complete money illusion. The fact that nominal wages are exogenous ensures the non–neutrality of money, since it can be shown that

$$\frac{\partial P}{\partial M} = \frac{\delta_1}{\delta_1 - \delta_2} < 1 \qquad [1.4]$$

Hence, monetary policy has real effects. In the 'monetarist' version adaptive expectations allow for the non–neutrality of money only in the short run. In the long run, the classical dichotomy holds and equation [1.3] is replaced by equation [1.3′]:

$$L_s(w) = F_L^{-1}(K,w) \qquad [1.3']$$

w = the real wage level
K = the stock of capital
L_s = labour supply

The real wage equals the marginal productivity of labour, and the level of employment is determined completely in the labour market. Given the level of real wages, real output is determined by equation [1.2]. Changes in M now only lead to equiproportionate changes in P, since Y is supply–determined.

1.4 The microfoundations debate

In the neoclassical synthesis, there is a clear analytical distinction between the analysis of resource allocation based on standard choice theoretic foundations, on the one hand, and the analysis of the determination of the level of aggregate output, on the other. This is not to say that macroeconomic models within the tradition of the neoclassical synthesis lack microfoundations (see Patinkin, 1956). The Arrow–Debreu model allows the analysis of microeconomic and macroeconomic phenomena. However, important phenomena like the level of aggregate output or the level of aggregate unemployment cannot be explained from choice theoretic foundations. In studying microeconomics it is assumed that the price mechanism coordinates economic activities well whereas in ('Keynesian') macroeconomics this mechanism is somehow not supposed to work. Underneath there is a more important difference, the distinction between theories that *assume* that the price mechanism ensures a socially efficient degree of coordination and those that do not. Following Weintraub (1979), we may observe that economists, in the tradition of the neoclassical synthesis, have tried to cut economic phenomena into micro and macro when, in fact, 'the appropriate "cut" is between models of coordination success and models of coordination failure,' as we argued in the first section of this chapter, but unfortunately 'the rules of the ADM modeling game ensure that coordination success will occur' (Weintraub, 1979, p. 75).

The insight that situations of non-market clearing cannot be analyzed adequately with a *Walrasian* general equilibrium model was taken up by and is essential in the work of Clower (1965) and Leijonhufvud (1968, 1981). It led to the development of the non-Walrasian fixprice general equilibrium approach. In chapter 3 a more detailed review of this literature is provided. In the non-Walrasian general equilibrium theory, false trading is allowed which creates the possibility of agents being rationed in their respective demands. As a result, excess demand functions not only include relative prices but quantities constraints as well. This implies the incompatibility of (the notional version of) Walras' Law and the existence of quantity-constrained equilibria. According to Leijonhufvud (1968), which elaborates upon the work of Clower, the analysis of Keynes' GT leads to the following conclusions.

(1) Keynes' GT is perfectly compatible with a standard choice theoretic framework; (2) price incentives are important in the GT; (3) the ranking of price and quantity adjustment is reversed in Keynes' GT (e.g. quantity adjustment occurs before price adjustment) and (4) it is by no means clear *how* these price incentives should lead to a degree of coordination that ensures full employment. 'The only thing which Keynes "removed" from the foundations of classical theory was the *deus ex machina* – the auctioneer which is assumed to furnish, without charge, all the information needed to obtain the perfect coordination of the activities of all traders in the present and through the future' (Leijonhufvud, 1981, p.15). On the other hand, it can be argued that the degree of coordination needed to establish non-Walrasian equilibria may even exceed the degree of coordination needed for the establishment of the Walrasian equilibrium. Hence, despite the fact that Leijonhufvud emphasized both the coordination failure argument and the rationing argument, the coordination failure argument was in fact sidestepped once more. The weakness of the non-Walrasian equilibrium approach is for a large part to be found in this area and not in the fixprice assumption, which was heavily criticized by new classical economists. The rise of the new classical economics meant a return to the ADM model from which Patinkin, Clower and Leijonhufvud tried to escape from. It is to these new classical theories that we now turn.

1.5 New classical and new Keynesian economics

Since the beginning of the 1970s a growing dissatisfaction with the weak or missing microeconomic underpinning of the conventional macroeconomic theory of changes in the level of economic activity has eventually resulted in the development of new classical macroeconomics. The approach was initiated by Lucas (1972, 1973), although Lucas and Rapping (1969) and Phelps (1968), both with adaptive expectations, can be regarded as immediate predecessors. New classical macroeconomics can be considered a straightforward application of general competitive equilibrium theory to the explanation of deviations of the level of economic activity from the natural level. The assumptions of competitive markets and rationally behaving agents have been maintained. The assumption of perfect information, however, has been relaxed, which enables the analysis of economic disturbances as a result of mistaken judgments by individuals.

Blanchard (1987) offers the following simple illustration of the implications of a new classical model. For the sake of simplicity, the microfoundation of the relationships is not considered explicitly. The natural level of output has been normalized at unity. Given the equilibrium condition that aggregate supply equals aggregate demand, the economy can be characterized by the following system of equations (in logs).

$$Y = \delta_1(M - P) \quad [1.4]$$

$$P_i = P + \varepsilon_i \quad [1.5]$$

$$Y_i = \delta_3(P_i - \mathrm{E}_i P) \quad [1.6]$$

$$\delta_1, \delta_3 > 0$$

$P_i =$ the commodity price in market i
$\varepsilon_i =$ white noise and uncorrelated across firms (i.e. a relative price shock)

It is assumed that each agent produces output in his own market. Both a global and a local shift variable, M and ε_i, respectively, are incorporated in the model, reflecting market-specific and economy-wide shocks respectively. Agents only observe local prices. Subjective expectations of P are formulated in line with equation [1.7].

$$\mathrm{E}_i P = \mathrm{E}M + \delta_4(P_i - \mathrm{E}M) \quad [1.7]$$

$$0 < \delta_4 < 1$$

The parameter δ_4 is dependent on the variances of the local and the global shift variables. In the absence of unanticipated shocks $\mathrm{E}_i P = \mathrm{E}M$. Substitution of [1.7] into [1.6] as well as aggregation over agents yields the aggregate supply curve [1.8].

$$Y = \delta_3(1 - \delta_4)(P - \mathrm{E}M) \quad [1.8]$$

From the equalization of aggregate supply and demand and some straightforward calculations it can be derived that

$$P = \delta_5 \mathrm{E}M + (1 - \delta_5)M \quad [1.9]$$

$$Y = \delta_1\delta_5(M - \mathrm{E}M) \quad [1.10]$$

$$\delta_5 = \frac{\delta_3(1-\delta_4)}{\delta_1 + \delta_3(1-\delta_4)}$$

In the absence of nominal surprises money is neutral and output is equal to its natural level. Unanticipated global shocks have a transitory impact on real economic activity through changes in relative prices as can be observed from equations [1.9] and [1.10]. Hence, it is shown that under conditions of general market clearing and rational expectations, unanticipated changes affect real economic variables.

It can be argued that the extension of the model above to a full-fledged model of the business cycle contains some serious drawbacks (see chapter 4). In order to tackle some of the issues, the real business cycle approach, following the pioneering articles by Kydland and Prescott (1982) and Long and Plosser (1983), has been expanding very rapidly during the 1980s. Real business cycle models are directed towards the explanation of empirical regularities within the context of a stochastic version of the neoclassical model of optimal capital accumulation. In addition, the propagation of the impulse can be generated in a multiperiod version of the model from the assumption of normal goods. With normal goods any favourable technology shift changes the intertemporal allocation of leisure and hence increases wealth, which implies that the expenditures on all goods (both for consumption and investment purposes) increase over the entire planning period. As a result, there is a positive relationship between fluctuations in the time patterns of employment and expenditure levels. Moreover, temporary movements are persistent. The analytical structure and the implications of the real business cycle theory are considered rather controversial (see chapter 2). For the moment, it is only emphasized that the general competitive equilibrium approach is only legitimate in situations where the coordination of individual activities has already been achieved or is of no interest to the problem at hand. The assumptions of continuous market clearing and homogeneity among agents do precisely establish these situations.

The popularity of new classical macroeconomics during the 1970s and 1980s, on the one hand, and the growing discomfort with the two aforementioned assumptions, on the other hand, have stimulated a recent outburst of analyses with a more Keynesian flavour directed towards the development of a microfoundation for market failures, given the assumption of rational expectations. According to Blanchard (1987), most of these theories have taken as a starting point that 'prices do not adjust fully and instantaneously to nominal money and focused on the reasons for and implications of imperfect price adjustment' (Blanchard, 1987, p.1). The major aim is to give a rationale for price rigidities in order to explain the non-neutrality of money and thereby to provide a rationale for stabilization policy. The assumption of imperfect competition is deemed necessary to counteract the classical argument that complete price flexibility ensures a Walrasian equilibrium with full employment and hence ensures the Quantity Theory of Money to hold. In chapter 4, we will consider the various manners in which the price (or wage) rigidities or fixed cost assumptions, like menu costs, are accounted for. At this place, the new Keynesian partial equilibrium approach can be summarized by observing that the various imperfectly competitive markets are characterized by some kind of inertial price behaviour and that aggregate demand is typically exogenous. The dismissal of the Walrasian auctioneer implies that agents do not only have imperfect information, but mostly asymmetric information as well. On the other hand, flexprice general equilibrium theories have been developed in which Keynesian results may arise because of the existence of many sectors and incomplete markets in economies. In these theories the absence of the Walrasian auctioneer leads to coordination failures; this absence implies that not all the available information is revealed to the market. Limitations in information dissemination can exist between agents, between sectors and between periods. Whether or not this may result in price rigidities is of secondary importance.

It can be observed that many of the new Keynesian partial equilibrium theories are analytically very similar to the new classical model. Just as in new classical theory, economy-wide phenomena are analyzed with the theory of the behaviour of the individual unit. Market failures arise and unemployment equilibria result because price and wage setting procedures prohibit the best possible outcome for the economy as a whole. In this respect, a more classical approach would offer similar results. Furthermore, the individual agent does not consider the impact of his activities on his environment. The issue of coordination is not addressed explicitly as it is in the coordination failure literature. On the other hand, the introduction of asymmetric information, besides the new classical concept of imperfect information as a rationale for price rigidities, represents an improvement in our opinion. Furthermore, the existence of asymmetric information implies heterogeneity, which is considered a prerequisite for analyzing the performance of the economy as a whole, although the heterogeneity concept as such is not used to analyze the interdependence between different agents or sectors, but is merely used to underpin price rigidities. This last characteristic represents a major improvement in comparison with fixprice non-Walrasian equilibrium theory. New Keynesian theories explicitly deal with the determination of market prices. Subsequently, theories of optimal price rigidities explain the existence of unemployment in the context of a full-fledged model of an economy. On the other hand, it may be ambiguous under which conditions a specific form of asymmetric information at the micro level, as for instance efficiency wages, can be generalized in order to apply to the economy as a whole.

In a number of ways general equilibrium theories of coordination failures are closer to Keynes' original coordination problem than the new classical theories or the new Keynesian partial equilibrium theories. As such, they represent a promising new field of economic research. At the present stage the coordination failure framework is fairly rudimentary and needs to be extended into a number of directions. One important argument that needs subsequent analysis deals with the concept of coordination in itself. In the coordination failure literature, multiple equilibria characterized by different levels of output are allowed. On the other hand, the establishment of these equilibria is taken for granted, which still presupposes a lot of (unexplained) coordination of individual activities to take place. The assumptions of market clearing and rational expectations are not derived from an optimizing framework. In that respect both new classical theories and new Keynesian theories cannot claim to provide a superior microfoundation of macroeconomics compared with those theories that do not belong to the realm of general equilibrium theory. At the present stage of theorizing, a more ambitious conclusion cannot be regarde as realistic.

1.6 Purpose and outline of this study

A major object of research of this study is concerned with the various explanations of different levels of aggregate output with the help of models, which are not at variance with microeconomic behavioural principles. In this introduction some important problems have been identified in this respect. In the first place, a central theme is whether the price mechanism may ensure a degree of coordination that leads to full employment. The mere assumption that coordination is perfect is very restrictive, even as a straightforward application of the *ceteris paribus* clause, since it neglects the implication of trade as a fundamental manifestation of the workings of a market economy. In the second place and related to the first observation, the heterogeneity of agents has to be considered more explicitly, either to underpin the implications of price setting procedures or to emphasize the interdependence between agents or sectors in the economy. In this respect, we will mainly confine ourselves to the first argument. In the third place, the adjustment processes that lead to the establishment of different equilibria need further consideration. Both new classical as well as new Keynesian theories take this establishment for granted. In this study, we will attempt to provide some insight on this subject by means of a sequential analysis.

The organization of this monograph will be as follows. A survey of the literature will be presented in the next three chapters. In chapter 2 we will consider flexprice models of economic fluctuations. The major characteristic of this approach is the assumption of perfect coordination. Deviations from the natural levels of output and employment are explained by introducing imperfect information. In chapter 3 and 4 we will discuss approaches that abandon the assumption of perfect coordination. Chapter 3 offers a review of fixprice models, whereas in chapter 4, on the one hand, new Keynesian explanations of price and wage rigidities are analyzed (partial economics) and, on the other hand, new Keynesian theories of coordination failures and indeterminacies are discussed. In chapter 5 we will extend the new Keynesian partial economic approach to the explanation of different levels of output by developing a small static macroeconomic model, which explains both real and nominal rigidities and inefficiently low equilibrium levels of economic activity. In the context of the model purely nominal shocks in aggregate demand affect the level of aggregate output, notwithstanding the complete rationality of individual decision making procedures. However, since the model is static, the adjustment processes toward a situation of equilibrium cannot be analyzed. To that purpose, a dynamic model will be developed in chapter 6 with the following characteristics. Time is divided in arbitrary small discrete periods. The agents' decisions in financial markets, on the one hand, and in the commodity and labour market, on the other hand, are intertwined and taken at the beginning of every unit period. Production takes one period and all commodities are stored. Sales are only made out of stock. The determination of commodity prices is analogous to Hahn (1978) and considers the implications of asymmetric information. The adjustment of wages in between periods rests upon the Phillips curve, whereas expectations are autoregressive. Despite the introduction of these two simplifications, the model cannot be solved analytically. The characteristics of the model have been studied by means of a number of simulation experiments. Results will be reported in chapter 7. Finally, chapter 8 will conclude this monograph with a number of observations on the relevance of the approach applied in this book, on the one hand, and on the relevance and scope of the microbased approach to the explanation of the performance of the economy as a whole in general, on the other hand.

2 Flexprice models of economic fluctuations

2.1 The principles of flexprice equilibrium theory

The concept of a general market clearing equilibrium has been formulated by Walras (1874). Wald (1936) was the first to prove the existence of a price vector that cleared all markets. More rigorous treatments of the existence of the Walrasian equilibrium followed (McKenzie, 1959, and Arrow and Debreu, 1954), which stimulated research in numerous directions.[1] Since this section contains only a description of the basic notions and concepts, the reader is referred to Arrow and Hahn (1971) for more detail. To describe the basic characteristics it is convenient to develop a special case of the general equilibrium theory, the pure exchange model. In a barter model all agents are consumers and the basic concern of the model is the allocation of scarce goods. Each agent holds an initial bundle of goods and participates in trade in order to maximize utility, given his or her endowments and given the prices of the goods. Goods are distinguished by time, location and state of the world. It is assumed that there exists a market for each good in which the price of that good is determined. Prices are completely flexible and each agent takes the market price as independent of his or her activities. It can be shown that, given some well-known regularity conditions on the agents' utility functions, there exists a non-zero price vector in the economy such that if agents were to simultaneously optimize at those prices, the total demand and supplies of goods that would result, entails the same set of prices. This set of prices, defined as the equilibrium price vector $\boldsymbol{p}^*$, reconciles 'the potentially conflicting choices of all the economic agents' (Weintraub, 1977, p. 9). The corresponding allocation of goods $\boldsymbol{A}^*$ is called a competitive allocation. A Walrasian (or a competitive) equilibrium is to be defined as a pair $(\boldsymbol{p}^*, \boldsymbol{A}^*)$ such that there is equality of demand and supply in all markets. Walrasian equilibria have the following properties. In the first place, it follows by Walras' Law[2] that if, at some non-zero price vector $\boldsymbol{p}$, n–1 markets clear, then the nth market must also clear. Another implication is that only relative prices can be determined by the equilibrium condition of market clearing. In the second place, Walrasian equilibria are Pareto efficient, i.e. there is no feasible allocation $\boldsymbol{A}'$ such that all agents prefer $\boldsymbol{A}'$ to $\boldsymbol{A}^*$ (a feasible allocation just uses up all the goods in the economy (Varian, 1984, p. 190)).

The extension of the above static economy to a time-dependent system[3] seems to be rather straightforward. Since goods can be distinguished by time, goods which are to be available at different moments should be regarded as different goods. Provided that there exists a complete set of spot and future markets, agents formulate demands and supplies at time 0 for all goods on the basis of intertemporal preferences for the complete future of the economy, given a complete set of current and future prices. An equilibrium price vector (of current and future prices) equilibrates supplies and demands for all (dated) goods. Goods are traded and paid for at time 0, whereas actual transactions can be carried out at some future date.

Up till now, we have not considered uncertainty to be an independent variable. In the context of general equilibrium theory, uncertainty is defined in a rather limited sense and refers to the existence of different subjective probability distributions about states of the 'world' at different future dates. The incorporation of uncertainty in general equilibrium models with a complete set of spot and future markets is rather straightforward (e.g. Arrow, 1970). Agents trade contingency contracts, i.e. contingent on the possible states of nature. Contracts for all states are traded and paid for at time t with certainty, but are carried out at time $t+j$ when the appropriate state of the world becomes reality. An equilibrium price vector can be defined as one where there is no excess demand for any contract. Hence, the standard framework under certainty can be completely maintained in terms of expected utilities.

> The assumption that all intertemporal and all contingent markets exist has the effect of collapsing the future into the present. (Hahn, 1984, p. 81)

The assumption that all markets are complete in the Arrow–Debreu sense can be criticized on empirical and theoretical grounds. It is obvious that in the real world future markets are quite rare. Moreover, if agents have different information, it is logically impossible that all the required markets exist (Radner, 1968). Next, 'if exchange is costly then certain markets will not open because it does not pay to do so' (Hahn, 1984, p. 81). Once there does not exist a complete set of spot and contingent future markets, trading will take place at every date (a sequence economy). In order to trade in the current period, agents will have to form beliefs about the possible occurrence of future events (states of the world) and about prices and future dates that will be determined given these events. Expected future prices have to be based on the expectations of *all* the agents about the prices of *all* goods, *each* period onward. Since it is logically impossible to require that the establishment of an equilibrium situation in the current period is dependent on the actual realization of expectations about activities in non-existing future markets, a current-period or temporary equilibrium can only be defined relative to the agents' expectations. Following Hicks, a temporary equilibrium is said to occur

> [W]hen all the "individuals" in [the economy] are choosing those quantities, which, out of the alternatives available to them, they prefer to produce and to consume.
> (Hicks, 1965, p. 15)

A Hicksian temporary equilibrium can be consistent with both flexible and rigid prices, which implies that we can define Walrasian as well as non-Walrasian temporary equilibria, depending on the market clearing impact of prices. The realization of exchange values in the current period does not have to be consistent with the expectations at the beginning of the current period concerning trade and prices in future periods. Hence, temporary equilibria can be accompanied by disappointed beginning-of-current-period expectations, which will lead to a revision of the latter at the beginning of the next period. It follows that for an equilibrium to be an intertemporal equilibrium,

> there must be equilibrium at every point of time within the period – an equilibrium which is of course based, as every point-of-time equilibrium must be based, upon its own expectations. But before period equilibrium there is the additional condition that these expectations must be consistent with one another and with what actually happens within the period. (Hicks, 1965, p. 24)

An intertemporal equilibrium is more than merely a sequence of temporary equilibria. Apart from the consistency of single period expectations with the outcomes of trade in each period, it is required that single period expectations related to different periods are consistent with one another. Note that, if the existence of a complete set of Arrow-Debreu markets is assumed, any equilibrium will be an intertemporal equilibrium.

In general, temporary equilibria are not efficient since these equilibria very much depend on the expectations of the agents. If expectations formation is taken as exogenous, only spot markets will be cleared by current prices. The establishment of market clearing prices will reveal new information which leads to a revision of expectations at the beginning of the next period. Hence, the price mechanism no longer ensures Pareto efficiency and the actual development of the economy is mainly determined by expectations formation. If expectations are rational, i.e. agents are forming forecasts of future spot prices in line with the conditional mathematical expectations that can be derived from the model, the efficiency of the resulting temporary equilibrium is ambiguous. Under specific conditions the equilibrium price vector $(\boldsymbol{p}^*, \mathbf{E}(\boldsymbol{p}^*))$, where $\mathbf{E}(\boldsymbol{p}^*)$ denotes the rational expectations of the set of future prices, will be a Walrasian equilibrium for the intertemporal economy. Grossman (1976, 1978) illustrates the efficiency properties of a rational expectations equilibrium. He considers a two-period economy with h agents who have different private information sets, a finite number of risky assets and one risk free asset. The agents exchange assets and bonds in the first period, but do not consume. In the second period there is no trade and agents consume their pro rate share of output of each of the assets. In order to maximize utility from consumption, every agent maximizes his wealth at the beginning of the second period. To solve this problem, every agent collects information about the asset prices in the second period, at the beginning of the first period. On the basis of this information agents then decide on their optimal portfolio, given the value of asset prices in the first period. An equilibrium price vector will take care of market clearing. Grossman refers to this situation as a 'naive equilibrium,' since agents do not take into account that market prices reflect other agents' information. If the establishment of this 'naive equilibrium' is replicated for a number of periods, agents will eventually learn the joint distribution of market clearing prices, private information and expected second-period prices since this is observable *ex post*. Agents realize that market clearing prices convey additional information to them and thus have the desire to recontract. On the other hand, if they optimally use all the information available, they will formulate their demand and supply schedules conditional to both private and public information, the latter being revealed by the market clearing asset prices in the current period. The equilibrium price vector which will be established in this situation describes a rational expectations equilibrium, since agents form the forecasts of future prices by taking conditional mathematical expectations with respect to the trading process that actually governs prices. Next, Grossman shows under which conditions the equilibrium price vector summarizes all the information available throughout the economy, i.e. under which conditions the price vector is a sufficient statistic[4] for all the private information scattered throughout the economy. In that situation each trader would find his own information to be redundant. Furthermore, if market prices reveal all the information needed to maximize individual utilities, it becomes impossible for a government to improve on that outcome. In this sense, rational expectations equilibria have a very strong welfare implication. However, the result is too strong. Grossman (1978) observes that if information is costly, subjects will have no incentive to collect information because the minute it is collected, it will be reflected by the equilibrium price vector so that everybody else will be offered a free ride. Hence, information will not be collected and the equilibrium price vector will reveal no information at all. Still, if no one is informed there remains an incentive to begin doing so. A competitive equilibrium cannot exist since there will always be someone who wants to change its position. To conclude, if information is a free good in the economy, rational expectations equilibria are Pareto efficient, which is a rather trivial observation because in that case we are back in the Arrow-Debreu world with perfect foresight. In case information can only be gathered at a price, it is logically impossible that rational expectations equilibria exist when the price system is totally informative. However, if the vector of market prices does not communicate all the information to the traders, agents have different information sets, which implies that rational expectations equilibria are generally not Pareto efficient in the Arrow-Debreu sense since the absence of some markets still prevents mutually advantageous exchanges between agents (Hahn, 1984, p. 82). Since non-rational expectations equilibria are generally not Pareto efficient as well, it can be observed that from a welfare-theoretic point of view the different characteristics of expectations formation are only of second order of importance.

In developing the arguments above, the pervasive role of the availability of information is obvious. The availability of information is also a prominent factor in the literature that studies the possibilities of generating fluctuations within the context of a competitive economy. In the next section, we will present a review of the most important developments in this flexprice approach to business cycles.

2.2 Macroeconomic flexprice equilibrium theory and the explanation of cyclical variations

2.2.1 *Introduction*

In the 1970s research directed toward the microeconomic underpinning of macroeconomics was stimulated due to a growing dissatisfaction with traditional macroeconomic theory, which studied fluctuations in aggregate output and employment in the context of an IS/LM model supplemented with a Phillips curve. A general feeling emerged that macroeconomic theory should be developed in line with the principles that underlie microeconomic theory. The approach that resembled closest the temporary general equilibrium model discussed in the previous section was initiated by Lucas (1972, 1973). It maintained the assumptions of perfectly competitive markets and completely rational behaviour. However, the assumption of perfect information was relaxed, which made it possible to relate economic disturbances to the mistakes people make in judging the impact of current developments, e.g. monetary shocks. In sections 2.2.2 and 2.2.3 this so-called monetary business cycle theory will be discussed.

Monetary business cycle models can be criticized by the fact that their results are highly dependent on the individual incapability of perceiving correctly aggregate data, such as the supply of money and the general price level. King (1981) argues that in developed economies data on monetary aggregates are available too promptly to be consistent with the assumption that agents are ignorant of contemporaneous monetary magnitudes. In answer to this criticism, a new major area of business cycle research has recently been developed, which exclusively focuses on the impact of real, as opposed to monetary, variables in order to explain fluctuations in output and employment. In the context of these real business cycle models, in particular technology shocks and changes in preference orderings do account for cyclical variations in economic activity. In section 2.2.4, the literature on real business cycle models will be reviewed. Finally, in section 2.2.5, we will evaluate the major observations of the monetary and real business cycle theories.

2.2.2 *Monetary business cycle theory*

Barro (1980) describes new classical macroeconomics as an attempt 'to understand business cycles from an equilibrium perspective in which imperfect information and rational expectations play a major role' (Barro, 1980, p. 39). More specifically, equilibrium business cycle models display the following characteristics.

i. Continuous market clearing. Actual combinations of prices and quantities are observed as intersection points of aggregate demand and supply schedules.

ii. Aggregate-relative confusion (Cukierman, 1984). Agents receive information on local prices and are unable to isolate relative price variation caused by market-specific factors from price variation resulting from aggregate demand fluctuations. They face a signal extraction problem,

because the current general price level is unobservable.
iii. A natural rate hypothesis, which implies that the decisions of rationally behaving agents depend on relative prices. Nominal surprises only have a temporary impact on real variables.
iv. Rational expectations.

The business cycle models developed by Lucas in two subsequent articles in 1972 and 1973 have served as a benchmark case for a large number of alternative versions, which all share the common features mentioned above (e.g. Lucas, 1975, Barro, 1976, 1981, Sargent and Wallace, 1975, Blinder and Fischer, 1981). Essentially, the more simple version of 1973 represents a standard IS/LM framework. In addition, Lucas assumes the aggregate demand curve is unit-elastic in prices, which implies that it can be written as (in logs)

$$Y_t = X_t - P_t \qquad [2.1]$$

Y_t = real aggregate demand for commodities
X_t = an exogenous shift variable, equal to the observable log of nominal income
P_t = the unobserved current general price level.

As a consequence, the log of nominal income has become exogenous to developments in the commodity market, which are reflected in movements in P_t. The decomposition of nominal income into real output and price changes is entirely related to supply considerations. All essential characteristics of the model can therefore be analyzed in terms of a model which only contains a description of the supply side of the economy. Lucas develops the following (log-linear, specification of supply (markets are indexed by i).

$$Y_t(i) = Y_{nt} + Y_{ct}(i) \qquad [2.2]$$

The quantity supplied in each market $Y_t(i)$ can be divided into a trend component Y_{nt} and cyclical component Y_{ct}, which is a function of perceived relative prices.

$$Y_{ct}(i) = \kappa_1 \left\{P_t(i) - {}_t\mathrm{E}(P_t\ /\Psi_t(i))\right\} + \nu Y_{c,t-1}(i) \qquad [2.3]$$

$$\kappa_1 > 0\ ,\ |\nu| < 1$$

$P_t(i)$ = the price observed in market i in period t
${}_t\mathrm{E}(P_t/\Psi_t(i)$ = the conditional expectation of P_t on the information available in market i, $(\Psi_t(i))$ i.e. the linear least square estimation of P_t on $\Psi_t(i)$.

The information set $\Psi_t(i)$ contains the following elements. In the first place, agents have information about past values of all variables. This information can be summarized in a 'prior' distribution on P_t, which is public. It is assumed that P_t follows a normal distribution with mean $\dot{P}$ and variance ρ_1^2. In the second place, agents observe current local prices $P_t(i)$. Local prices deviate from the unobserved general price level P_t by a proportion i, which is normally distributed, independent of P_t, with mean zero and variance ρ_2^2. Hence,

$$P_t(i) = P_t + i \qquad [2.4]$$

Equation [2.4] can be used to derive an estimation of the current general price level (Sargent, 1987, pp. 441–442). ${}_t\mathrm{E}(P_t/\Psi(i))$ is

$${}_t\mathrm{E}\left[P_t/\Psi_t(i)\right] = {}_t\mathrm{E}\left[P_t/P, P_t(i)\right] = (1-\rho_3)\ P_t(i) + \rho_3 P \qquad [2.5]$$

where

$$\rho_3 = \rho_2^{\,2}/(\rho_1^{\,2} + \rho_2^{\,2}) \qquad [2.6]$$

Substitution of [2.3] and [2.5] into [2.2] yields

$$Y_t(i) = Y_{nt} + \kappa_1\ \rho_3\ \left(\ P_t(i) - P\ \right) + \nu Y_{c,t-1}(i) \qquad [2.7]$$

Finally, averaging over markets (integrating $Y_t(i)$ over the distribution of markets) gives aggregate supply Y_t

$$Y_t = Y_{nt} + \kappa_1\ \rho_3\left(P_t - P\right) + \nu\left(Y_{t-1} - Y_{n,t-1}\right) \qquad [2.8]$$

The natural rate property can be illustrated by solving [2.8] for P_t–P and subtracting P_{t-1} from both sides.

$$P_t - P_{t-1} = \frac{1}{\kappa_1\rho_3}\left\{ Y_t - Y_{nt} - \nu\left(Y_{t-1} - Y_{n,t-1}\right)\right\} + (P - P_{t-1}) \qquad [2.9]$$

Equation [2.9] can be regarded as a Phillips curve which directly relates the gap between the actual current price and the perceived current price to output. Output positively responds to a positive gap between P_t and P because as $P_t > P$ real wages decline, workers suffer from aggregate–relative confusion as well, labour demand increases and output expands. Expected inflation ($P - P_{t-1}$) is completely passed on to realized inflation without any impact on relative prices and real economic activity. Equation [2.8] can be rewritten as:

$$(1-\nu \mathrm{L})Y_t = \kappa_1\rho_3(P_t - P) + (1-\nu \mathrm{L})Y_{nt} \qquad [2.10]$$

L = the lag operator

The solution of this linear first order difference equation equals

$$Y_t - Y_{nt} = (Y_0 - Y_{n0})\nu^t + \kappa_1\ \rho_3 \sum_{j=1}^{t} \nu^{t-j}\ (P_j - P) \qquad [2.11]$$

Real aggregate output is not correlated with anticipated movements in the general price level but with unanticipated movements. Anticipated exogenous shifts in demand (ΔX_t), such as a publicly announced monetary impulse, only affect the general price level without any impact on real economic activity.

The slope of the Lucas supply curve equals $\rho_3\kappa_1$. If changes in individual prices generally reflect changes in the general price level and hence ρ_2^2 is small, $\rho_3\kappa_1$ will be small. In that situation, the aggregate supply curve will be nearly vertical at the level of aggregate permanent output. If, on the other hand, the general price level is considered stable (ρ_1^2 is small), $\rho_3\kappa_1$ will be close to κ_1, which is the local price elasticity of demand. In this case, a change of policy regime will be very effective since agents perceive a change in the general price level as local price variation. Consequently, real aggregate output will be adjusted. To conclude, the invariance proposition does not suggest that a favourable trade off between inflation and employment cannot exist across different aggregate demand regimes. Only a systematic policy will have this result.

2.2.3 *Some critical observations*

According to Sheffrin (1983), the following critical arguments can be observed with respect to the characteristics of Lucas type business cycle models. As a first characteristic the assumption of continuous market clearing has been mentioned. A discussion about the implications that follow from the introduction of sticky prices will be postponed to the next chapter. Here, we will confine ourselves to the observation that since the mid-seventies a large number of articles have appeared which develop rational theories of price and wage rigidity (e.g. Bailey, 1974, Azariadis, 1975, Fischer, 1977, Barro, 1977, and Taylor, 1980). Essentially, rational contracts are compatible with the invariance propositions, if the economy consists of a complete set of Arrow-Debreu markets (e.g. Sargent, 1987, ch. XVIII). To the extent that there are costs involved in writing, monitoring and enforcing contracts, a rationale for some degree of price stickiness may exist. In the second place, the neutrality proposition itself can be considered a characteristic element of the analysis. Two remarks are relevant in this context. First, in a world with government debt denominated in money terms, monetary shocks are nonneutral unless future tax payments, necessary to service the interest on bonds, are fully discounted by the public in the calculation of its net worth. Indeed, a similar argument underlies the debt-neutrality literature (e.g. Barro, 1974), which provides a rationale for the ineffectiveness of fiscal policy. Second, monetary business cycle models do not consider the possibility of a persistent impact of the rate of growth of money on the trend component of real aggregate output. As Tobin (1965) showed, the rate of monetary growth may affect the rate of capital accumulation through portfolio adjustments. More recently, Fischer (1979) has provided evidence that supports Tobin's argument. Hence, it is not likely that money will be superneutral. In the third place, some doubts can be expressed concerning the persistence of the shocks in aggregate output that are generated by monetary business cycle models. Since the forecast errors are orthogonal to the agents' information sets that contain the forecast errors in the past, knowledge of past mistakes does not contain any information about current mistakes. This may imply that levels of aggregate output are serially uncorrelated as well. If in the context of the model developed in the preceding section ν equals zero, the model does not produce cycles but only random fluctuations in output, since a mechanism to propagate shocks is lacking.[5] In that situation, the current level of aggregate output is equal to its natural level Y_{nt} and a scalar times the current-period forecast error (equation [2.8]). In a situation where $\nu > 0$, serial correlation in output exists. However, observe that an explanation, why ν should exceed zero, has not been offered yet. Cukierman (1984) provides a rather complete enumeration of the propagation mechanisms as developed in the literature. The author himself stresses the importance of the 'permanent–transitory' confusion in this respect. Agents' beliefs about the persistence of economic developments affect their decisions. People make mistakes in forming these judgments, which creates an independent source of confusion in the economy. Unlike the aggregate–relative confusion, the permanent–transitory confusion does not disappear as economic processes evolve, which creates a channel for persistent expectational errors. However, it can be argued that, as agents take their supply and demand decisions with respect to local prices, permanent–transitory confusion can only apply to local prices. Consequently, uncertainty about the persistence of changes in relative prices does not explain fluctuations in output and employment on an economy wide scale. To allow business cycles, nominal price uncertainty has to be introduced, which takes us back to the original aggregate–relative signal extraction problem.

Another source of persistence can be found in the observation that there exists a time lag between the firm's decision to invest and the actual utilization of the desired productive capacity. To explain these time lags, reference can be made to costs of adjustment and to gestation lags in production. In case costs of adjustment (e.g. installation costs) increase with the desired change in capacity, it can be profitable to firms to adjust capital stocks adaptively. In that situation, it is possible that unanticipated temporary shocks in the price level change the rate of capacity growth for several periods ahead. The resulting changes in capacity levels induce changes in labour demand and commodity supply, which creates a channel for persistence. However, as Barro (1980) observes, the cyclical variability of changes in productive capacity alone will probably not be sufficient to account for the empirically observed cyclical patterns of output and employment. To that purpose, additional propagation mechanisms have to be introduced. By relying on different costs of adjustments, the extension to a number of propagation mechanisms is relatively straightforward. Sargent (1987, chapter XVIII) points at the costs of adjusting labour inputs. Many kinds of labour can be regarded as quasi–fixed production factors. With costs of adjusting the amount of labour (e.g. turnover costs, training costs) it can be profitable to change labour inputs in an adaptive way. Blinder and Fischer (1981) have developed a channel for persistence by considering the existence of inventories. The existence of inventories itself is motivated by referring to adjustment costs in production which rule out the instantaneous response of output to fluctuations in demand. Suppose the economy experiences a nominal demand shock. Because of aggregate–relative confusion, part of the increase is considered an increase in relative prices. Output is expanded and inventories are lowered to satisfy demand. As agents become aware of their mistakes, they plan to return to natural levels of output and inventories. However, these adaptations cannot be realized simultaneously since production has to exceed its natural level in order to restore the natural level of inventories. As a result, serially uncorrelated shocks in demand create serially correlated shocks in output and employment.

It can be argued that the incorporation of adjustment costs in order to explain persistence in fluctuations in output, is more or less at variance with the initial impact effects of a random shock (Barro, 1980, p. 49 and Blanchard, 1987, p. 26). Costs of adjustment, included to model a propagation mechanism, tend to lessen the quantitative importance of intertemporal substitution impulses, which determine the size of the initial effect of the shock. To conclude, it can be observed that cost-of-adjustment type business cycle models are able to generate serially correlated fluctuations in output. It can be doubted, however, whether the cyclical potential of these models is large enough to account for the empirically observed variability of aggregate output and employment.

Models that focus on gestation lags as a channel for persistence do not suffer from the shortcomings mentioned above. However, since persistence in this case is directly related to the structure of technology in the economy, and hence independent from sources like aggregate demand or money, explanations of this type characterize a different class of models. In the next section, we will discuss these real business cycle models in more detail.

2.2.4 *Real business cycle models*

Real business cycle theory has been one of the most rapidly expanding areas[6] of economic research in recent years. Following the pioneering articles of Kydland and Prescott (1982) and Long and Plosser (1983), a large number of studies have been published directed towards the explanation of empirical regularities within the context of the standard neoclassical model. Although the analytics of the approach are rather complicated in many cases, the main arguments are very simple. The standard dynamic version of the neoclassical model of economic growth, which matches up with general competitive equilibrium theory (e.g. Solow, 1956, Lucas and Rapping, 1969), always serves as a frame of reference. In this respect, King, Plosser and Rebelo (1988) mention as the basic limitations of the neoclassical model, the strictly Harrod neutral character of technical progress, the fact that steady states are only feasible if all real variables grow at the exogenously specified rate of labour (measured in efficiency units) and that the supply of labour cannot grow in the steady state, apart from the demographically determined rate of population growth, notwithstanding the rising marginal productivity of labour, due to technical progress, which implies that the (intertemporal) income and substitution effects of increasing real wages are assumed to exactly cancel out in steady states. Furthermore, in standard growth theory, technical progress is assumed to be a smooth, permanent, and deterministic process (King, Plosser and Rebelo, 1988, p. 196). In real business cycle theory, this last assumption is amended by the introduction of uncertainty. On the one hand, uncertainty is introduced in the form of temporary, as opposed to permanent, productivity shocks; on the other hand, uncertainty is incorporated by unanticipated shocks in preference orderings. The fluctuations in the data generated by the augmented neoclassical model, can be looked upon as resulting from these shocks in productivity and preference orderings. A first important implication of this line of reasoning is that fluctuations in economic activity represent equilibrium phenomena. At any moment in time, markets are cleared and agents are choosing the quantities they prefer. Real business cycle models do not contain externalities. Equilibria are competitive and agents are not subject to signal extraction problems which characterized the Lucas-type explanations of business cycles. A second conclusion is that the behaviour of real wages and output is determined independently of the processes that govern the behaviour of nominal prices. Monetary considerations do not play a part in these models. The behaviour of the real economy can be explained by taking into account real factors only.

To illustrate the above, it is convenient to develop a simple model, which incorporates many of the characteristics mentioned before. The model developed and the derivations are taken with only minor adaptations from Sargent (1987) chapter XVIII. For the sake of simplicity, we formulate the central planner's version of the problem in this section. Sargent describes a full-fledged competitive economy. It can be shown that the two alternative specifications are completely analogous. Consider a stationary Robinson Crusoe economy, which consists of a single infinite-lived individual, with given labour endowments, preferences and production possibilities. The objective is to maximize life-time utility by the choice of a consumption-production plan for the whole time period. Crusoe takes his decisions with respect to the following quadratic utility function.

$$U_t = {}_t\mathrm{E} \sum_{j=0}^{\infty} b^j \left\{ \kappa_2 C_{t+j} - \left(\kappa_3 + \varepsilon_{1,t+j}\right) L_{t+j} - 1/2\ \kappa_4 L_{t+1}^2 \right\} \qquad [2.12]$$

$$0 < b < 1,\ \kappa_2,\ \kappa_3, \kappa_4 > 0$$

C_{t+j} = consumption in period $t+j$
L_{t+j} = employment in period $t+j$
b = the discount factor

The utility function expresses that consumption yields a positive utility, whereas employment is valued negatively. In this respect, the operator ${}_t\mathrm{E}$ denotes the conditional expectation at time t of life time utility. The linear-quadratic specification is chosen for the sake of simplicity. One should be aware that the results derived here, cannot be generalized easily to alternative specifications of the decision problem. The parameter b represents the discount factor. The process $\left\{\varepsilon_{1,t+j}\right\}_{j=0}^{\infty}$ is a stochastic process, i.e. an unanticipated sequence of random shocks in preference orderings. The choice of a contingent consumption-leisure plan is constrained by the following linear-quadratic production technology.

$$C_{t+j} = (\kappa_5 + \varepsilon_{2,t+j}) L_{t+j} - \frac{1}{2}\ \kappa_6 L_{t+j}^2 - \frac{\kappa_7}{2}\left(L_{t+j} - L_{t+j-1}\right)^2 \qquad [2.13]$$

$$\kappa_5\ ,\ \kappa_6\ ,\ \kappa_7 > 0\ ,\ L_{t-1} \text{ given},\ j = 0,\ 1,\ 2,\ \ldots$$

Production does not involve the use of capital goods. Again, the linear-quadratic production structure is only chosen for the sake of simplicity and certainly does not represent a common characteristic of the real business cycle approach. In fact, most real business cycle models stay closer to the basic neoclassical model. The sequence $\{\varepsilon_{2,t+j}\}_{j=0}^{\infty}$ represents an indexed collection of random shocks in labour productivity, to express uncertainty about the development of technology. The last term on the right-hand side of equation [2.13] specifies the adjustment costs, resulting from a change in the equilibrium level of employment. The agent's decision problem is now to maximize utility [2.12] subject to the production constraint [2.13]. The first-order condition for this problem is:

$$\kappa_2(\kappa_5 + \varepsilon_{2,t+j}) - (\kappa_3 + \varepsilon_{1,t+j}) - (\kappa_2\kappa_6 + \kappa_4) L_{t+j} -$$
$$\kappa_2\kappa_7(L_{t+j} - L_{t+j-1}) + b\kappa_2\kappa_7({}_{t+j}\mathrm{E}\ L_{t+j+1} - L_{t+j}) = 0$$

$$j = 0,\ 1,\ 2,\ \ldots \qquad [2.14]$$

Collecting terms gives

$${}_{t+j}\mathrm{E}\ L_{t+j+1} + \Lambda L_{t+j} + b^{-1}L_{t+j-1} =$$

$$-\ (b\kappa_2\kappa_7)^{-1}\{\kappa_2(\kappa_5 + \varepsilon_{2,t+j}) - \kappa_3 - \varepsilon_{1,t+j}\} \qquad [2.15]$$

$$\Lambda = -(b\kappa_2\kappa_7)^{-1}\{\kappa_2(\kappa_6 + \kappa_7(1+b)) + \kappa_4\} \qquad [2.16]$$

$$j = 0,\ 1,\ 2,\ ..$$

To solve this second order difference equation, two boundary conditions have to be satisfied. On the one hand, the exogenously given value of L_{t-1} satisfies one boundary condition. On the other hand, the transversality condition has to be fulfilled to assure the convergence of the utility function. The transversality condition in this infinite horizon problem can be formulated as $\lim_{T\to\infty} (\partial U_{t+T}/\partial L_{t+T})L_{t+T} = 0$, where T denotes the time horizon. Sargent, 1987, p. 201) derives the restrictions on the sequences $\{L_{t+j}\}$, $\{\varepsilon_{2,t+j}\}$ and $\{\varepsilon_{1,t+j}\}$ for the transversality condition to be fulfilled. In order to solve equation [2.15], it is convenient to write it as

$$(1 + \Lambda\mathrm{L} + b^{-1}\mathrm{L}^2)_{t+j}\mathrm{E}L_{t+j+1} = -\ (b\kappa_2\kappa_7)^{-1}\Big\{\kappa_2(\kappa_5 + \varepsilon_{2,t+j}) -$$

$$\kappa_3 - \varepsilon_{1,t+j}\Big\} \qquad [2.17]$$

where L is a lag–operator defined by $\mathrm{L}_{t+j}\mathrm{E}Z_{t+j} = {}_{t+j}\mathrm{E}Z_{t+j-1}$. To find the roots of the difference equation define

$$1 + \Lambda\mathrm{L} + b^{-1}\mathrm{L}^2 \equiv 1 - (\nu_1 + \nu_2)\ \mathrm{L} + \nu_1\nu_2\mathrm{L}^2$$

Then $\nu_2 = (\nu_1 b)^{-1}$ and ν_1 has to satisfy

$$b\nu_1 + \nu_1^{-1} = \frac{\kappa_2(\kappa_6 + \kappa_7\ (1+b)) + \kappa_4}{\kappa_2\kappa_7}$$

The function $b\nu + \nu^{-1}$ attains a local minimum if $\nu = (\sqrt{b})^{-1}$,[7] in which case the function itself has a value of $2\sqrt{b}$. Since $0<b<1$, $2\sqrt{b} < 1+b$ and hence, as κ_2, κ_6, κ_4, $\kappa_7 > 0$, $2\sqrt{b}<\kappa_4(\kappa_2\kappa_7)^{-1} + \kappa_6\kappa_7^{-1} + 1 + b$. This assures that the roots ν_1 and ν_2 are real and distinct. Furthermore, if $\nu=1$, $b\nu + \nu^{-1} = 1+b$, which implies $\nu<1$, to make $b\nu + \nu^{-1} = \kappa_4(\kappa_2\kappa_7)^{-1} + \kappa_6\kappa_7^{-1} + 1 + b$. On the other hand, if $\nu = b^{-1}$, $b\nu + \nu^{-1}$ also equals $1+b$, which implies $\nu>b^{-1}$, to make $b\nu+\nu^{-1} = \kappa_4(\kappa_2\kappa_7)^{-1} + \kappa_6\kappa_7^{-1} + 1 + b$. To conclude, the difference equation [2.15] has two real and distinct roots. One root is stable, the other is unstable. Without loss of generality, we can assume ν_1 to denote the stable root (see also Sargent, 1987, p. 202).

Now, we can write the difference equation as

$$(1 - \nu_1 L)(1 - \nu_2 L)\ {}_{t+j}E\ L_{t+j+1} = (b\kappa_2\kappa_7)^{-1}\left\{\varepsilon_{1,t+j} + \kappa_3 - \kappa_2(\kappa_5 + \varepsilon_{2,t+j})\right\} \qquad [2.17]$$

Since $\nu_2 > 1$, in order to satisfy the restrictions that underlie the transversality condition (Sargent, 1987, p. 201), the unstable root has to be solved forward. Operating on both sides of the equation with $1/(1-\nu_2 L) = -(\nu_2 L)^{-1}/(1 - (\nu_2 L)^{-1})$ gives:

$$(1 - \nu_1 L)\ {}_{t+j}E\ L_{t+j+1} = -(\nu_2 L)^{-1}/(1 - (\nu_2 L)^{-1})$$

$$(b\kappa_2\kappa_7)^{-1}\left\{\varepsilon_{1,t+j} + \kappa_3 - \kappa_2(\kappa_5 + \varepsilon_{2,t+j})\right\} + \kappa_8 \nu_2^{\ t}$$

where κ_8 is a constant. Since $\nu_2 > 1$, $\kappa_8 = 0$ in order to satisfy the terminal condition. The difference equation can be solved to obtain a bounded sequence $\{L_{t+j+1}\}_{j=0}^{\infty}$.

$$L_{t+j+1} = \nu_1 L_{t+j} - (b\kappa_2\kappa_7)^{-1} \sum_{i=0}^{\infty} \left(\frac{1}{\nu_2}\right)^i\ {}_{t+j+1}E$$

$$\left\{\varepsilon_{1,t+j+1+i} + \kappa_3 - \kappa_2\kappa_5 - \kappa_2\varepsilon_{2,t+j+1+i}\right\} \qquad j = -1, 0, 1, 2, ..$$

Suppose that shocks in preference orderings and productivity are serially uncorrelated (${}_tE\ \varepsilon_{1,t+1} = 0$ and ${}_tE\ \varepsilon_{2,t+1} = 0$). This implies that employment can be written as (remember that $1/\nu_2 = b\nu_1$)

$$L_{t+j+1} = \nu_1 L_{t+j} - (b\kappa_2\kappa_7)^{-1}\left\{\varepsilon_{1,t+j+1} - \kappa_2\varepsilon_{2,t+j+1}\right\} + \frac{(b\nu_1)^{-1}}{1 - (b\nu_1)^{-1}}(b\kappa_2\kappa_7)^{-1}\left\{\kappa_3 - \kappa_2\kappa_5\right\} \qquad [2.18]$$

which is a first–order Markov process with decay parameter ν_1. From equation [2.18] it can be observed immediately that random fluctuations in technology and tastes have a prolonged impact on employment and hence on output. A productivity shock instantaneously increases the equilibrium level of output and employment (through the intertemporal substitution of leisure for labour), a temporary increase in the valuation of leisure has the opposite effect. By drawing temporary shocks from the exogenously given distributions of technology patterns and preference orderings, one can simulate the development of employment in time with the help of equation [2.18].

The next step is then to compare the simulation results with the actual time series of the relevant variables. As has already been stressed, the model described here is too specific to generate employment patterns that can stand a comparison with reality. However, more sophisticated real business cycle models have shown some remarkable results in this respect, which according to Long and Plosser supports the argument that since real business cycle models are capable of generating business-cycle-like behaviour, 'models of this type provide a well-defined benchmark for evaluating the importance of other factors in actual business-cycle episodes' (Long and Plosser, 1983, p. 67).

Usually, new theoretical developments are controversial. In this respect, real business cycle theory is not the exception that proves the rule. In an excellent review of real business cycle models McCallum summarizes the main counter arguments (McCallum, 1988). In the first place, it can be argued that representative agent models are misrepresentations of actual economic systems since they imply that all households are alike and in that situation it is impossible to have externalities in the economy, an argument which also applies to the monetary equilibrium business cycle models, whereas the government sector can only be incorporated on a per household basis. In the second place, considerable scepticism can be expressed with regard to the potential of shocks in technology and preference orderings to account for the amplitude of cyclical fluctuations as experienced in the real world economies. As shocks in technology and preference orderings cannot be observed, real business cycle theorists simply choose the parameterization necessary to explain real world observations, e.g. Kydland and Prescott (1982) and Long and Plosser (1983). In the third place, output is only determined by current labour and capital. In case also earlier vintages are used in production, real business cycle models tend to overestimate the magnitude of technical change. A related argument refers to the heterogeneity of technology in different sectors of production. Technological shocks in different sectors will probably be highly independent, which implies that the aggregate variability of technological shock may be rather small. In the fourth place, there is one important aggregate supply side disturbance which cannot be incorporated in real business cycle models. Since these models do not have a foreign sector, shifts in the real price of imported raw materials are only shown as changes in the residual term of the production function. Given the significance of these shifts for the performance of the real world economies in recent years, a substantial share of the variance in output can only be attributed to unexplained residual shifts in the production function in real business cycle models. In the fifth place, money is omitted in real business cycle models. Now it would be wrong to argue that real business cycle theorists deny the correlations between monetary and real variables. Yet they claim that causality runs the other way round, i.e. from real variables towards monetary variables (reverse causation viewpoint). On the one hand, evidence to support this proposition has been delivered by Sims (1980a, 1980b) who demonstrated that changes in the stock of money have little explanatory power when a nominal interest was included in the system, whereas Nelson and Plosser (1982) showed that cyclical fluctuations in output were trend dominated. However, as McCallum (1987, pp. 30–32) argues, these favourable arguments suffer from a mistaken interpretation of estimation results, on the one hand, and from the application of insufficiently discriminating causality tests, on the other hand. At this stage it is not possible to settle this issue in a definite and unambiguous way. In the sixth place, there is the relationship between economic growth and cyclical fluctuations in real business cycle models. Traditionally the dividing line between the neoclassical theory of economic growth and the theory of business cycles rests on the assumption that growth theory deals with the economic consequences of technical progress and the accumulation of production factors, whereas business cycle theory analyzes the implications of the utilization of fixed stocks of capital and labour. In the context of real business cycle models however, cycles and growth should simultaneously be accounted for since technology shocks are the principal driving force behind cyclical variation. In that case, these models can be criticized because they abstract from economic growth since only detrended data series are taken into account. Subsequently, there is no reason to assume that exogenous technical progress represents the best description of real world experience in this respect. Real business cycle models which incorporate endogenous technical progress have only been developed very recently and do not permit any conclusions to be drawn at this moment.

To conclude, real business cycle analysis represents a fascinating and rapidly expanding area of economic research. Yet, despite the considerable amount of effort and ingenuity which characterizes the approach, many topics remain to be settled. Therefore, the conclusion that real business cycle models provide a well-defined benchmark for subsequent research of business cycles, seems at least premature and at this stage cannot be supported by unambiguous theoretical and empirical findings.

2.3 Some final observations

In this chapter, a survey of equilibrium business cycle models has been presented. After outlining the basic notions and concepts of dynamic general equilibrium theory, it has been emphasized that these models are very much akin to the basic temporary equilibrium model, since the fundamental assumptions of perfectly competitive markets and completely rational behaviour of agents have been maintained. It has been emphasized that economic fluctuations result from erratic shocks under optimal individual decision making, i.e. cycles are random deviations from equilibrium paths. The monetary misperception approach to business cycles relaxes the assumption of full information, in order to be able to consistently assure the emergence of economic disturbances. In doing so, a possible inconsistency concerning the existence of rational expectations equilibria in the presence of a fully informative equilibrium price vector and costly acquisition of information, an argument developed by Grossman and discussed in section 2.1, can be circumvented. On the other hand, the performance of monetary business cycle models with respect to the propagation of shocks appears to be less convincing, as can be concluded from the analysis presented in section 2.2.3. In addition, it can be argued that information on monetary aggregates is available too promptly, to warrant the fundamental assumption concerning the ignorance of individuals on empirical grounds. The desire to meet these objections has led to the development of real business cycle models directed towards the explanation of empirical regularities within the context of the standard dynamic version of the neoclassical model of economic growth. Although these models do not possess all the *ad hoceries* that characterize monetary equilibrium business cycle models, a definite answer to the usefulness of the real business cycle approach cannot be given either, as has been argued in the previous section. To conclude, flexprice equilibrium business cycle models do not provide a rigorous explanation of economic fluctuations.[8] The claim that fluctuations in output and employment can be analyzed adequately in the context of a perfectly competitive economic system cannot yet be justified.

Notes

1. As a very brief selection out of the numerous extensions that followed the publication of the Arrow–Debreu–McKenzie model, we refer to analyses that deal with a meaningful incorporation of money in the general equilibrium theory, *e.g.* Hahn (1965) and Gale (1983), with the introduction of transaction costs, *e.g.* Ulph and Ulph (1975) and with intertemporal uncertainty, *e.g.* Grandmont and Younes (1973), as well as the modeling of economic activity without a definite beginning and end (the development of overlapping generations models, *e.g.* Samuelson (1958) and Diamond (1965)).

2. Walras' law states that aggregate excess demand equals zero in case each individual satisfies his budget constraint, i.e. the value of individual excess demand equals zero.

3. The incorporation of time in general equilibrium theory is based upon a sequence–analytical notion of the economy, in accordance with Hicks' (1939) interpretation of Lindahl's (1930) and Ohlin's (1937) contributions to economic theory. Economic processes are described as a succession of periods. A period is an interval of time in which prices and plans remains unchanged. These variables are only allowed to change at the junction of two subsequent periods (see also chapter 6).

4. A sufficient statistic is defined as a partition of a sample from a known distribution which summarizes all the information available in the sample.

5. In this context McCallum (1984) observes that the mere fact that the early rational expectations theorists ignored serial correlations does not indicate that the authors denied the existence of these effects. Their main interest at the time was to explain a trade–off between nominal and real variables in the context of a general equilibrium model (McCallum, 1984, p. 398).

6. Recently the editor of the Journal of Monetary Economics has dedicated an entire volume to a discussion of real business cycle models (Journal of Monetary Economics, 1988, vol. 21).

7. A local maximum is attained for $\nu = -(\sqrt{b})^{-1}$. The function itself has a value of $-2\sqrt{b}$ in that case. Since $\dfrac{\kappa_2(\kappa_6 + \kappa_7\,(1+b)) + \kappa_4}{\kappa_2\kappa_7} > 0$ this possibility does not need further consideration.

8. In this respect, it can be observed that in 1939 Keesing wrote a thesis on the unhappy relationship between of equilibrium analysis and the need for dynamic economic theory. Until now, his optimism, expressed on the last page of the book, concerning the solution of this problem has not been confirmed by actual theoretical developments (Keesing, 1939, p. 192).

3 Fixprice models and economic fluctuations

3.1 Introduction

From the analysis of the equilibrium business cycle theory, it has been concluded that models, which maintain the fundamental assumptions underlying the competitive equilibrium, perfect flexibility of market prices and hence general market clearing, have not succeeded in offering a convincing explanation of the existence of persistent economic fluctuations. In this chapter, we will consider alternative analyses of output and employment variability, which allow prices to be fixed at non–market clearing levels. An immediate implication of this last assumption is that rationing appears. Agents take decisions with respect to price *and* quantity signals, which extends the 'Walrasian tool kit' of notions and concepts in a number of directions. In the first place, the Walrasian demand and supply schedules have to be adapted to account for the impact of quantity signals (the theory of effective demand and supply). In the second place, expectations formation has to be related to price and quantity rationing. In the third place, the organization of exchange processes in markets has to be considered more explicitly. In the fourth place, temporary equilibria are established with respect to prices and quantities.

In the literature (e.g. Benassy, 1987), the arguments in favour of the development of fixprice models arise from empirical as well as from theoretical considerations. On the one hand, perfect markets with completely flexible prices appear to be quite rare in real world economies. The existence of implicit and explicit contracts, administered prices and asymmetries in the fluctuations of prices does prohibit the establishment of general market clearing in many situations. On the other hand, as has been argued in the preceding chapter, many macroeconomic features (e.g. the magnitude of fluctuations in economic variables or the a-cyclical movement of real wages) are difficult to reconcile with the major characteristics of competitive equilibrium theory.

Economists who initiated research in the area of non-Walrasian general equilibrium theory are Patinkin (1956), Clower (1965) and Leijonhufvud (1968), although Samuelson (1947) and Tobin and Houthakker (1951) already considered the impact of quantity rationing at an earlier stage. Barro and Grossman (1971) integrated the models of Clower and Patinkin, which led to the first non-Walrasian general equilibrium model. Drèze (1975) and Benassy (1975) provided the generalization to an economic system with many markets, whereas Barro and Grossman (1976) and in particular Malinvaud (1977) have been the first economists to show the macroeconomic implications of the new approach in great detail. Subsequent developments focus on intertemporal considerations (e.g. Böhm, 1978, Honkapohja, 1979, Malinvaud, 1980, Kuipers, 1981, 1988), the impact of quantity constraints on expectations formation (e.g. Neary and Stiglitz, 1983) and the incorporation of price setting in non-Walrasian general equilibrium models (e.g. Hahn, 1977, 1978, Negishi, 1979) and in macroeconomic models (e.g. Woglom, 1982, Blanchard and Kyotaki, 1987). This last extension will be discussed in chapter 4. In this chapter, we will review the developments in fixprice general equilibrium theory. In section 3.2, the principles of fixprice general equilibrium models will be discussed. Fixprice macroeconomic models with quantity rationing will be dealt with in sections 3.3 and 3.4. This chapter is concluded with some final observations on fixprice disequilibrium theory in section 3.5.

3.2 The concepts of non-Walrasian general equilibrium theory[1]

As in flexprice general equilibrium theory, each agent maximizes utility given his endowments by formulating demands and supplies in all the markets of the economy. Prices are also assumed to be taken as given by the individual agent. However, as trade takes place at false prices, demands and supplies cannot be reconciled. A first implication is that transactions must be distinguished from demands and supplies. The latter variables represent signals sent to the market before exchange takes place. Transactions denote actual purchases and sales. The latter must necessarily sum to zero in each market. A rationing scheme is proposed as a description of the organization of the exchange process in each market, in order to generate consistent transactions out of possibly conflicting demands and supplies in each market. Rationing schemes have the following properties. In the first place, exchange is voluntary. No agent can be forced to trade more than he wishes to trade. In the second place, if markets are efficient, subjects on the short side of the markets always realize their net demands (the short side rule). In addition, rationing schemes can be distinguished with respect to their manipulability; this is the possibility that agents can improve their level of transaction in a particular market by increasing their net demands in that market. For instance, proportional rationing schemes are manipulable; uniform schemes are not. Under the assumptions of voluntary exchange and of the short side of the market realizing its intentions, agent h's transactions in market i can be determined according to equation [3.1].

$$t_{hi} = min\left\{d_{hi},\ max(\overset{*}{t}_{hi},\ -s_{hi})\right\} \qquad [3.1]$$

$$d_{hi} = G^d_{hi}(\overset{*}{t}_{-hi}) \qquad [3.2]$$

$$-s_{hi} = G^s_{hi}(\overset{*}{t}_{-hi}) \qquad [3.3]$$

t_{hi} = net transaction of agent h in market i
$\overset{*}{t}_{hi}$ = net demand (demand–supply) of agent h in market i
d_{hi} = the perceived upper bound on agent h's purchases in market i
s_{hi} = the perceived upper bound on agent h's sales in market i
$\overset{*}{t}_{-hi}$ = net demand (demand–supply) of all other agents in market i

Equations [3.2] and [3.3] represent h's expected constraints on purchases and sales, respectively. Perceived constraints depend on the planned activities of all other agents in a particular market, or in case of a multimarket framework and given the mutual interdependence of individual economic decisions, on planned activities of all other agents in all the markets of the economy. In a situation where agent h's net demands in market i are positive ($\overset{*}{t}_{hi} > 0$), d_{hi} may be a binding constraint on purchases. On the other hand, in a situation where agent h is a net supplier in market i ($\overset{*}{t}_{hi} < 0$), $-s_{hi} < 0$ may represent a binding constraint on planned sales. Equation [3.1] reflects this impact of constraints on agent h's transactions. Equations [3.4], [3.5] and [3.6] determine agent h's transactions in a multimarket framework.

$$t_h = F_h(\overset{*}{t}_h, \overset{*}{t}_{-h}) \qquad [3.4]$$

$$d_h = G^d_h(\overset{*}{t}_{-h}) \qquad [3.5]$$

$$s_h = G^s_h(\overset{*}{t}_{-h}) \qquad [3.6]$$

t_h = vector of net transactions of agent h in all markets
$\overset{*}{t}_h$ = vector of net demands of agent h in all markets
$\overset{*}{t}_{-h}$ = set of vectors of net demands of all agents except h in all markets
d_h = the perceived upper bound on agent h's purchases in all markets
o_{-h} = the perceived upper bound on agent h's sales in all markets

This system can be solved for given values of $\overset{*}{t}_{-h}$ and given prices after the vector of net demands of agent h in all markets ($\overset{*}{t}_h$), has been determined. To determine this vector, the individual decision problem has to be considered.

As mentioned before, demands and supplies are signals sent to the markets in order to obtain the best possible vector of transactions. This vector can be derived from the (identical) agent's decision problem. It represents the utility maximizing vector of transactions given the agent's budget constraint, as a function of prices and perceived constraints. Such a vector will exist if the usual regularity conditions on the utility functions are fulfilled. However, transactions are determined in markets, whereas agents formulate only demands and supplies. For instance, notional demands and supplies achieve the best possible transactions in a situation where there are no binding constraints perceived. On the other hand, effective demands and supplies correspond to the best possible transactions in situations with binding perceived constraints. The problem with this set-up, which is similar to Drèze (1975), is that the correspondence between net demands and best possible transactions is not unique. As soon as one constraint becomes binding, any net demand will achieve the best possible transaction, which equals the level of the constraint in that situation. Furthermore, since agents maximize utility by choosing the best possible transactions in the Drèze model, net demands are not signaled to the market when there is a binding constraint perceived. Hence, the resulting Drèze-equilibria do not offer a measure of the degree of excess demand in a particular market. Furthermore, Drèze-equilibria are not invariant to the rationing scheme chosen. To meet these objections, Benassy (1975) proposes a more straightforward interpretation of Clower's dual decision hypothesis by assuming that agents, in formulating utility maximizing net demands in a particular market, only take account of the constraints perceived in other markets. Repeating this procedure sequentially for all markets in the economy results in the agent's effective net demand vectors. It can be argued that these net demand vectors always lead to the vector of best possible transactions (Benassy, 1977, 1982). Indeed, excess demands have a more natural interpretation and are signaled to the markets. Finally, after having determined the agent's individually rational net demands, equilibria (K-equilibria) can be derived with the help of equations [3.4], [3.5] and [3.6] for all agents. Benassy defines a K-equilibrium with rationing as a consistent set of individually rational net effective demands, best possible transactions and perceived constraints, for given prices and rationing schemes in all markets. The perceived constraints described in equations [3.5] and [3.6] result from the exchange process. In equilibrium, perceived constraints correspond to actual constraints. They need not be identical, since there exists only a *correspondence* between individually rational demands and best possible transactions as well. Furthermore, the latter relationship is rather *ad hoc*, since it is dependent on the particular specification of the rationing schemes, although the principles of voluntary exchange and non-manipulability are met.

The conceptual framework of the non-Walrasian general equilibrium theory developed in this section, permits the following questions and observations. In the first place, how can constrained equilibria be brought about (Nagatani, 1981)? The actual allocation of quantities is dependent on the rationing scheme imposed. On the assumption that markets are efficient, only long sides get rationed in the markets of the economy. It is not hard to imagine that in order to establish such an efficient allocation of quantities, the informational requirements are tremendous and by no means smaller than in a competitive economy. Therefore, the Walrasian auctioneer cannot be dismissed in fixprice models. His job has only been given a new content, which implies that markets are still perfect in the non-Walrasian economy. Except for the fact that prices are determined outside the system, there are no reasons to expect equilibria to be different from the competitive alternative. In the second place, what keeps the economy at a constrained equilibrium? In general, fixprice equilibria are not Pareto optimal, notwithstanding the efficiency of the exchange process (Benassy, 1987, pp. 30-37). On the other hand, Laroque (1978) showed that in a multi-commodity, multi-agent exchange model, it is possible for constrained agents to be better off in an equilibrium with rationing, rather than in a Walrasian equilibrium. However, Laroque's conception is limited to exchange processes with opposite situations of excess demand in the two separate markets. In situations with general excess demand fixprice equilibria are not constrained Pareto optimal. Pareto improving trades are possible but arbitrarily prohibited, since agents are not allowed to signal packages of mutually interdependent net demands to separate markets. In the third place, the Benassy model does not provide an unambiguous measure of the degree of excess demand as well. Because of the sequential character of the agents' maximization procedure, it is not guaranteed that feasibility conditions are met. Consequently, the agent's vector of net demands may not satisfy the budget constraint. In that situation, the difference between the aggregate of effective net demands and the actual transactions in a particular market cannot serve as a correct measure of the degree of excess demand in that market. To solve this problem, models with stochastic constraints have been introduced in the literature (e.g. Gale, 1979, Green, 1980, Hey, 1981, and Svensson, 1980, 1981). In these models agents observe, besides prices, the *aggregate* disequilibrium signals that go with these prices in the markets they visit before decisions on demands and supplies are taken. On the other hand, subjects are uncertain about the relationship between these aggregate disequilibrium signals and the perceived constraints they will face at the micro level. The knowledge about this relationship is limited to the probability distributions of the quantity constraints, which implies that in case expected constraints come true, the agent's vector of net demands will on average satisfy the budget restriction. Thus, a more consistent measure of excess demand over transactions is obtained. A central assumption with respect to this approach is of course the observability of the aggregate disequilibrium signals even before exchange takes place, an assumption which will be hard to rationalize in a world without (stochastic) perfect foresight. Moreover, the fact that aggregate disequilibrium signals cannot be manipulated crucially depends on the absence of monopoly power in the economy, which is merely an assumption rather than an implication of the theory.[2] Nevertheless, non-Walrasian models with stochastic rationing can be considered useful extensions of the deterministic varieties[3] and have resulted in interesting analyses, in particular in the field of macroeconomics (e.g. Ito and Honkapohja, 1985).

3.3 Fixprice macroeconomics

Non-Walrasian general equilibrium theory has provided a rigorous frame of reference for a large number of macroeconomic models based on the fixed price approach (Van der Ploeg, 1987, is a recent survey of macroeconomic models, with emphasis on the disequilibrium analyses of open economies whereas Drazen (1980) and Gordon (1981) take a more general approach in their reproduction of the literature). In general, the analyses concentrate on the characteristics of quantity-constrained equilibria in labour and product markets of monetary economies.[4] Combining states of excess demand in the markets makes it possible to categorize the resulting quantity constrained equilibria according to their rationing properties. Four regimes are distinguished, Keynesian and classical unemployment, repressed inflation and underconsumption (e.g. Malinvaud, 1977, Muellbauer and Portes, 1978, and Benassy, 1977 and 1982). Keynesian unemployment or general excess supply provides a microeconomic rationale for demand-induced involuntary unemployment. Classical unemployment, a situation where households are rationed in both markets, is only possible if households can neglect income constraints by drawing on accumulated real balances. Inventories have likewise buffer stock characteristics in a situation of underconsumption, which is the opposite extreme of classical unemployment. Finally, repressed inflation characterizes an economy with positive excess demands in both markets. To[5] relate these four regimes to each other consider the following illustration.

In a macroeconomic three (agents) by three (goods) by three (markets) framework, households demand commodities and real balances and supply labour. Real balances reflect the indirect utility of future consumption. It is assumed that the demand for real balances is derived from intertemporal preferences. Firms sell commodities out of stock and buy labour for production purposes. The government sector wants commodities and finances these purchases through taxation and the creation of money. On the assumption that all profits (*PRF*) are completely taxed away (*PRF* = *PT*), the sectorial budget identities are summarized in the following equations.

Households:	$WL \equiv PC + S$	[3.7]
Firms :	$PSA - WL \equiv PRF$	[3.8]
Government:	$S \equiv PG - PT$	[3.9]

with

$$S \equiv M_d - \bar{M} \equiv PG - PT \equiv PG - PRF \qquad [3.10]$$

PRF = aggregate end-of-period profits
PC = aggregate nominal consumption expenditures
WL = aggregate nominal labour income
PT = aggregate current-period nominal taxes
PG = nominal government expenditures
PSA = aggregate current-period nominal sales
S = aggregate nominal savings or the current-period mutation in households' money balances
M_d = end-of-period aggregate stock of money balances
$\bar{M}$ = beginning-of-period aggregate stock of money balances

In the absence of rationing, the representative household maximizes utility $U = U(c,l,m_r)$, where c, l and m_r denote the agent's actual current-period consumption, employment and real balances respectively, subject to the budget constraint, $wl + \bar{m}_r = c + m_r$ ($\bar{m}_r$ denotes the agent's beginning-of-period real balances). Maximum utility is achieved when the marginal rate of substitution between consumption and real balances equals unity and when the marginal rate of substitution between consumption and leisure equals the real wage. In that situation, the notional demand for commodities c_d and real balances m_{rd}, on the one hand, and the notional supply of labour l_s on the other hand, is represented by equations [3.11], [3.12] and [3.13], respectively (on the assumption that the agent's time endowment has been normalized at unity).

$$c_d = c_d(\overset{+}{w}, \overset{+}{\bar{m}_r} + w) \qquad [3.11]$$

$$m_{rd} = m_{rd}(\overset{+}{w}, \overset{+}{\bar{m}_r} + w) \qquad [3.12]$$

$$l_s = l_s(\overset{+}{w}, \overset{-}{\bar{m}_r} + w) \qquad [3.13]$$

The signs above the equations indicate sign–characteristics of the first order derivatives. It is assumed that the substitution effect dominates the income effect in [3.13].

In the presence of a labour market constraint, households' effective demand for commodities c_{de} maximizes $U(c_{de}, l, \bar{m}_r + wl - c_{de})$, where l is equal to employment, given the demand constraint in the labour market. Effective demand for commodities is given by

$$c_{de} = c_{de}(\overset{+}{l}, \overset{+}{\bar{m}_r} + wl) \qquad [3.14]$$

In case aggregate commodity demand exceeds supply, households perceive a constraint in the commodity market. In that situation, the effective supply of labour l_{se} maximizes $U(c, l_{se}, \bar{m}_r + wl_{se} - c)$, where c is equal to actual consumption given the rationing scheme in the commodity market.

$$l_{se} = l_{se}(\overset{+}{c}, \overset{+}{w}, \overset{-}{\bar{m}_r} - c) \qquad [3.15]$$

Firms maximize the aggregate vf of real current profits (prf) and discounted future profits. It is assumed that discounted future profits can be conveniently expressed by a value[6] function v with the end-of-period commodity stock inv as argument.

$$vf = prf + v(inv) \qquad [3.16]$$

$$inv = inv_0 + f(l) - sa \qquad [3.17]$$

$$prf = sa - wl \qquad [3.18]$$

$$v' > 0 \; v'' < 0, \; f' > 0, \; f'' < 0$$

sa = real current–period sales
$f(l)$ = current–period production
inv_0 = the beginning of period commodity stock.

Maximizing profits by choosing current–period sales and production levels, yields two first–order conditions, $v' = 1$ and $f'(l) = w$, respectively. In the absence of constraints, the notional demand for labour l_d is equal to

$$l_d = l_d(\overset{-}{w}) \qquad [3.19]$$

Production is given by

$$q = f(\overset{+}{l}_d) \qquad [3.20]$$

and intended sales by

$$sa_s = inv_0 + q - inv^* \qquad [3.21]$$

inv^{*} = the optimal notional level of the end-of-period commodity stock (derived from $v' = 1$).

Equation [3.21] indicates that firms may choose to hold a precautionary commodity stock. In the presence of a perceived constraint in the labour market, the effective intended sales sa_{se} maximize $vf = sa_{se} - wl + v(inv_0 + f(l) - sa_{se})$.

$$sa_{se} = sa_{se}(\overset{+}{inv_0}, \overset{+}{l}) \qquad [3.22]$$

In this situation, l denotes the labour market transaction that can be realized given the rationing scheme in the labour market. On the other hand, if firms perceive a demand constraint in the commodity market, the effective demand for labour l maximizes $vf = sa - wl_{de} + v(inv_0 + f(l_{de}) - sa)$.

$$l_{de} = l_{de}(\overset{-}{inv_0 - sa}, \overset{-}{w}) \qquad [3.23]$$

In equation [3.23], sa represents the highest possible transaction in the commodity market that does not exceed the rationing scheme perceived in that market.

After aggregation of the agents' demand and supply schedules (capitals denote aggregate variables), the conditions for market clearing can be derived in the different regimes. As usual, it is assumed that the government sector cannot be rationed. A situation of general market clearing, a Walrasian equilibrium (WA) is characterized by equations [3.24] and [3.25].

$$C(w, \bar{M}_r + w) + G = INV_0 + F(L_d) - INV^{*} \qquad [3.24]$$

$$L_s(w, \bar{M}_r + w) = L_d(w) \qquad [3.25]$$

Equations [3.24] and [3.25], respectively, describe commodity and labour market equilibria in situations without rationing. Note that equation [3.24] is downward sloping in a $\bar{M}_r - w$ space, whereas equation [3.25] is upward sloping. Equilibrium in the commodity market in a situation with excess supply of labour is given by equation [3.26]. In a $\bar{M}_r - w$ space the slope of [3.26] is steeper than [3.24], since with excess supply of labour a reduction of real wages has a smaller depressing impact on the effective demand for consumer goods, which implies that the compensating increase of real money balances can be smaller as well.

$$C_{de}(L, \bar{M}_r + wL) + G = INV_0 + F(L) - INV^{*} \qquad [3.26]$$

$$C(w, \bar{M}_r + w) + G = SA_{se}(INV_0, L) \qquad [3.27]$$

In a situation where firms are rationed in the labour market, the commodity market equilibrium locus is described by equation [3.27]. With excess demand for labour, firms will have to diminish intended sales, given a desired level of the precautionary commodity stock. Equilibrium in the commodity market thus implies a lower level of aggregate demand which, when compared to a situation where constraints are absent and given the level of real wages, can be brought about by a lower level of real balances. As a result, the effective commodity market equilibrium locus will be sloped more steeply than its notional image.

Equilibrium in the labour market with excess supply in the commodity market is given by equation [3.28].

$$L_s(w, \bar{M}_r + w) = L_{de}(INV_0 - SA, w) \qquad [3.28]$$

When compared with a situation where constraints are absent, it can be observed that a reduction of real wages will not boost production considerably. As a result, the compensating reduction of real balances needed to choke off the impact of the real wage decrease can be smaller as well. Hence, the slope of the effective labour market equilibrium locus with excess commodity supply will be larger. On the other hand, with excess commodity demand the labour market equilibrium locus is given by equation [3.29].

$$L_{se}(C, w, \bar{M}_r - C) = L_d(w) \qquad [3.29]$$

In this situation households cannot realize their intention in the commodity market which implies that the supply of labour will be lowered. To restore equilibrium in the labour market, real wages have to increase, given the level of real balances. Consequently, the effective labour market equilibrium locus with excess commodity demand will have a steeper slope.

The equilibrium loci derived above can be depicted in a $w-M_r$ space in order to partition this space into five regimes. This is done in figure 3.1. Remember that labour market loci are upward sloping, whereas commodity market loci are downward sloping. Effective loci are represented by solid lines. The Walrasian regime WA is described by the intersection point of notional (and effective) labour and commodity market equilibrium loci. The regime of Keynesian unemployment KU (general excess supply) is bounded by equations [3.26] and [3.28], classical unemployment CU (households rationed in both markets) by equations [3.26] and [3.29], repressed inflation RI (general excess demand) by equations [3.27] and [3.29] and, finally, underconsumption UC (firms rationed in both markets) by equations [3.27] and [3.28].

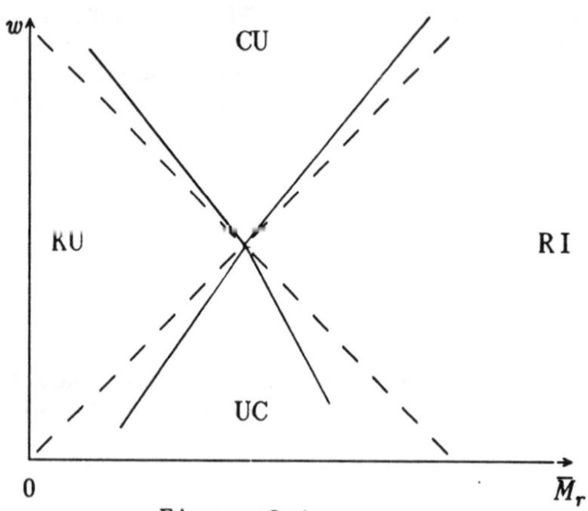

Figure 3.1

Multipliers that relate changes in sales and employment to changes in the exogenous variables w, $\overline{M}_r$ and G are regime-specific. In a situation of classical unemployment fiscal ($\frac{dSA}{dG}$ and $\frac{dL}{dG}$) as well as monetary policy multipliers ($\frac{dSA}{d\overline{M}_r}$ and $\frac{dL}{d\overline{M}_r}$) are equal to zero since actual transactions in the commodity market and in the labour market are given by the right-hand side of equations [3.24] and [3.25], respectively, which reflects the fact that unemployment is caused by too high real wages in this situation. In a situation of Keynesian unemployment fiscal and monetary policy multipliers in the commodity market are $1/(1 + L_{de,1}(C_{de,1} + wC_{de,2}))$ and $C_{de,2}/(1 + L_{de,1}(C_{de,1} + wC_{de,2}))$ respectively, since in that situation actual transactions are equal to the left-hand side of equation [3.26]. Employment in a situation of Keynesian unemployment is equal to labour demand (the right-hand side of equation [3.28]). In this respect $C_{de,1}$ and $C_{de,2}$ denote first order partial derivatives of the consumption function. $L_{de,1}$ (and $L_{de,2}$) has (have) a similar meaning in case of the employment function. As the multipliers are greater than zero (on the assumption that $0 < -L_{de,1}(C_{de,1} + wC_{de,2}) < 1$, i.e. the marginal propensity to consume is smaller than unity), both fiscal and monetary policy have a positive impact on actual sales in a situation of Keynesian unemployment. The fiscal and monetary multipliers in the labour market are $-L_{de,1}/(1 + L_{de,1}(C_{de,1} + wC_{de,2}))$ and $-L_{de,1}C_{de,2}/(1 + L_{de,1}(C_{de,1} + wC_{de,2}))$ respectively, as employment in a situation of Keynesian unemployment is equal to labour demand (the right-hand side of equation [3.28]). Actual transactions are equal to the left-hand side of equation [3.26]. As $L_{de,1} < 0$ and $0 < -L_{de,1}(C_{de,1} + wC_{de,2}) < 1$, the two multipliers have positive values as well. Both fiscal and monetary expansion have positive employment effects. The impact of real wage changes on employment in a situation of Keynesian unemployment is ambiguous. A wage increase has a positive effect on employment through increased spending $(-L_{de,1}C_{de,2}L/(1 + L_{de,1}(C_{de,1} + wC_{de,2})) > 0)$. On the other hand, the costs of labour will rise as wages increase. This will have a negative impact on employment $(L_{de,2} < 0)$. If the spending effect dominates, wages move pro-cyclical. The multipliers for the remaining regimes can be derived as above. Van der Ploeg (1987) provides the complete picture.

The model above has two independent sources of dynamics. First, real wages may change between periods. However, in the context of fixprice models it is unclear how and as a consequence of what, real wage changes may come about. To enable the study of the impact of price changes in the fixprice model, additional *ad hoc* rules dealing with the determination of real wages have to be formulated. At the end of this section, the implications of a number of alternative assumptions are illustrated, although a discussion of optimal price setting in disequilibrium models is postponed to the next chapter. Second, household savings may change. Since positive savings imply the accumulation of real balances, every change in savings behaviour has real effects. In general, the introduction of stocks in a disequilibrium model is important for the following reason. If trade is allowed at false prices, errors are made, which result in unintended changes in stocks (money, inventories, capacity). However, these errors do not show in fixprice equilibria, since only flows are taken into account. Hence, the incorporation of the dynamics of stocks represents a natural extension of the fixprice approach (see also Nagatani, 1981, and Drabicki and Takayama, 1979). Only zero savings will result in the establishment of a stationary state in this model (see also Böhm, 1978, and Honkapohja, 1979, for a similar framework, as well as Böhm (1987, for a more rigorous treatment in the context of a general equilibrium model with overlapping generations). In addition, it is only by accident that the Walrasian equilibrium lies on the stationary time path. With positive savings the Walrasian equilibrium eventually enters the regime of repressed inflation. A decline in real balances causes the Walrasian equilibrium to end up in a Keynesian regime.

On the assumption that the Walrasian equilibrium has positive savings, the following intertemporal characteristics can be derived from the model. In a situation of Keynesian unemployment, real aggregate household savings are given by equation [3.30].

$$S_r = wL - C_{de}(L, \overline{M}_r + wL) \qquad [3.30]$$

Furthermore, the level of employment L is determined in the commodity market [3.26].

$$F(L) = C_{de}(L, \overline{M}_r + wL) + G + INV^* - INV_0 \qquad [3.31]$$

Total differentiation of [3.30] with respect to $\overline{M}_r$ and w, along an iso-savings curve $S_r = 0$ gives

$$dS_r|_{S_r=0} = \frac{\partial S}{\partial \overline{M}_r} d\overline{M}_r + \frac{\partial S}{\partial w} dw \qquad [3.32]$$

From [3.30] it can be derived that

$$\frac{\partial S_r}{\partial \overline{M}_r} d\overline{M}_r = \left\{ \left[w - (C_{de,1} + C_{de,2}w) \right] \frac{\partial L}{\partial \overline{M}_r} - C_{de,2} \right\} d\overline{M}_r \qquad [3.33]$$

$$\frac{\partial S_r}{\partial w} dw = \left\{ L - C_{de,2}L + \left[w - (C_{de,1} + C_{de,2}w) \right] \frac{\partial L}{\partial w} \right\} dw \qquad [3.34]$$

From equation [3.31] it can be derived that

$$\frac{dL}{d\overline{M}_r} = \frac{C_{de,2}}{(dF/dL - (C_{de,1} + wC_{de,2}))} \qquad [3.35]$$

$$\frac{dL}{dw} = \frac{C_{de,2}L}{(dF/dL - (C_{de,1} + wC_{de,2}))} \qquad [3.36]$$

Substitution of equation [3.35] into equation [3.33], on the one hand, and of equation [3.36] into equation [3.34], on the other hand, followed by some straightforward calculations results in

$$\left.\frac{dw}{d\overline{M}_r}\right|_{S_r=0} = - \frac{-(dF/dL - w)C_{de,2}}{L(dF/dL - C_{de,1} - C_{de,2}dF/dL)} \qquad [3.37]$$

Observe that $C_{de,2}$, $dF/dL - w$, $dF/dL - C_{de,1}$ (because the marginal propensity to consume < 1), $L > 0$. Furthermore, presumably $C_{de,2}$ will be small for high levels of wealth. For a given level of $\overline{M}_r$ this assumption implies that $dw/d\overline{M}_r$ will probably be positive for high wages and possibly negative for low wages.[7] In a situation of underconsumption, household savings are given by

$$S_r = wL - C_d(w, \overline{M}_r + w) \tag{3.38}$$

whereas actual employment can be derived from

$$F(L) = C_d(w, \overline{M}_r + w) + G + INV^* - INV_0 \tag{3.39}$$

By proceeding as above, it can be calculated that in a situation of underconsumption

$$\left.\frac{dw}{d\overline{M}_r}\right|_{S_r=0} = \frac{(dF/dL - w)C_{d,2}}{LdF/dL - (dF/dL - w)(C_{d,1} + C_{d,2})} \tag{3.40}$$

Since $dF/dL - w$, $C_{d,2}$, L, $C_{d,1} > 0$ and $\partial C/\partial w$ is small for high wages, $dw/d\overline{M}_r$, will be positive for high wages and possibly negative for low wages. In a situation of repressed inflation, aggregate savings are given by

$$S_r = wL(C, w, \overline{M}_r - C) - C \tag{3.41}$$

whereas aggregate production is described by

$$SA + INV^* - INV_0 = F(L(C, w, \overline{M}_r - C)) \tag{3.42}$$

As $SA \equiv G + C$, equation [3.42] can be written as

$$G + INV^* - INV_0 = F(L(C, w, \overline{M}_r - C)) - C \tag{3.43}$$

From equation [3.41] and [3.43], it can be derived that

$$\left.\frac{dw}{d\overline{M}_r}\right|_{S_r=0} = - \frac{-(dF/dL - w)L_3}{L(1 - dF/dL(L_1 - L_3)) - (dF/dL - w)L_2} \tag{3.44}$$

On the plausible assumption that the supply of labour is relatively inelastic with respect to the binding constraint on consumer goods, the real wage rate and beginning-of-period real money balances, both $L_1 - L_3$ (= $\partial L/\partial C$) and L_2 (= $\partial L/\partial w$) will be small. We will restrict $L_1 - L_3$ to be smaller than $1/(dF/dL)$.[8] In that case, $dw/d\overline{M}_r < 0$ for high wages and possibly negative for low wages in a regime of repressed inflation.

If we combine the results from the analysis of equations [3.37], [3.40] and [3.44], the iso-savings curve $S_r = 0$ can be drawn in the w–$\overline{M}_r$ space of figure 3.1. This is done in figure 3.2.

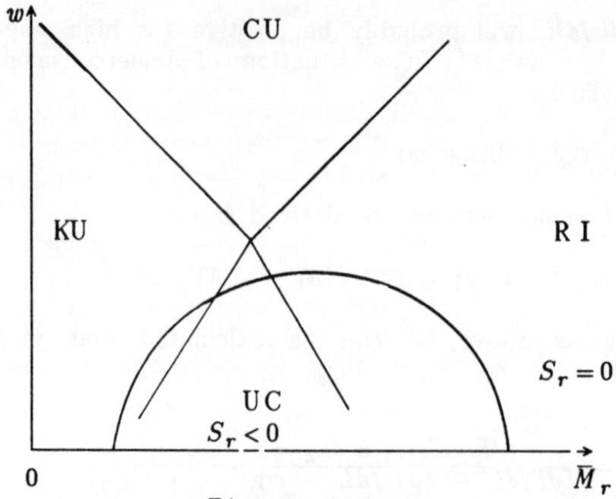

Figure 3.2

Below the iso–savings curve, households dissave and hence the government budget shows a surplus. Above the curve households accumulate real balances and hence the budget will be in deficit. Since positive/negative savings imply by definition accumulation/decumulation of real balances, it immediately follows that situations of repressed inflation are locally unstable, whereas situations of Keynesian unemployment and under consumption may be locally stable. Hence, the conclusion drawn in the literature (e.g. Böhm, 1978, Honkapohja, 1979, and Malinvaud, 1977) that there can be observed a medium–run tendency in the economy to settle down in a situation characterized by general excess supply, depends, among other things, on the assumption that commodities cannot be stored. Furthermore, the stability characteristics are dependent on the initial $(w, \bar{M}_r)$ combination, which the analysis takes as a starting point. Finally, in case the Walrasian regime is characterized by dissaving and the regime of classical unemployment has to be considered, the abovementioned conclusions no longer hold as well.

The analysis of the dynamics of savings has been carried out on the assumption that prices and wages are rigid for some time. Clearly this assumption is *ad hoc* and needs to be abandoned. In case the Walrasian auctioneer still does the job, nominal prices and wages are adjusted with respect to the state of excess demand in the commodity and the labour market, respectively. However, in the framework developed above it is the adjustment of real wages that drives the economy, which implies that additional assumptions about the relative speed of adjustment in prices and wages have to be made. The implications of several alternative assumptions have been studied in this respect (e.g. Böhm, 1978, 1987, Honkapohja, 1979, 1980, and de Lorie, 1978). Böhm (1978), for instance, observes that in a situation where nominal wages are more rigid than prices the time path of the economy may be cyclical around the Walrasian equilibrium. On the other hand, if real wages fall in an unemployment situation and rise in a state of excess demand in the labour market, the economy will be saddle point stable in the intercept of the iso–savings curve $S_r = 0$ and the borderline between the Keynesian regime and the regime of underconsumption. In general, the assumptions made determine to a very large extent the conclusions drawn. To overcome this unfortunate characteristic, a more general analysis may be developed with additional endogenous dynamics. However, very soon this analysis will become very complicated, which makes it impossible to study the impact of more dynamic features in the context of the model developed.

To quote Hénin and Michel

> 'Sur le plan formel d'abord, les contributions se distinguent pour la choix des variables dont la dynamique est explicitée, salaire, prix, en caisse, stock de capital, prévisions de demande, de profitabilité ou d'inflation. Il est clairement impossible de traiter rigoreusement le modèle général qui incluerait tous ces adjustements.' (Hénin and Michel, 1982, p.14).

For that reason, additional dynamic considerations described in the literature will be reviewed separately in the next section.

3.4 More dynamics

3.4.1 *Physical capital accumulation*

Up to now changes in the level of productive capacity have not been considered in the analysis. Models that do take account of the capacity effects of investment have only rarely been developed in the economic literature. Notable exceptions are Ito (1980), Kuipers (1981, 1988) and Malinvaud (1980). Kuipers (1988) and Malinvaud (1980) restrict the analysis to economic behaviour in the medium run whereas Ito (1980) and Kuipers (1981) also deal with full substitutability between factors of production as a long-run phenomenon.

Malinvaud (1980) focuses on the relationship between profitability and unemployment. More in particular, the question is analyzed which rate of profits permits a rate of capital accumulation, characterized by neither shortage of capacity nor excess capacity. The time dimension involved in this question necessarily extends the model to be developed beyond the immediate short run. On the other hand, the theory of economic growth with its natural inclination toward the long run, assumes instantaneous adjustment of prices, which Malinvaud considers to be at variance with real world experience. Hence, a medium-term model is developed, which is characterized by the absence of growth, rigid prices and wages in the short run (the unit period) accompanied by competitive adjustments in between two unit periods, strict complementary factors and an exogeneously determined distribution of income. Moreover, investments have only spending effects in the short run, whereas both physical and financial capital accumulation, together with the adjustments in prices and wages, define the dynamic links between two unit periods. Expectations are static expectations. The conventional typology of regimes applies to the equilibria in the short run with the addition that the structural situation of the economy (labour versus capital shortage) has to be accounted for in this respect. From the subsequent study of the dynamic paths in each regime, Malinvaud concludes that only a Keynesian stationary state is stable in the medium run, a conclusion which can be drawn only because of the assumption of a constant real wage rate in a situation of Keynesian unemployment. In a situation of classical unemployment in the short run, downward real wage adjustments in the medium run depress aggregate consumption demand more than that they stimulate employment through increased investments. Hence, a Keynesian stationary state will eventually emerge. In a situation of (repressed) inflation, real wages drift upward by assumption, which makes capacity fall.

Furthermore, rising prices cause a decline in aggregate demand because of the Pigou effect and because of capital decumulation. Finally, the economy will end up in a Keynesian regime, possibly by moving through a classical phase in the first place.

In a similar framework as described above, Kuipers (1988) more explicitly studies the cyclical characteristics of the adjustment paths. In addition, there is a perfectly competitive bond market incorporated into the model to consider portfolio behaviour. Finally, Kuipers follows Witteveen (1956) in his observation that the characteristics of the trade cycle are different because of the structural discrepancies (capital and labour shortage) involved. For that reason, the theoretical explanation of cyclical patterns has to be dependent on these structural characteristics as well. Kuipers concludes that Witteveen's synthesis of over- and underinvestment theories continues to hold if a *dis*equilibrium model is chosen as a frame of reference. However, Witteveen's assessment that the underinvestment theories, on the one hand, and the overinvestment theories, on the other hand, are not fundamentally different in their explanation of the lower turning point, cannot be supported.

The previous two studies have been confined to the analysis of the medium run. Considerations related to the theory of economic growth, in fact the complete substitutability of factors of production (ex post and ex ante), as well as the adjustment of expectations concerning the choice of the optimal production technique have been explicitly taken into account by Ito (1980) and Kuipers (1981). Ito studies capital accumulation in a conventional one-sector neoclassical growth model where the flexibility of the real wage is assumed to be imperfect. As a result, only transactions in the labour market are determined by quantity rationing. Given this constraint, savings behaviour is regime-dependent, which implies, since investments are supply determined in a neo-classical world, that capital accumulation will be regime-dependent. In case, the average propensity to save out of wage income is smaller than out of non-wage income (the Kaldor hypothesis), the time pattern of the disequilibrium system will oscillate around the Walrasian equilibrium, which resembles the existence of a (trade) cycle. On the other hand, if the Kaldor hypothesis is not fulfilled, the economy is stable and will converge toward the Walrasian steady state.

In contrast with Ito (1980), where only labour market transactions are determined by quantity rationing, Kuipers (1981) extends Malinvaud (1980) by supplementing it with a long period. In the long run, the choice of the production technique is considered with respect to the long-run development of price expectations. However, this problem is considered only after that in the medium run existing excess capacity or capacity shortages have been eliminated through price adjustments. Price adjustment in the medium run are a response to fixprice short-run equilibria. In the short and medium run the level of long run expectations is exogenous. Since in that situation, the productive capacity is fully utilized at the end of the medium run, Keynesian unemployment cannot exist in the long run which is defined as a sequence of medium-run periods. This conclusion illustrates that Malinvaud's observation about the inherent convergence towards a Keynesian stationary state in the economy, is heavily determined by the assumed strict complementarity of factors. However, the use of the Marshallian period analysis by Kuipers implies a clear analytical distinction between short- and long-run expectations. In particular, it is unclear how long-run expectations may change *after that* in the medium run full utilization has been achieved, except for reasons not incorporated in the model. Technological developments, for instance, are exogenous and can lead to adjustment of expectations. However, there is no uncertainty concerning the development of technology assumed so that there is no evidence which will lead to adjustment of long-run expectations. Hence, the establishment of the long run as a whole remains rather ambiguous in Kuipers's analysis.

In general, all the conclusions that are derived in the context of the models discussed in this section, depend to a very large extent on the assumptions made. The assumptions were partly needed to simplify the analytics involved, whereas their theoretical implications were only relevant in the second place. For that reason, the conclusions drawn cannot be disentangled from the 'economy' from which they are derived which limits their scope considerably. On a more fundamental level, doubt can be expressed concerning the stability results derived in Malinvaud (1980) and Kuipers (1981, 1988). As Ito (1980) and Van den Heuvel (1983) have argued the conventional conditions for stability are not sufficient if the economy is a 'patched' system. In particular, the fact that stability can be proven for each regime does not imply stability of the 'patched' system as a whole. Hence, subsequent research in the field of disequilibrium growth theory is necessary and should be stimulated given the essentially dynamic character of economic processes.

3.4.2 *Expectations*

Any model that deals with intertemporal considerations has to deal with the consequences of expectations formation. The theories discussed in the previous two sections treat expectations on an *ad hoc* basis, which implies that either simple adaptive mechanisms are incorporated to determine the behaviour of expected prices and wages or that expectations are static expectations. Moreover, expectations concerning the future development of the economic system as a whole, which can be ambiguous in a disequilibrium model, are not considered. In an excellent paper, Neary and Stiglitz (1983) have considered the impact of expectations in disequilibrium models more systematically. In particular, they have analysed the impact of expected intertemporal spill-over effects. Intertemporal spillovers arise in case the expected future constraints affect the characteristics of the equilibria to be established in the current period.

The effect of expected future constraints on the nature of current- period equilibrium are explored in a two-period model of temporary equilibrium with rationing. The model describes the behaviour of households, firms and the government sector with respect to commodities, labour and real balances and analyses the situations in the labour and the commodity market. Optimal household and firm behaviour in the distinguished markets is formulated with respect to current and future prices and real wages, on the one hand, and current and future quantity constraints, on the other. In order to reduce the dimension of the problem only the impact of changes in current period nominal wages W_t and next period commodity prices P_{t+1} are analysed. Furthermore, the intertemporal substitution of leisure is not considered, which implies that the supply of labour is inelastic with respect to P_{t+1} in each period, wheras the particular formalization of the firms' profit maximization problem allows to abstract from the possibility that P_{t+1} influences the demand for labour. In figure 3.3 the notional and effective current-period equilibrium loci of the commodity market and the labour market that can be derived from these assumptions are represented in a $W_t - P_{t+1}$ space (Neary and Stiglitz, 1983, p.208). It is assumed that all markets are expected to clear at notional levels in the second period.

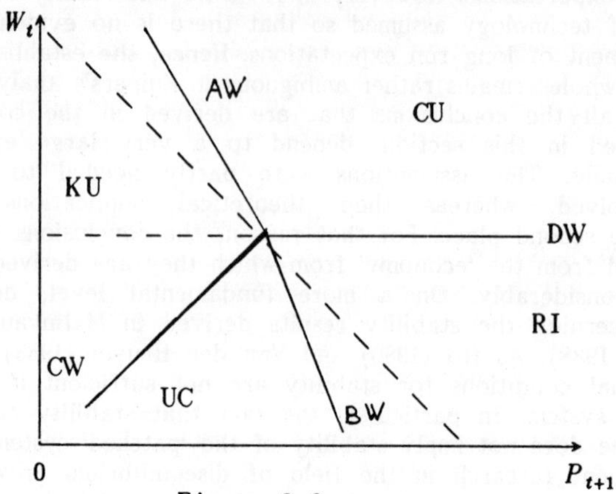

Figure 3.3

Effective (solid lines) and notional (dashed lines) commodity market equilibrium loci for the current period are downward sloping because an increase in P_{t+1} increases current-period demand (the intertemporal substitution effect dominates) which has to be offset by an increase in supply. To enforce the latter, the real wage has to fall, which for a given level of P_t can be brought about by a reduction of W_t. Effective commodity market equilibrium loci (AW and BW) have a steeper slope than notional loci, since with excess supply of labour in the current period (locus AW) the lower effective level of consumer demand implies that the notional equilibrium locus (which reflects the higher unconstrained demand for consumer goods) has to fall in the area of excess commodity supply. A situation of excess demand for labour in the current period (locus BW) implies a constrained and lower level of commodity supply. Hence the notional equilibrium locus (which reflects the higher unconstrained supply of commodities) has to fall in the area of excess commodity demand.

Since there is no intertemporal substitution of leisure and because of the particular formalization of the firms' profit maximization problem, the notional labour market equilibrium locus is only dependent on current-period commodity prices and nominal wages, and thus independent of P_{t+1}. In case firms face a supply constraint in the commodity market, the demand for labour will be decreased. To clear the labour market W_t has to be lower, given P_{t+1}, which implies that the effective labour market equilibrium locus CW will be below the notional labour market equilibrium locus. Furthermore, CW is upward sloping since an increase in P_{t+1} increases current-period consumption demand, which stimulates effective labour demand. To restore equilibrium in the labour market the supply of labour has to rise which calls for an increase in the nominal wage given P_t. Furthermore, a sales constraint in the commodity market implies a higher (forced) level of investments. The end-of-period commodity stock will be higher than in the absence of a sales constraint in the current period. As BW is characterized by the absence of a sales constraint, the level of investment at locus CW is higher than at locus BW. Since a higher level of investment implies a higher level of supply in the next period, the level of P_{t+1} has to be lower in order to restore commodity market equilibrium in the next period (remember that the analysis assumes Walrasian expectations). Hence the locus CW lies to the left of the locus BW. In between the two loci the regime of underconsumption can be found. Finally, a situation of excess commodity demand in the current period does not affect the equilibrium in the labour market DW since the supply of labour is inelastic with respect to P_{t+1}.

Next, it is shown that the picture changes in a situation where quantity constraints are to be expected in the markets in the second period. To illustrate the implications, Neary and Stiglitz confine the analysis to the impact on the commodity market equilibrium loci in situations of excess supply of current period labour. Hence, only the implications for the borderline between classical and Keynesian unemployment AW are considered. With excess supply of labour expected in the second period, households expect a decline in real wealth which depresses current-period consumption demand. To maintain equilibrium, commodity supply has to fall which calls for a higher real wage level, given P_{t+1}. Hence the notional commodity market equilibrium locus, given an expected supply of labour in the second period, lies to the right of the notional commodity market equilibrium locus with equilibrium in the labour market expected in the second period. This shift to the right is indicated in figure 3.4 as a rightward shift of the dashed lines. In this respect, the dashed curve to the left in figure 3.4 coincides with the notional commodity market equilibrium locus of figure 3.3. In a situation of expected Keynesian unemployment, the commodity market displays excess supply in the second period as well, however only in case the second-period price exceed a minimum level P_{t+1}^{min}, which indicates a minimum profitability constraint. This expected excess supply in the second period stimulates firms to increase current-period supply, thereby enlarging the region of excess supply in the current period. In figure 3.4 this enlargement causes the commodity market equilibrium locus given an expected excess supply of labour to pivot further to the right around the intersection point of this locus and the vertical line P_{t+1}^{min}. On the other hand, a situation of expected classical unemployment in the next period is characterized by expected excess commodity demand in the next period, however only below a second-period commodity price level P_{t+1}^{max}. Above P_{t+1}^{max} it is expected that a situation of excess demand cannot exist. A situation of expected excess commodity demand encourages firms to transfer commodities to the second period, thereby cutting supply in the current period. Hence, in a situation of expected excess commodity demand, the commodity market equilibrium locus, given the expected excess supply of labour, pivots to the left, around the intersection point of the commodity market equilibrium locus, given an expected excess supply of labour, on the one hand, and the vertical line P_{t+1}^{max}, on the other. Finally, effective current period commodity market equilibrium loci with expected classical unemployment AWCU2 on the one hand, and with expected Keynesian unemployment AWKU2, on the other hand, are steeper than notional loci for reasons explained earlier (see figure 3.3). The horizontal curve in figure 3.4 depicts the labour market equilibrium locus.

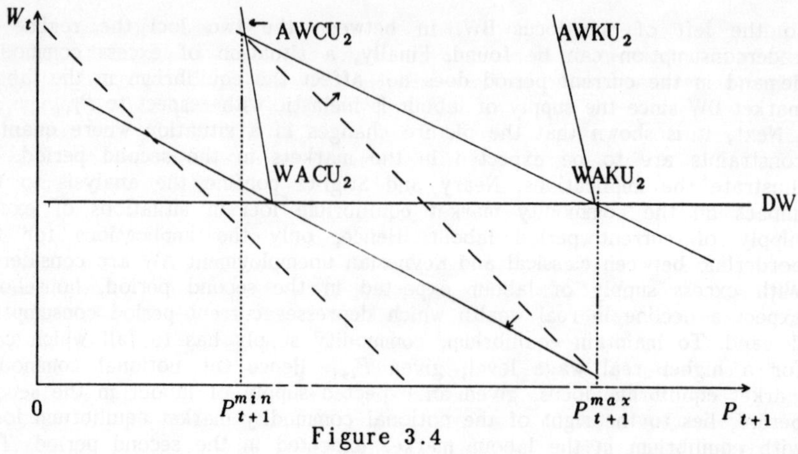

Figure 3.4

Figure 3.4 permits the following conclusions. In the first place, the competitive price vector is not unique but dependent on the constraints expected in the second period. In the second place, there exists a region (between AWCU2 and AWKU2) where effective equilibria are not uniquely determined by the prevailing wage–price combination, but are dependent on the set of expectations as well. In the third place, expectations imply a bootstrap effect since the region of current period Keynesian unemployment is considerably enlarged if Keynesian unemployment is expected to prevail tomorrow. A similar argument applies in a situation of expected classical unemployment.

In the analysis above, expectations concerning future constraints are arbitrary expectations. To relieve this arbitrariness, Neary and Stiglitz consider situations in which the expected future constraints come true (rational constraint expectations). It is shown that the bootstrap property continues to hold. If Keynesian unemployment is rationally expected tomorrow it is more likely to occur today, since firms will increase current–period supply in case excess commodity supply is rationally expected to prevail tomorrow as well. Hence, the region of current period excess supply expands. Furthermore, it can be shown that in a situation of Keynesian unemployment in the current period, the employment multiplier is greater with rational constraint expectations (KU2) than with arbitrary expectations of Keynesian unemployment or Walrasian equilibrium tomorrow (Neary and Stiglitz, 1983, pp. 221–224) which emphasizes the observation that the policy conclusions drawn by the advocates of the REH approach do not depend on the rationality of behaviour of agents, but rather on the assumed flexibility of prices and the validity of the efficient market hypothesis.

3.5 Conclusions

In this survey we have chosen an analytical approach to present the main characteristics of fixprice disequilibrium theory. In doing so, it is easy to focus on the large number of more or less arbitrary assumptions necessary mainly because of the analytical complexity of the analysis. In general, the desire for generality and completeness has stressed the limitations of the non–Walrasian approach. Nevertheless, on a conceptional level disequilibrium theory has much appeal and has enriched economic analysis with new arguments and methods to study the adjustment processes toward equilibria and the equilibria themselves. Moreover, the main argument continues to hold. In case the markets in the economy are characterized by imperfections there is not necessarily a tendency toward the establishment of a Walrasian equilibrium to be perceived in the economy. Note that it does not have to be assumed that prices are rigid. The analyses presented in sections 3.3 and 3.4.1 have illustrated that sticky prices are sufficient for the justification of the main conclusions. Of equal importance is the observation by Neary and Stiglitz presented in section 3.4.2 that non–Walrasian equilibria do not originate from irrational behaviour or expectations formation, which emphasizes the importance of the perfect market assumption in the flexprice models of economic fluctuations.

Ironically, the weakness of the approach is to be found in the field of microfoundations. The informational requirements needed for the establishment of non–Walrasian equilibria even exceed those in flexprice models so that markets, although cleared by quantity rationing, need to be highly efficient. On the other hand, despite the assumed capacity of information dissemination in the economy, agents are only allowed to trade on a market–by–market basis and cannot signal demand packages concerning more than one market at the same time. Finally, the stickiness in prices and real wages does not originate from the behaviour of individuals but is clearly *ad hoc* which is probably the main theoretical objection to the fixprice assumption. In order to relieve this objection, a by now comprehensive literature about the incorporation of imperfect competition in disequilibrium theory has been developed. We will review this literature in the following chapter.

Notes

1. Section 3.2 is based on Benassy (1987).

2. In my opinion, Drazen (1980) misses the main argument since with stochastic manipulable rationing rules it is assumed that the individual cannot manipulate the aggregate disequilibrium signal. Hence, it is impossible to break one's restriction (Drazen, 1980, p. 289).

3. In this respect, the virtual price approach developed by Neary and Roberts (1980) is an interesting alternative framework.

4. Korliras (1984) and Miller (1982) have extended the analysis by considering a non–clearing bond market, which increases the complexity of the analysis considerably since with 3 non–clearing markets the model incorporates 27 alternative equilibrium situations. On the other hand, Knoester (1979 and 1984) has considered the impact of a non–clearing money market (the buffer stock approach to monetary economics).

5. The analytical framework is similar to Van der Ploeg (1987).

6. For an explicit analysis of inventory dynamics see Honkapohja and Ito 1980.

7. Böhm (1978) makes a similar assumption [Böhm (1978), p. 193].

8. Böhm (1978) and Honkapohja (1979) make similar assumptions.

9. Persson and Svensson (1983) have applied the analysis of future constraint expectations to open economies.

4 Trade without an auctioneer and economic fluctuations

4.1 Introduction

In the preceding two chapters, alternative explanations of fluctuations in output and employment have been investigated. Flexprice and fixprice methods have been distinguished with respect to the rationing mechanism imposed. On the other hand, there are many similarities between the two methods. Both methods preserve the fundamental principles of general equilibrium theory. All goods are homogeneous, there is a large number of agents, prices are given to the individual agent, individuals optimize and markets are auction markets.

In this chapter we will discuss some recent developments in economic theory, which aim at a theoretically sound explanation of observed variations in economic activity and real wages. All analyses look away from the presence of an auctioneer who reconciles demand and supply in the markets: the consequences for output and employment levels are analysed in an economy, which in the absence of an auctioneer is characterized by imperfect and/or asymmetric information. Following Roberts (1987), three major lines of research can be distinguished. In the first place, a large number of articles have been published that focus on a microfoundation of the rigidities in prices and wages. Several explanations of real wage rigidity will be reviewed in section 2, whereas alternative approaches to commodity price rigidity will be dealt with in section 3. The consequences of optimal real wage and price stickiness in the context of a macroeconomic model will be analysed in section 4. In the second place, we will touch upon the work on conjectural Keynesian equilibria (e.g. Hahn, 1977, 1978), which allows for flexible prices, endogenous price determination and binding quantity constraints in the context of a general equilibrium model. In the third place, we will discuss the merits of the theory of non-cooperative behaviour as a starting point of the analysis of variations in output and employment. This line of work focuses on the possibility of macroeconomic coordination failures. A macroeconomic coordination failure is defined as a situation where the economy 'can get stuck at an inefficient equilibrium with a low level of "economic activity," even though a better equilibrium exists' (Cooper and John, 1988, p. 448). Macroeconomic coordination failures may arise in the context of search processes or imperfect competition. In section 5 we will review this approach. Finally, section 6 concludes this chapter with some final observations.

4.2 Real wage rigidities

4.2.1 *Implicit contract theory*

One of the main impulses to the development of modern macroeconomic theory has been the discomfort with the classical analysis of labour market phenomena, which is considered to be at variance with the 'stylized' facts in labour markets. These 'facts' indicate that over the 'typical' business cycle money wages tend to fluctuate less than total employment and that there is a strong contribution to lay-offs (instead of quits) to unemployment. Since the mid-seventies a new theoretical approach has tried to address the observed phenomena through the introduction of an insurance element in labour market decisions (excellent surveys of the literature are Azariadis, 1979, Hart, 1983, Rosen, 1985, and Stiglitz, 1986). In (implicit) contract theory the employment relationship is viewed as a long-term attachment. Workers are taken to be more risk averse than firms with respect to fluctuations in income across states of nature, since they do not have likewise possibilities to compensate these losses through portfolio management. External insurance is blocked because of monitoring problems. Hence, firms are the natural trading partners to negotiate income risks in addition to labour services. As a result, real wages do not only coordinate labour decisions but reflect an insurance component as well, which implies that real wages no longer equalize the marginal rate of transformation and the marginal rate of substitution between consumption and leisure. Because of the insurance element the decision concerning wages is separated from the employment decision, which offers the opportunity to analyse the stylized facts above in a theoretically consistent way.

To illustrate these arguments, consider the following contract model, which can be derived from Azariadis (1975) (see also Cooper, 1987). In an economy with risk-neutral firms and risk-averse workers, real wages and employment are determined through contracts. It is assumed that work sharing is impossible and that firms do not pay severance payments to laid-off workers. Firms maximize profits across states. Suppose, only two states can be realized, each with a probability of occurrence of one half. In that situation, expected firm profits across states can be denoted by equation [4.1].

$$\mathbf{E}prf = \frac{1}{2}\{p^{+}f(l^{+}) - w^{+}l^{+} + p^{-}f(l^{-}) - w^{-}l^{-}\} \qquad [4.1]$$

where a superscript + denotes a favourable state and a superscript − denotes a bad state. In this respect, p is the real price of output in terms of a numeraire. The production function $f(l)$ is assumed to be strictly concave.

Similarly, w stands for the real wage. Workers derive utility from consumables and finance their purchases out of labour income or out of an unemployment allowance obtained from the government. Workers will only sign contracts if the feasibility condition [4.2] is fulfilled.

$$\frac{1}{2}\left\{(l^{+}/\tau_1)U(w^{+}) + (1 - l^{+}/\tau_1)U(d) + (l^{-}/\tau_1)U(w^{-}) + (1 - l^{-}/\tau_1)U(d)\right\}$$
$$\geq \bar{U} \qquad [4.2]$$

where τ_1 denotes labour time per worker, U utility, l employment, d the unemployment allowance and $\bar{U}$ the reservation level of utility. The feasibility condition [4.2] will always be met with equality, since otherwise firms are able to reduce wage offers without any consequence for the employment decision of workers. The optimal contract maximizes [4.1] subject to [4.2], by choosing optimal levels of w^{+}, l^{+}, w^{-}, l^{-}. An optimal contract has to satisfy the following two conditions.

$$U'(w^{+}) = U'(w^{-}) \qquad [4.3]$$

$$pf'(l) = w - \frac{U(w) - U(d)}{U'(w)} \qquad [4.4]$$

$$p = p^{+}, p^{-}; l = l^{+}, l^{-}; w = w^{+}, w^{-}$$

Equation [4.3] is the condition for optimal risk sharing. The marginal utility of income is equalized across states. An employed worker will receive equal pay in good and in bad states. Hence, real wages are completely rigid. Equation [4.4] shows that real wages have a fixed insurance component and a state dependent productivity component. Workers are insured against fluctuations in the real wage rate. Since real wages are completely rigid, the right hand side of equation [4.4] has a fixed value. Because of $p^{+} \geq p^{-}$, on the one hand, and decreasing marginal returns, on the other hand, it can be concluded that employment is lower in the bad state than in the good state. Hence, in this situation the employment risk is completely passed on to the workers. However, alternative solutions are possible as well. To see this, we substitute $p = p(st)$ and $l = \Theta(st)\tau_1$ in equation [4.4]. Here, st denotes a particular state drawn from a given distribution of possible states and $\Theta(.)$ the employment risk that is passed on to workers as a function of states. In case $\Theta(st) = 1$ for all possible states, workers are completely insured against fluctuations in income and employment. Note that $\Theta(st)$ is manipulable to a firm. Furthermore, there exists a negative relationship between Θ and w. Consider the following illustration. With $l = \Theta(st)\tau_1$ the feasibility condition [4.2] can be written as

$$\mathrm{E}\left\{\Theta(st)U(w(st)) + (1 - \Theta(st))U(d)\right\} \geq \bar{U} \qquad [4.2a]$$

Given st, $\bar{U} \geq U(d)$, since otherwise no one will work. Furthermore, $w \geq d$, since otherwise no worker will sign a contract. Starting from an equilibrium situation, it can be observed that in case Θ is increased given st, the left hand side of equation [4.2a] will exceed the right hand side. Under competitive conditions this implies that wages will be lowered. At the expense of higher real wages in all states, firms can manipulate the level of Θ so as to gain lay-off possibilities in adverse states. Workers will not object to these strategies as long as the firm is willing to pay more (in terms of higher wages and by taking account of condition [4.4]) to reduce employment in adverse states than workers require as a compensation (by taking account of condition [4.2*a*] for the extra employment risk). Hence, a contract with unemployment in adverse states can be preferred to a contract with full employment in all states by all agents participating in the contract.

An important argument against contract models as above has been the observation that the optimal contract results in higher employment in bad states than the corresponding competitive solutions (*e.g* Cooper, 1987, and Frank, 1986). In a situation of unemployment, the level of employment in a *competitive* labour market l_s will be determined from

$$p(st)f'(l_s(st)) = d \qquad [4.5]$$

On the other hand, the level of employment in a *contract* model $l(st)$ follows from equation [4.4] with $p = p(st)$ and $l = l(st)$. Subtraction of equation [4.5] from equation [4.4] yields equation [4.6].

$$p(st)f'(l(st)) - p(st)f'(l_s(st)) = w - d - \frac{U(w) - U(d)}{U'(w)} \qquad [4.6]$$

The employment level in the contract model will exceed the employment level in a competitive labour market in case

$$U'(w) < \frac{U(w) - U(d)}{w - d} \qquad [4.7]$$

Condition [4.7] will be satisfied if workers are risk-averse, since in that situation utility functions are strictly concave. Hence, the contract model does not provide a convincing explanation for equilibria with inefficiently high levels of unemployment. In order to provide a more satisfactory explanation for the establishment of these levels of unemployment, economic theory has proceeded by putting restrictions on the availability of information. The informational requirements of contract models are very high indeed. All agents must be able to observe without costs, the complete distribution of states *ex ante* as well as the particular realization of some state *ex post*. In contract models with asymmetric information (e.g. Azariadis, 1983, Azariadis and Stiglitz, 1983, Grossman and Hart, 1983), it is assumed that only firms can observe the realization of a particular state *ex post*, whereas workers know that firms possess this superior information. The analyses focus on the characteristics of the contracts that are implementable under these conditions. In order to develop the argument, consider figure 4.1.

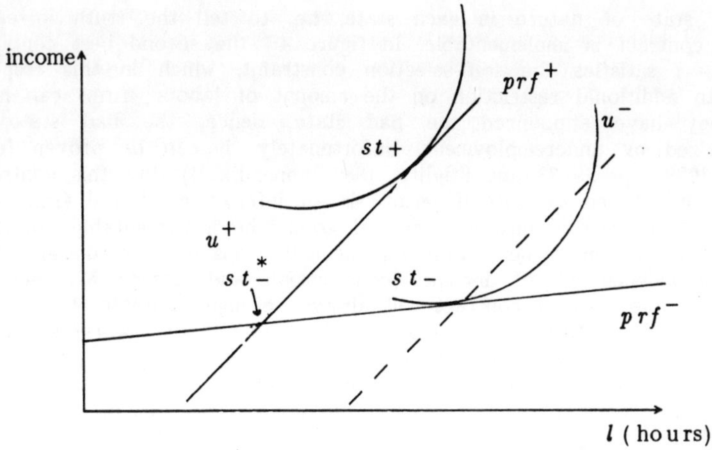

Figure 4.1

In figure 4.1, the following situation is depicted. Risk-neutral firms maximize expected profits across two equally possible states by choosing optimally the level of real wages and the level of working hours per worker in each state. Again the favourable state is denoted with a superscript +, the bad state with a superscript −. Variations in employment show up as variations in working hours in this context (work sharing). Risk-averse workers, on the other hand, derive a positive utility from income and leisure in each state. The optimal contract maximizes expected profits subject to the workers' feasibility condition, in each state. Necessary conditions for the existence of the optimal contract are the equality of the marginal utilities of income across states, on the one hand, and the equality of marginal rates of transformation and substitution across states, on the other hand. The marginal utility of substitution in each state is equal to the slope of the indifference curve in each state in figure 4.1. The slopes of the iso-profit curves are equal to the marginal rates of transformation across states. In figure 4.1, which is with some minor adaptations taken from Stiglitz (1986), the optimal contract is shown as the combination (*st*+, *st*−), where the firm's iso-profit curve and the worker's iso-utility curve are tangent in each state. Note that we have assumed a non-linear technology i.e. the number of workers is constant and every possible choice of working hours is implementable in the production process. Furthermore, profits in the good state are positive, whereas in the bad state they are negative, since in the favourable state firms obtain a positive profit (i.e. a negative wage income) even in a situation where working hours are reduced to zero. In the bad state profits are negative in that situation. The interesting question in this context is whether the optimal contract will be implementable in a situation of asymmetric information as defined above. The answer has to be in the negative. Firms will always have an incentive to announce the bad state, since in doing so they move to a higher iso-profit curve in case the favourable state will be perceived *ex post*. Hence, it pays firms to cheat. However, since workers know that firms will have and exploit superior information, the optimal contract cannot be realized. To put it differently, the optimal contract is not incentive-compatible: it does not satisfy self-selection or truth-telling constraints. Only if firms have no incentive to misrepresent the true state of nature in each state, i.e. to tell the truth in each state, a contract is implementable. In figure 4.1 the second best contract (*st*+, *st*–) satisfies the self-selection constraint, which in this respect implies an additional restriction on the amount of labour, firms can hire after they have announced the bad state. Hence, the bad state is characterized by underemployment. Unfortunately, it can be proven (*e.g.* Cooper, 1986, pp. 29–33 and Stiglitz, 1986, appendix B) that this contract will only be chosen *ex ante* if leisure is an inferior good and firms are risk-neutral. In case leisure is a normal good, the implementable contract will display overemployment with risk-neutral firms. If the demand for leisure is independent of income (consumption and leisure are perfect substitutes), the optimal contract will always be implementable. Under the assumption that firms are more risk-averse than workers, also underemployment becomes a possibility if leisure is a normal good (e.g. Stiglitz, 1986, pp.19–20). However, this assumption is almost nonsensical in a world with more or less efficient capital markets. Hence, it can be concluded that only under very restrictive and unrealistic assumptions implicit contract theory succeeds in providing an explanation for the mutual establishment of real wage rigidity and underemployment.

An additional line of criticism focuses on the enforceability of contracts. So far, it has been assumed that contracts are binding. However, what mechanisms force participants to stick to an agreement that may prove to be a second best solution *ex post*? Workers can easily break the contract in favourable states, whereas firms can exert downward pressure on wages in bad states by referring to the un(under)employment pool. In the literature, the impact of reputation mechanisms has been proposed as a solution to the enforcement problem (e.g. Holstrom, 1983). Analytically, the incorporation of the future consequences of current behaviour implies the introduction of multi-period contracts and bonding systems (e.g. Hall and Lazear, 1984, and Ioannides and Pissaridis, 1983), which supports the view that implicit contracts 'represent perfect equilibrium (wage, employment) strategies in a repeated game between employers and employees' (Stiglitz, 1986, p.32, see also Shaked and Sutton, 1984, for a similar approach). However, a problem with this approach is that although it may be possible to analyse the consequences of reputation effects, it is impossible to endogenize the size of these effects. To conclude, literature has not yet provided an unambiguous answer to the question whether reputation effects can enforce the fulfilment of implicit contracts. All in all, we believe that contract theory has not produced robust results, neither with respect to the determination of real wages nor with respect to the explanation of under- or unemployment. In the next section we will present an alternative approach to the explanation of real wage rigidity and unemployment, the efficiency wage theory.

4.2.2 *Efficiency wage theory*

Efficiency wage models are founded on the hypothesis that firms have imperfect information about the performance of workers on the job. However, firms perceive that the on-the-job performance can be improved by enlarging the difference between the real firm wages and incentives that can be obtained elsewhere in the economy. Labour productivity is assumed to increase with the real relative wage paid (see Summers, 1988, for interesting similarities between efficiency wage models and insider-outsider models of wage determination, e.g. Lindbeck and Snower, 1986). As real wage cuts harm productivity, cutting real wages may raise labour costs, thus providing firms with an argument to resist real wage cuts in the presence of unemployment. In this section, we will first develop the basic structure of the 'efficiency wage models of unemployment' (Yellen, 1984, Stiglitz, 1987, and Akerlof and Yellen, 1986, are good surveys of the main arguments in this area). Next, we discuss several microfoundations of the efficiency wage model and describe the main implications in this respect.

According to the efficiency wage hypothesis[1] real wage cuts may harm productivity. Let e denote the effort per worker and q the firm's commodity output, then the short-run production function implied by the efficiency wage hypothesis, is given by

$$q = f(e(w)l) \qquad [4.8]$$

Consider an economy with identical, perfectly competitive firms (in the commodity market). Each firm has a production function as [4.8] above. Maximizing real firm profits ($f(e(w)l) - wl$) gives the following first order conditions.

$$f'(e(w)l)e(w) - w = 0 \qquad [4.9]$$

$$l(f'(c(w)l)e'(w) - 1) = 0 \qquad [4.10]$$

Conditions [4.9] and [4.10] are fulfilled if firms offer a wage w^*, which satisfies the condition that the elasticity of effort with respect to the wage equals unity ($e'(w)w/e(w) = 1$). This wage w^* is known as the efficiency wage and minimizes labour cost per efficiency unit (Solow, 1979). Labour is hired up to the point where its marginal product equals the real wage w^* ([4.9]). As long as w^* exceeds the workers' reservation wage and aggregate demand for labour falls short of supply there will be unemployment in the economy. Real wage reductions are not considered by firms because the implied reduction of the productivity of employees already on the job will exceed the gain from lower wages. In that situation, cutting wages raises the costs of labour. A wage-productivity curve ($e(w)$) as depicted in figure 4.2 achieves this result. Here, the specific shape of the wage-productivity curve will not be investigated in any detail (see Stiglitz, 1987, for a justification).

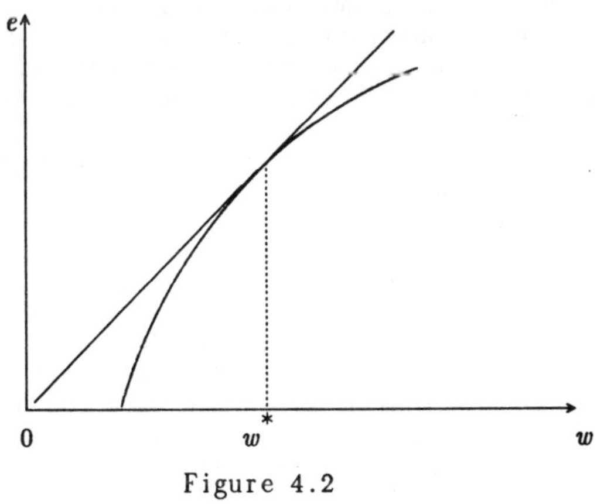

Figure 4.2

The efficiency wage model above can be extended in order to develop more explicit behavioural foundations of the basic relationships. In the shirking model (Shapiro and Stiglitz, 1984), efficiency wages are paid because of imperfect monitoring possibilities of workers' on-the-job performance. To induce its workers not to shirk, a firm is prepared to pay more than the going wage, which creates a penalty to job loss (cheat-threat). However, if it pays one firm to raise its wage, it is profitable to all. Consequently, the incentive not to shirk disappears. But as all firms raise wages, the aggregate demand for labour decreases and unemployment arises. The emergence of unemployment provides an individual with an incentive not to shirk. The equilibrium rate of unemployment just offsets the workers' marginal temptation to shirk rather than to work. Hence, there will be noshirking in the economy. Note that unemployment in the shirking model does not result from lay-offs because of shirking but from too high real wages. The shirking model has been criticized because more ingenious contracts with seniority schemes, bonding systems or employment fees (e.g. Eaton and White, 1982) are able to lower the wage to market clearing levels. However, in the context of this last set of models, apart from the complexity, the problem of moral hazard may render impossible the enforceability of these ingenious contracts. Hence, the arguments against the shirking model have not proven to be very convincing. In the labour turnover model (e.g. Salop, 1979), firms offer wages in excess of market clearing to induce workers to be more reluctant to quit, so that labour turnover is reduced. Labour turnover can be particularly costly if the firm invests in on-the-job training. Again, if all firms are identical, equilibrium is characterized by a real wage rate in excess of the market clearing rate with positive unemployment to diminish labour turnover. However, it has been observed that seniority wage schemes may effectively lower real wages, by taking account of the differences of skill. The moral hazard problem is less serious in this context, since wage profiles, training facilities and efforts can be assessed unambiguously and contracted explicitly between workers and firms. In the adverse selection approach (e.g. Weiss, 1980), a positive relationship is assumed between the quality of the worker and his reservation wage. Firms with higher wages will attract more able workers. On the other hand, the willingness of an individual to work for less than the going wage will strengthen the firms' expectation that he is a lemon. Therefore, firms will optimally turn away applicants offering to work for less than the efficiency wage. Finally, in the sociological models of efficiency wages (e.g. Akerlof, 1982), wages higher than market clearing are paid to induce loyalty to the firm. Each worker's effort depends on the work conventions and norms of the group he participates in. The firm may be able to raise group work norms and average effort by paying workers in excess of the minimum required.

Efficiency wage theory opens the possibility to analyse a number of characteristics of modern labour markets. In the first place, the existence of a dual labour market can be explained since efficiency wage considerations may be important in some productive sectors but not in others (e.g. Bulow and Summers, 1986). In the second place, a stable prior distribution of wage offers which is assumed *ad hoc* in search models, can follow from different wage-productivity relationships in different sectors. However, empirical evidence (e.g. Katz, 1986, and Krueger and Summers, 1988) suggests that, although there is a substantial dispersion in real wages across industries, it is rather ambiguous in as far as these wage differences can be attributed to unobserved quality differences as is stressed by efficiency wage theories. In the third place, efficiency wage models are able to explain unemployment rates that exceed the competitive natural rate. Furthermore, these models are able to predict real wage stickiness in the face of real productivity shocks and, hence, the existence of unemployment. However, as an independent explanation of business cycle fluctuations efficiency wage models are inadequate, since cycles may be demand–determined and *nominal* shocks cannot be analysed. To enable the study of demand shocks, an explanation of commodity price stickiness has to be considered as well. In the next section, alternative explanations of price rigidities are described.

4.3 Commodity price rigidities

4.3.1 *Stocks*

The existence of storage possibilities can give rise to sticky prices, because firms can mitigate the impact of demand shocks by transferring commodities to the future. As such, inventories serve as a buffer to smooth production over the cycle. Additionally, inventories may serve as built–in stabilizers of the economy since their presence allows firms to benefit from intertemporal fluctuations in factor prices. With regard to this last characteristic, evidence suggests that stocks are highly volatile and move procyclical, which suggests that the stabilizing impact of stocks cannot be observed. On the other hand, the first characteristic has been studied rather extensively in recent years (e.g. Amihud and Mendelson, 1983, Blinder, 1982, 1985, Reagan, 1982, and Reagan and Weitzman, 1982). The basic argument, as put forward by Reagan and Weitzman (1982), is the following. Consider a competitive firm, which faces a production–lag of one period in the production of storable output, unit production costs in competitive factor markets, constant marginal productivity and constant returns to scale. The production decision has to be taken with respect to next period demand conditions which are uncertain. Reagan and Weitzman show that a rational expectations equilibrium can be established in the commodity market if the production and sales decisions taken by identical firms are such that the subjective distribution of future prices is consistent with the true distribution of prices. No agent will have the desire to change its choice in that situation. The existence of an equilibrium can be illustrated with the following arguments. In case of a tempory fall of the current–period commodity price below the current–period production costs, firms will choose to store all goods since in that situation the gain from not producing is larger than the loss from not selling. On the assumption that prices approach infinity if supply approaches zero, current–period commodity prices will at least equal production costs. On the other hand, if commodity prices temporarily exceed production costs in the current period, firms will choose to sell all available stock since selling now, in combination with producing now, is more profitable than selling stocks in the future. Hence, the commodity price equals the maximum of unit production costs and the price that could be obtained if the complete stock is sold out in the current period. However with a production lag, inventory levels have to be determined before commodity prices are available. In that situation, it can be argued that the optimal size of the stock just equalizes the maximum of the discounted values of future prices, as above determined, and current period production costs (Reagan and Weitzman, 1982, pp. 417 – 419). An immediate implication of this result is that price adjustments are asymmetric since the commodity supply curve is backward–L–shaped (see also Amihud and Mendelson, 1983). Deficient demand shocks are followed by quantity adjustments, whereas prices are rigid. Favourable shocks are reacted upon with price adjustments. It can be shown that in the analysis above, the lag structure in production and the characteristics of the commodities are particularly important for the conclusions obtained. Moreover, the analysis breaks down in case of a non–linear technology. Blinder (1982) develops a more general framework in order to study the impact of stocks on price and quantity adjustments. He concludes that, given the shape of the marginal revenue and marginal costs schedules, with storable commodities both price and quantity adjustments (in production) are smaller if demand shocks are less persistent, on the one hand, and if output is more storable (e.g. because of lower storage costs), on the other hand. In general, the analyses of inventory behaviour can be criticized on the following arguments. In the first place, with lump sum inventory costs, production does not respond to fluctuations in demand. Hence, prices are rigid but there is no link between output and demand fluctuations. On the other hand, with increasing inventory costs, prices and sales will respond to demand fluctuations, but employment will not. The interplay between demand and employment adjustments is missing in inventory models. In the second place, inventory models are homogeneous of degree zero with respect to nominal shocks. If all prices (and costs) double nothing happens, which implies that only real rigidities can be explained.

4.3.2 *Menu costs and near–rational behaviour*

The menu costs approach (e.g. Mankiw, 1985, Ball and Romer, 1987a) and the near–rational behaviour approach (Akerlof and Yellen, 1985a) explicitly address the possibility of nominal rigidities as a response to shocks in demand. Both theories argue that sticky prices can be privately efficient and socially inefficient at the same time. On the one hand, the existence of small costs to changing prices (e.g. reprinting catalogs or informing salesmen) can make these changes unprofitable. On the other hand, it can be shown that under some conditions rules of thumb (near–rational behaviour) produce, results which are privately efficient but socially inefficient. The impact of menu costs can be illustrated with the help of the following diagram (Mankiw, 1985, p. 532). It is assumed that firms face a linear downward sloping demand schedule and constant real average total production costs. Furthermore, firm prices as well as nominal average total production costs positively depend on the level of a nominal scale variable (aggregate demand, the general price level or the money stock). Real prices and average total production costs (k) are invariant to a (correctly perceived) change in the level of this scale variable, which implies that the profit maximizing level of the firm's output is invariant to this change as well. Commodities are perishable, which implies that production equals sales. What will be the impact of an adverse demand shock in this framework?

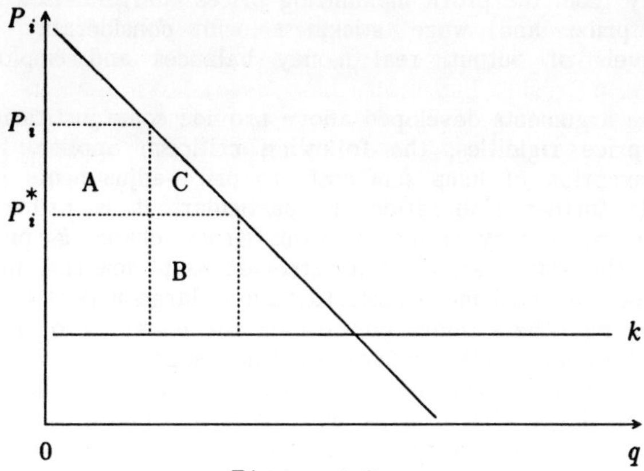

Figure 4.3

Mankiw argues that in case a nominal shock is correctly perceived, its impact is neutral since all prices (including average production costs) are affected equiproportionally. On the other hand, if *aggregate* demand expectations appear to be too optimistic, the observed firm (or local) price P_i will be above the firm's profit maximizing price P_i^* ($P_i = P_i^* (x^e/x)$ where x^e and x denote the expected and the observed level of the nominal scale variable, respectively). The profit maximizing price equals the commodity price that would have been set, had the demand shock been perceived correctly. Since $x^e > x$, the situation illustrates an adverse demand shock. In that case (see figure **4.3**), the loss in profits (the producer's loss) is equal to the surface B minus the surface A. Total welfare on the other hand, decreases by the surface B plus the surface C, where B + C > B – A. In case B + C > *mct* > B – A, where *mct* denotes the menu costs to price changes, it is an optimal policy of the firm not to adjust its price *ex post* although it is socially profitable to do so. Hence, prices can be rigid in the presence of adverse demand shocks. In addition, Mankiw illustrates that in case favourable demand shocks are followed by price adjustments *ex post* social welfare may be reduced, which implies that the welfare properties of the pricing behaviour of firms are asymmetric (ibid. p. 534).

The concept of near-rational behaviour can be used to provide a better microfoundation of the menu costs argument above. By the envelope theorem (Varian, 1984, pp. 327 – 329) it can be shown that, since optimal choice implies indifference at the margin, an agent who is inert to a shock makes an error which is of first order (proportional) and suffers a loss only proportional to the squared deviation of the error (second order). However, on an economy wide scale the consequences of these errors are of first order. In a situation where first-order consequences are relatively large compared to the second-order consequences, it can be argued that only small deviations from optimal choices have a large impact on the economy. Relatively small menu costs result in relatively large fluctuations in output and employment. Akerlof and Yellen (1985a) provide several examples where first-order errors are large in comparison with second-order errors. Particularly if markets are characterized by monopolistic competition, inertial behaviour has only small consequences for the profits of near-rational agents, since sales do not fall excessively as prices depart only marginally from the profit maximizing prices charged elsewhere. On the other hand, price and wage stickiness will considerably affect the equilibrium levels of output, real money balances and employment (see section 4.4.2).

Although, the arguments developed above provide some justification for the existence of price rigidities, the following criticism applies. In the first place, the assumption of lump sum costs to price adjustments is rather *ad hoc* and needs further elaboration. In particular, it is rather ambiguous whether menu costs may withhold firms from changing prices if the fluctuations in the state variable are perceived as permanent. In the second place, the scope for small menu costs to have a large impact on output and employment among others things depends on the elasticity of labour supply (Blanchard and Kyotaki, 1987, p.664). Evidence suggests that this elasticity is generally very low. Indeed, menu costs alone do not provide a convincing explanation for large fluctuations in quantities unless the analysis is supplemented with additional real wage rigidities (see section 4.4). In the third place, the private costs from holding a price different from its optimal market clearing level are only of second order in a situation where commodity market equilibrium served as a starting point. In the fourth place, since it is just another application of the envelope theorem the near-rationality concept does not make clear why firms will choose prices to be rigid in an situation where they do not maximize profits with respect to prices but with respect to quantities instead. For instance in a framework where firms behave as Cournot-Nash maximizers the near-rationality concept would imply that errors in optimal quantity adjustments are of a second order of magnitude. As a result, quantities may be rigid instead of prices.

4.3.3 *Imperfect information*

The connection between imperfect information and imperfect competition has been recognized long ago (e.g. Scitovsky, 1950, and Arrow, 1959). The first author, who formally deals with the consequences of incomplete information is Stigler (1961). His analysis focuses on the dispersion of prices as a manifestation of consumer ignorance about current price quotations. Households know the objective distribution of prices but they have to search for low-price firms. If search is costly, consumers limit their search activity. The degree of price dispersion then depends on the firms' cost functions. If firms have identical costs, the equilibrium has a unique market price, otherwise there will be some dispersion of market prices in equilibrium. Rothschild (1973) has argued that in Stigler's model the variety of price *offers* is not explained from the optimizing behaviour of the firms on the markets. Furthermore, if search activity reduces price variability, if it is successful, it is not needed. There is a free rider problem in this context. If I know that everyone else will reduce the variability in price, by doing a lot of comparative shopping there is no need for me to do any comparative shopping myself. With every subject reasoning in this way, the market will support more variability. On the other hand, if households take decisions under conditions of incomplete information firms possess monopoly power. A firm will not lose all its customers if it raises its price, nor will it gain the whole market instantly, if it cuts its price. In fact, Rothschild has shown that in Stigler's model only the monopoly price is sustainable in a situation where all households have positive search costs. Several economists have investigated the implications of this property for the firms' optimal pricing policy and the characteristics of market equilibrium. Phelps and

Winter (1970) consider the firm to be a monopolist in the short run but a perfect competitor in the long run. This asymmetry emerges as a result of the increasing diffusion of information on price differentials over time through markets. An individual firm cannot set its price permanently above or below the going market price. In equilibrium, there is no net in– or outflow of consumers for every firm, so each firm perceives its price to equal the prices charged elsewhere in the market. Because of imperfect information this market equilibrium is neither a competitive nor a monopolistic equilibrium. Phelps and Winter argue that the resulting market price is below the monopoly price but above the competitive, so that compared to a competitive equilibrium situation there will be some excess capacity. Fisher's (1972) analysis does end up in a competitive equilibrium, but this result is mainly due to the fact that he assumes firms to be price takers. However, competitive firm behaviour in a world with not completely informed consumers can be considered suboptimal. In Diamond's (1971) analysis, firms act rationally in this respect, since they consider the complete demand schedule as relevant for their optimal pricing policy. His approach results in a unique monopoly price. Diamond assumes that firms know the objective demand curve. However, given the different experiences subjects have from previous transactions, it is more likely that, in the first place, firms have different perceptions of the true demand curve and, in the second place, that true demand curves will shift over time as a result of consumer search. Finally, an equilibrium distribution of prices will result if firms only take account of their perception of local demand (Hey, 1974). In this respect, the importance of the informational requirements is emphasized because if firms were to know each other's prices at a moment in time, a unique market price would result.

Until now, we have assumed that asymmetries in information are absent. However 'the assumption that all those who would be moved to action by knowledge of a price also possess that knowledge is seldom justified. The whole market responds to a price increase, only part of it responds to a decrease' (Scitovsky, 1978). The reason for this asymmetry is that if a firm contemplates raising its price relative to a uniform equilibrium price, all customers with a certain level of search costs will leave since they only need one search effort to find a low–price firm. On the other hand, if a firm contemplates lowering its relative price it may not attract an equal number of new customers since with increasing marginal search costs it may take too many searches to locate the low–price firm (e.g. Stiglitz, 1979, 1987). As a result, the price elasticity for price decreases is smaller than for price increases in a situation with increasing marginal search costs, which implies that commodity prices will, under some conditions, not respond to changes in marginal production costs. In general, the assumptions made with respect to the specification of search costs and the search procedure have a large impact on the nature of the market equilibrium (see also Braverman, 1980).[2] Consider the following illustration of the arguments above (Stiglitz, 1987, pp. 1053–1054).

Firms maximize the profits $(P_i - k)vc(P_i)$, where v denotes the number of customers, P_i the firm's price, k average total production costs and $c(P_i)$ the household's demand function. Profit maximization implies

$$(P_i - k)/P_i = 1/\theta \qquad [4.11]$$

$$\theta = -\left\{\frac{d\ ln\ v}{d\ ln\ P_i} + \frac{d\ ln\ c}{d\ ln\ P_i}\right\} \qquad [4.12]$$

θ = the price elasticity of firm demand

In equation [4.12], $d \ln v / d \ln P_i$ denotes the in(out)flow of customers following a price-de(in)crease. In a monopolistic situation this factor will be zero, it approaches infinity in case of perfect competition (in the absence of search costs). With asymmetric information the level of $(d\ln v/d\ln P_i)$ will be dependent on whether an increase or a decrease in prices is analysed. In order to illustrate the possibility of rigid commodity prices Stiglitz makes the following assumptions.[3] The starting point of the analysis is a symmetric equilibrium with f firms and h households. Each firm sells to $v = h/f$ customers at the equilibrium price P_i^*. Furthermore, it is assumed that search takes place without replacement (a customer cannot return to the original firm after a search effort) and that search costs approach infinity for more than two searches. Consider a firm that contemplates raising its price ($P_i > P_i^*$). All customers know that on the next search, they will find a low-price firm. A particular customer will search as long as the costs associated with this additional search effort are less than the expected gain in utility from consumption at a lower price. In case the indirect utility function (V) is separable in prices and income this condition can be written as

$$V(P_i^*) - V(P_i) = \bar{s}(P_i) \qquad [4.13]$$

which illustrates that all individuals with search costs $s < \bar{s}$ will leave the firm. After raising its price a firm will only sell to

$$v = h/f(1 - F(\bar{s}(P_i))) \qquad [4.14]$$

customers, where $F(\bar{s}(P_i))$ the fraction of customers with search costs up to $\bar{s}(P_i)$.

$$\frac{dv}{dP} = -\frac{h}{f}f(\bar{s}(P_i))c(P_i) \qquad [4.15]$$

where, $f(\bar{s}(P_i))$ denotes the density function and $c(P_i)$ equals ds/dP_i which follows from a straightforward application of Roy's identity (Varian, 1984, p.126). By multiplying equation [4.15] with P_i/v and by considering that in equilibrium $v = h/f$, we obtain

$$\frac{d \ln v}{d \ln P_i} = -f(0)c(P_i)P_i \qquad [4.16]$$

$$\left(f(\bar{s}(P_i)) = f(0)\right)$$

which implies that the price elasticity of demand in case of a price increase equals

$$\theta^+(P_i^*) = -\left\{\frac{d \ln c}{d \ln P_i} - f(0)c(P_i^*)P_i^*\right\} \qquad [4.17]$$

On the other hand, assume that a firm contemplates lowering its price. Every customer who happens to select a high-price firm from the initial distribution knows that at least one of the other $f - 1$ firms charges a lower price. From his search technology he has one additional search left. Hence, the probability to find the low-price equals $1/(f-1)$. A customer at a high-price store will start searching as long as

$$\frac{V(P_i) - V(P_i^*)}{f-1} \geq \bar{s}(P_i) \qquad [4.18]$$

The low-price firm knows that from all people searching only $1/(f-1)$ will succeed in finding the firm. Hence, the number of customers after lowering its price will be

$$v = h\left\{\frac{1}{f-1}F(\bar{s}(P_i)) + \frac{1}{f}\left(1 - \frac{1}{f-1}F(\bar{s}(P_i))\right)\right\} \qquad [4.19]$$

The term between braces indicates the following. The first argument times h denotes the number of searchers who have succeeded in finding the low-price firm. The second argument times h denotes all other customers, where it is assumed that every firm attracts an equal proportion of this latter group. From straightforward calculation it can be concluded that

$$\frac{d\ ln\ v}{d\ ln\ P_i} = -\frac{f(0)c(P_i)P_i}{f-1} \qquad [4.20]$$

which implies that the elasticity of demand in case of a price decrease equals

$$\theta^-(P_i^*) = -\left\{\frac{d\ ln\ c}{d\ ln\ P_i} + \frac{f(0)c(P_i^*)P_i^*}{f-1}\right\} \qquad [4.21]$$

From [4.17] and [4.21] it immediately follows that the downward elasticity of the demand is smaller than the upward elasticity of demand. With a convex search technology the demand curve is kinked, which implies that commodity prices are rigid. Since the distribution of prices is not changed if all prices change equiproportionally, only real price rigidities can be explained in the context of the model above. In the next chapters, we will develop a model with a kinked demand curve that allows the explanation of nominal rigidities. Furthermore, the location of the kink falls outside the scope of the model, since the analysis starts from a symmetric equilibrium situation. Moreover, an explanation of the initial distribution of prices is missing as well. Efficiency wage considerations, which allow for different wage productivity relationships across firms can be of help in this respect. However, such an analysis implies that the partial equilibrium model of this section has to be incorporated in a model, which allows for the interplay between different markets. In the subsequent chapters, we will attempt to develop a model which takes account of the aforementioned asymmetries in information in the commodity market. In this chapter, we will proceed with a number of alternatives in that direction.

4.4 More markets

4.4.1 *Conjectural equilibria*

This section discusses the contributions of Benassy (1977), Grandmont and

Laroque (1977) and Hahn (1977, 1978), who prove the existence of a general equilibrium in a multi-market setting. The analyses are distinguished by their different behavioural assumptions. On the one hand, Benassy and Grandmont and Laroque analyze markets of monopolistic and monopsonistic competition, whereas Hahn does not 'want to make imperfect competition intrinsic to the model' (Hahn, 1978, p. 2). Subjects set prices with respect to a perceived demand curve. If expectations do not come true, agents are confronted with quantity rationing.

Grandmont and Laroque use a fixprice temporary equilibrium model of a monetary economy to prove the existence of an intertemporal equilibrium, which is characterized by general excess supply. Within elementary periods quantities change, between periods subjects decide about prices and expectations. Each period ends up in a temporary equilibrium. These equilibria are Drèze-equilibria. Optimal prices are set by firms in all goods markets with respect to perceived demand schedules. The planning period consists of two elementary periods. Sales are only made out of stock. Production takes one period. Productive capacity cannot be changed. The decision problem at the beginning of each planning period aims at maximizing profit at the end of the planning-period by choosing the price and quantity supplied of the latter of the two elementary periods, given all available information and expectations at the beginning of the planning period and also given the prices of the first elementary period. This decision simultaneously fixes production and employment in the first elementary period. Consumers have the same planning period. Their problem is to maximize utility at the end of each planning period, by choosing the optimal wage and related labour supply, given expectations and information available at the beginning of the planning period and also given the stocks of real balances at the beginning of the planning period. Consumers treat expected prices as parameters, whereas firms do the same with respect to the expected wage. Furthermore, agents take into account the expected quantity restrictions in *all* markets.

The analysis of Grandmont and Laroque permits the following observations. First, subjects can only take account of discrepancies between expectations and reality with a delay of one elementary period. The model does not explain this suboptimal behaviour. Secondly, and related to the first problem, subjects are not allowed to manipulate quantity restrictions in the first elementary period by changing prices and wages in that period. Thirdly, it is not clear how subjects receive information on true demand and supply conditions, because in formulating their decisions, they take notice of the quantity restrictions in *all* markets (see the preceding chapter). Finally, the auctioneer cannot be missed, when it comes to establishing a fixprice equilibrium.

Benassy assumes goods markets to be characterized by monopolistic competition. In contrast to the former analysis there is no labour market. Benassy develops a monetary temporary equilibrium model. Production and sales take place within the same period. Within the period only quantities can change. Markets are visited sequentially within the period. At the end of every period a K-equilibrium results (see the preceding chapter). Between periods prices and expectations can change. Consumers maximize end-of-period utility with respect to given prices and expectations. Discrepancies between realized and expected values give rise to new information and thus to changes in expectations at the beginning of the next period. Firms manipulate quantity restrictions on sales by their price. In order to find the profit maximizing price-sales combination, firms have to perceive the demand curve at the beginning of each period, as well as the quantity restrictions in other markets during the period. It is assumed that the actual price–quantity combination of the previous period is a point on the true demand curve. By looking at the past, firms learn to understand the future. If subjects do not have to revise their estimates of within–period quantity restrictions and beginning–of–period expectations of demand and prices, then at the beginning of the next period, one can speak, on the basis of the actual transactions at the end of the period under consideration, of an intertemporal equilibrium. It can be proven that in such a situation the monopolist will always meet the observed commodity demand.

The main objection to be raised against the analysis of Benassy is related to the way the production processes are modeled. Production is timeless and does not incorporate labour. An improvement compared to the theory of Grandmont and Laroque is that subjects do take account of the result of the immediately previous period.

The analyses of Hahn (1977, 1978) are directed toward the existence of non–Walrasian equilibria in an economy that also includes the competitive equilibrium. Hahn argues that in a non–Walrasian equilibrium there are additional Pareto–superior transactions possible, because by enlarging the transactions in markets where one is not constrained, agents make it possible for other agents to relieve the quantity constraints on markets where one is actually restricted. Why do subjects refrain from these transactions as they do in fixprice models? To answer this question, one has to dispense with the auctioneer and to allow for price setting. Hahn's description of individual behaviour centers round the notion of 'conjecture.' A conjecture is defined as the subjectively perceived relationship between the vector of (relative) market prices and individual excess demands, given the actual price–quantity combinations in the markets. It is assumed that the initiative to change prices can only be undertaken by the constrained market side. A conjectural equilibrium is established if neither supplying nor demanding agents want to change prices in all markets. In a conjectural equilibrium there are no net–transactions possible and market prices have their optimal values. Hahn formulates sufficient conditions for the co–existence of several conjectural non–Walrasian equilibria and one conjectural Walrasian equilibrium.

It can be argued that the introduction of conjectures or perceived demand curves does not represent a major improvement of economic theory since, although the market price is endogenous, the analysis now aggravates to the specification of the conjectures and, as Hahn shows, it is fairly difficult, if not impossible to derive a relationship between the properties of the conjectures and the resultant conjectural equilibrium. Almost any specification of conjectures is consistent with a certain equilibrium situation ('The circumstance that the market signals that the agent has not made a mistake does not ensure that he is in fact not mistaken.' (ibid., p. 1). Another point of criticism applies to the informational restrictions that are implicitly used in Hahn's analysis. As has already been stated, only the restricted market side can manipulate prices. This assumption requires the other market side not to take notion of the quantity–constrained position of price–setting subjects. In reality this assumption will not be met. Generally, both sides of the market will influence prices, unless markets are characterized by imperfect competition. Thus, Hahn's assumption about the price–setting behaviour of agents is rather arbitrary. The analysis of individual behaviour in disequilibrium situations in a competitive economy still awaits a firm microeconomic foundation.

4.4.2 *Macroeconomic approaches*

Initially, contract models have been developed to provide a microfoundation for price and wage rigidities in the context of a macroeconomic model, directed toward the analysis of the consequences of stabilization policy and the neutrality proposition of new classical economics. Fischer (1977) considers the macroeconomic implications of two-period wage contracts. Contracts are written in nominal terms. It is not surprising that in contrast to one-period contracts, policy choices affect output and employment. However, with full indexation (real wage contracts) past nominal shocks (and hence previous policy choices) loose their relevance for the current period, which implies that the policy neutrality results are restored. Gray (1976, 1978) analyses real (productivity) shocks as well. She addresses the optimal degree of indexation in the presence of shocks: nominal shocks, full indexation, real shocks and zero indexation. Taylor (1980) focuses on the implications of non-synchronized wage contracts. He argues that relative wages are relevant to agents, which implies that contractants take account of previously negotiated contracts. The effectiveness of policy in his framework is completely dependent on the arbitrarily selected staggered structure of wage contracts. To conclude, as has already been emphasized, implicit contract theory cannot provide a well-defined microfoundation of (real) wage rigidities and employment fluctuations. With respect to the macroeconomic contract models above it can furthermore be observed that they are not optimal contracts, since there are unexplained inefficiencies *ex post* (Barro, 1977).

In the context of the menu costs approach a number of articles have been published recently, which apply menu costs, on the one hand, and near-rational behaviour, on the other hand, to the analysis of fluctuations in employment and output and the effectiveness of (monetary) policy (*e.g.* Blanchard and Kiyotaki, 1987, Ball and Romer, 1987a, and Van de Klundert and Peters, 1988). However, as has already been observed in section 4.3.2, menu costs alone are not capable of explaining large fluctuations in employment, since the observed wage elasticity of labour supply is too low. In order to develop a macroeconomic model, which enables the study of large fluctuations in output, menu costs have to be linked with alternative characteristics that explain real wage rigidities. Akerlof and Yellen (1985b) (see also Ball and Romer, 1987c) have introduced the efficiency wage hypothesis to characterize labour market behaviour in the context of a macroeconomic model with near-rational behaviour in the commodity market. The model has the following basic features. Firms are efficiency wage setters in the labour market and monopolistic competitors in the commodity market. In the long run, wages and prices are set by all firms in an optimal way. In the short run, some firms keep nominal wages and prices constant while others choose these variables optimally in response to a deviation from the long run equilibrium position caused by a shock in aggregate demand. The behaviour of the non-maximizing firms is near-rational. The consequence of this inertial wage-price behaviour is that changes in money supply cause changes in employment, output and profits. Each identical firm faces the following demand curve.

$$q = \left(\frac{P_i}{P}\right)^{-\theta}\left(\frac{M}{fP}\right) \qquad [4.22]$$

$$\theta > 1$$

with,

q	=	demand for commodities of firm i
P_i	=	the commodity price charged by firm i
P	=	the aggregate price level
M	=	the aggregate supply of money
f	=	the number of firms
$-\theta$	=	the price elasticity of demand

Note that $P_i = P$ implies $Pfq = M$. In a long-run equilibrium with all firms charging the same price, [4.22] is consistent with the quantity theory. Output is produced according to the following production function.

$$q = (e(w)l)^{\tau_2} \qquad [4.23]$$

$$0 < \tau_2 < 1$$

Nominal profits of each firm are given by

$$PRF_i = P_i q - wPl \qquad [4.24]$$

Maximizing profits ([4.24]) by taking account of [4.22] and [4.23] with an initial money supply M_0 and the long-run equilibrium condition $P_i = P$, yields the following equilibrium price.

$$P^* = \tau_3 M_0 f^{-1} \qquad [4.25]$$

with,

$$\tau_3 = \left\{\theta w^* / \left(\tau_2(\theta - 1)e(w^*)\right)\right\}^{(\tau_2/(1-\tau_2))} \qquad [4.26]$$

Substitution of [4.23] and [4.25] into the quantity theory equation $Pfq = M$ gives firms' long run equilibrium employment, l^*.

$$l^* = \tau_3^{-1/\tau_2}/e(w^*) \qquad [4.27]$$

Now, consider the following description of short-run behaviour. Suppose that the money supply changes by a fraction τ_4, so that $M = M_0(1+\tau_4)$. In the short-run equilibrium the key endogenous variables are determined by equations [4.28] to [4.32] (the index n denotes a variable chosen by a non-maximizing firm, the index m denotes the choice of his maximizing competitor). Equation [4.28] shows that non-maximizing firms continue to set the same nominal price.

$$P_n = P^* \qquad [4.28]$$

$$P_m = P^*(1 + \tau_4)^{\tau_5} \qquad [4.29]$$

$$P = P^*(1 + \tau_4)^{(1-\tau_6)\tau_5} \qquad [4.30]$$

$$w_m = w^* \qquad [4.31]$$

$$w_n = w^*(1+\tau_4)^{-(1-\tau_6)\tau_5} \qquad [4.32]$$

Maximizers calculate the price P_m (equation 4.29) by setting the derivative of the profit function [4.24] with respect to P_m equal to zero. The optimal price is obtained by solving this first order condition with $w=w^*$, $P = (P_n)^{\tau_6}(P_m)^{(1-\tau_6)}$ (the average price is the geometric mean of actual market prices), $P_n = P^*$ and $M = M_0(1+\tau_4)$. τ_5 stands for a constant ≤ 1 and denotes the optimal shift in prices after a change in the money supply considering that only a fraction τ_6 of the firms are non-maximizers (Akerlof-Yellen, 1985b, p. 833). τ_5 equals unity if τ_6 equals zero. Note that in that situation a change in the money supply is neutral in the short run. Equation [4.30] follows from the substitution of equations [4.28] and [4.29] into $P = (P_n)^{\tau_6}(P_m)^{(1-\tau_6)}$. Equation [4.31] expresses that maximizing firms set wages optimally in line with thecondition that the elasticity of effort with respect to the real wage w_m equals unity in equilibrium. Finally, equation [4.32] shows that the money wage paid by non-maximizing firms is unchanged at its initial value W_0. The real wage (W_0/P) can be rewritten as (W_0/P^*) (P^*/P). The first term (W_0/P^*) equals the efficiency wage w^*, the second term equals $(1+\tau_4)^{-(1-\tau_6)\tau_5}$, after substitution of [4.30] into (P^*/P).

Employment in the short-run is obtained by taking account of the quantity theory equation. Substitution of equation [4.30] as well as $M = M_0(1+\tau_4)$ into $Pfq = M$ gives

$$P^*fq = M_0(1+\tau_4)^{1-\tau_5(1-\tau_6)} \qquad [4.33]$$

Substitution of equations [4.23], [4.25] and [4.26] into [4.33] and some rewriting yields

$$l = \left\{\tau_3^{-1}(1+\tau_4)^{1-\tau_5(1-\tau_6)}\right\}^{\frac{1}{\tau_2}} e(w^*)^{-1} \qquad [4.34]$$

Division of equation [4.34] by equation [4.27] gives the level of short run employment relative to its long run equilibrium level per firm.

$$l/l^* = (1+\tau_4)^{(1-\tau_5(1-\tau_6))^{1/\tau_2}} \qquad [4.35]$$

Note that if τ_4=0, l/l^*=1. In the absence of changes in the money supply there is no difference between the long-run and the short-run equilibrium level of employment. If all firms are maximizers (τ_5=1 and τ_6=0), short-run and long-run employment will be equal as well. Changes in the money supply are neutral in that situation. However, with some firms acting as non-maximizers changes in the money supply affect real output. In the vicinity of τ_4=0, we have

$$\lim_{\tau_4 \to 0} \frac{\partial(l/l^*)}{\partial \tau_4} = \left(1-\tau_5(1-\tau_6)\right)^{1/\tau_2} \qquad [4.36]$$

Because of $0 \leq \tau_5 \leq 1$, $0 \leq \tau_6 \leq 1$ and $0 < \tau_2 < 1$, equation [4.36] has a positive value, if some firms are non-maximizers. This implies that an increase in the growth of money supply has a positive impact on employment and output. Herewith, Akerlof and Yellen have shown that changes in the money supply can be nonneutral in the short run if some agents behave near-rational. However, the fact that firms choose price stability instead of employment stability (see section 4.3.3) still awaits a satisfactory explanation.

4.5 Coordination failures and indeterminacies[4]

All the explanations discussed in this chapter have one important characteristic in common. The absence of a Walrasian auctioneer implies that not all the available information is revealed to the market. Limitations in information dissemination can exist between agents, between sectors and between periods. As a result, coordination failures may arise because the assumptions that agents make about the mutual interdependence of their trading activities, define the perceived scope for their trading possibilities. These assumptions may cause the economy to end up in an equilibrium with low levels of output and employment although equilibria with higher levels of output and employment exist as well. In this section, we discuss the analysis of Cooper and John (1988) where it is argued that coordination failures can arise with flexible and with sticky prices (e.g. Blanchard and Kiyotaki, 1987), in the context of a competitive search model (Diamond, 1982) or in case markets are characterized by imperfect competition (e.g. Hart, 1982, Weitzman, 1982).

Cooper and John attempt to provide a general microeconomic framework which allows for the establishment of 'Keynesian results.' In general, these results 'are generated from the inability of agents to coordinate their activities successfully in a many-person, decentralized economy' (ibid., p. 442], which is characterized by incomplete information. The analysis exacerbates the discussion of two important concepts, spill-overs on the one hand, and strategic complementarity, on the other hand. Spill-over effects arise in the context of the model if an increase in the effort of one agent affects the pay-offs of other agents. In case of strategic complementarity, an increase in effort of an agent increases optimal efforts of other agents (Bulow, Geanakoplos and Klemperer, 1985). To illustrate how these concepts are related to the establishments of 'Keynesian results,' such as multiple equilibria and multiplier processes, a static non-cooperative game is developed. Agents are Nash-competitors, which implies that in deciding about the level of activities, they assume that their activities do not affect the activities of other agents. To analyse the implications of this kind of strategic behaviour, define $V(e_i, e)$ as the pay-off of agent i when all other agents choose e. Cooper and John observe that e may represent some aggregate index of effort put forward by the other agents and stress the relevance of incorporating macroeconomic variables in microeconomic behavioural relationships (ibid., p 461]. Let e_i^* be the optimal response of agent i when all other agents select e. At a symmetric Nash equilibrium, all agents choose the same optimal action. Hence, the reaction function of agent i can be defined as $V_1(e_i, e) = 0$, where V_1 denotes the first-order derivative with respect to the first argument of the pay-off function. Positive spill-overs arise if $V_2 > 0$. On the other hand, strategic complementarity implies $V_{12} > 0$. If other agents increase their activities, the marginal returns of agent i increase, which implies that it is optimal for i to increase his activities as well. Reaction functions are upward sloping. Strategic complementarity is a necessary, but not sufficient condition for multiple equilibria, the multiple intersections of reaction functions, which are characteristic for Keynesian-type analyses. A sufficient condition in the context of the model is $-V_{12}/V_{11} > 1$, which is implied by the strict concavity of the pay-off function, on the one hand, and by the assumptions that ensure the existence of an interior maximum, on the other hand (ibid., pp. 444–446). Furthermore, in the presence of positive spill-overs or externalities, symmetric Nash equilibria will always be inefficient, since by definition the positive impact from individual activities on the pay-offs of other agents is not considered. With positive spill-over effects, equilibria with higher levels of activity will be preferred by all agents, which in case of multiple equilibria opens the possibility for coordination failures. Finally, in the context of the present framework, multiplier effects may arise, in case an exogenous shift stimulates an increase in individual activities. With strategic complementarity, the aggregate response to the shift will dominate the individual initial response to the shift. Relatively small changes in parameters may be able to induce big shocks in the aggregate variables.

A second method of analyzing the existence of socially inefficient equilibria in a flexprice general equilibrium model is to drop the ADM-assumption of a complete set of future markets in order to introduce the indeterminacy of one or more variables in the model. Within any Keynesian type of overlapping generations (OLG) model these indeterminacies are present and these OLG models underpin the heterogeneity of agents (see Geanakoplos and Polemarchakis (1986). The indeterminacy of one or more variables necessitates the analysis of the process of expectations formation. In Keynes' GT the role of expectations is essential, in particular those expectations that govern the rate of investment. In OLG theories markets are incomplete by definition and expectations do matter. As is shown in, for instance, Garretsen and Janssen (1989), John (1988) and Chatterjee and Cooper (1989) the OLG model can be used to amend the coordination failure argument which is essentially static and devoid of expectations. Both the indeterminacy argument and the coordination failure argument may lead to Keynes' conclusion that the classical separation of demand and supply does not hold for the economy as a whole and that therefore the assumption of a unique equilibrium is not a good starting point for the analysis of the level of aggregate output and employment. The endogeneity of aggregate variables and the absence of the Walrasian auctioneer creates the possibility that in the presence of multiple Nash equilibria the economy can get 'stuck' at an equilibrium which is Pareto dominated by another equilibrium (Cooper, 1987a, p.1). However, the strength of the multiple equilibria approach is a serious weakness at the same time. Theories of multiple or even of a continuum of equilibria do provide conditions 'for the *existence* of multiple equilibria but do not provide insights into the question which of the equilibria is more or less likely to be observed' (ibid. p.2). This also explains why these theories are not yet very suitable for the analysis of policy effectiveness. The mere fact that multiple equilibria exist, does not imply that there is any scope for policy, since it is ambiguous whether the authorities are able to relieve the limitations on information in the economy. Subsequent research should be directed towards the analysis of these issues and should therefore be especially directed towards the development of theories that shed some light on the question what equilibrium (or what class of equilibria) is more likely to occur (see, for instance, Cooper, 1987a, for an attempt in this direction).

Some of the arguments that were mentioned in our criticism of the microfoundation of new classical macroeconomics also apply to those new-

Keynesian theories that belong to the coordination failure framework. The assumptions of market clearing (equilibrium) and of rational expectations are not derived from choice theoretic foundations. However, there are also important differences with the new classical framework. The coordination failure literature does not assume the unicity of a market–clearing equilibrium in which coordination is perfect and in which the socially efficient situation does not differ from the individually efficient situation. The introduction of heterogeneity among agents and of incomplete markets makes the analysis of *non*–cooperative equilibria possible. The coordination failure literature does ***not*** take for granted that the exchange process achieves the coordination of individual activities and therefore does not need a separate theoretical treatment. As such the analysis of multiple (or a continuum of) equilibria does not cast macroeconomic problems in terms of microanalogies. The theories discussed in this section do, however, not really analyze the exchange process. It is only emphasized that the absence of the assumption of perfect coordination implies the possibility of the exchange process leading to non–cooperative outcomes. But the question how a non–cooperative Nash ***equilibrium*** comes about is left unanswered. It is simply assumed that an individual agent knows that all other agents 'play Nash' (see Bernheim, 1984). The assumption of cooperative behaviour is replaced by the assumption of non–cooperative (Nash) behaviour. In this respect there is a fundamental difference between the concept of coordination failures in the work of Leijonhufvud and Hayek and the concept of coordination failures as discussed in this section. Leijonhufvud, for instance, explicitly refers to the question of ***how*** a coherent outcome (whether cooperative or non–cooperative) may be achieved.[5]

Another drawback of the coordination failure literature (and in fact of all general equilibrium theories) is that it is essentially concerned with real economies; money has no proper place of its own in these models. The existence of strategic complementarities or spill–over effects does not depend on the presence of money. Cooper and John (1988, p.462) suggest to extend the coordination failure analysis with the introduction of menu–costs in order to arrive at the non–neutrality of money. In line with Buiter (1989) we do not think that this is a fruitful approach because the menu cost approach only gives us a theory of nominal stickiness if prices are set in terms of money. If some bundle of real goods were the numeraire and if the cost of changing prices applied to price changes in terms of this real numeraire, there would be no nominal stickiness. The unmotivated assumption that prices are set in money terms is therefore a crucial one. 'Until we have a theory of money, we are unlikely to see a theory of nominal inertia' (Buiter, 1989, p.16). The problem is, however, that in general equilibrium theories like the new classical and the new Keynesian theories money is in fact unessential. In these models the demand for money is not explained but simply assumed by putting money into the utility function or by some cash–in–advance constraint. We believe that as a possible restriction to the number of alternative equilibria it may be fruitful to incorporate the role of institutions and conventions. Money can be considered to be a convention that reduces uncertainty. In this respect, the post–Keynesian contribution to the microfoundations debate, which aims to provide a macroeconomic (or better monetary) foundation for microeconomic theory may offer some interesting starting points (e.g. Kregel, 1987, Davidson, 1978). Anyhow, the coordination failure framework is yet a rather rudimentary and elementary one. It needs to be extended in a number of directions to incorporate more (institutional) characteristics of modern economies. In this respect, the analysis may benefit from insights that have been developed outside the scope of general equilibrium theory.

4.6 Some final observations

Now that we have arrived at a point where this survey of recent developments in macroeconomic stabilization theory can be concluded, it is useful to summarize the main arguments that we have put forward in this and the preceding two chapters. In the context of the flexprice method, *persistent* fluctuations in economic activity arise as an equilibrium response to stochastic fluctuations in technology and preference orderings. Although the method has analytical appeal, it can be criticized on theoretical and empirical grounds. Representative agent models do not leave scope for the presence of externalities. On the other hand, the successful coordination of individual activities is assumed rather than explained. Furthermore, if the process of obtaining knowledge is monotonic or if technology shocks are not economy-wide, the rationale for fluctuations disappears altogether. With respect to the empirical arguments, it has been discussed in chapter 2 that real business cycle theory cannot explain large fluctuations in output together with relatively small fluctuations in real wages. Hence, the claim that fluctuations in output and employment can be analysed in the context of a perfectly competitive system cannot be confirmed. Unfortunately, the alternative fixprice method suffers from some serious drawbacks as well, as has been put forward in chapter 3. Although this approach is more in line with empirical observations, it can be argued that the analysis is incomplete where it concerns the fixprice assumption and inconsistent with respect to the assumptions underlying the dispersion of information. The following arguments apply. In the first place, the behaviour of prices is not explained. Individuals formulate demands and supplies *at given prices* and perceived constraints, whereas the auctioneer reconciles potentially conflicting choices by means of a rationing scheme *at given prices*. In particular, it is not explained why agents refrain from price adjustments to relieve perceived constraints, since the assumption that agents behave as if they can trade whatever they wish at given prices no longer holds (Arrow, 1959). In the second place, it can be argued that Pareto improving trades are prohibited because agents do not take account of all the consequences of their behaviour. Agents only consider the impact of a perceived constraint in a particular market on their own behaviour in other markets. However, in a situation of general excess supply, the activities of one agent may have a non-negligible impact on the behaviour of other agents. Yet, strategic behaviour is not considered in fixprice models, which in the presence of an auctioneer who guarantees by assumption the successful coordination of individual activities (perfect information), can only follow from *ad hoc* limitations of the process of information dispersion. To conclude, fixprice general equilibrium theory does not provide a convincing explanation of fluctuations in output and employment.

With respect to the analyses discussed in this chapter, we believe that a definite conclusion cannot be drawn yet. As argued above, the approach dealt with in this chapter considers trade in non-auction markets. The absence of an auctioneer who reconciles demand and supply, implies the introduction of incomplete information in the economy. Contrary to the monetary approach to business cycles of chapter 2, the presence of imperfect information implies that although individual activities are privately efficient, agents may not be able to coordinate their activities successfully in a decentralized economy. As a result, individual activities may not be socially efficient and the economy may get *stuck* in an equilibrium with a low level of economic activity. Prices do not reveal all available information about relative scarcities and may signal additional information beside scarcity relationships at the same time, as in the theory of implicit contracts and the efficiency wage theories. However, prices are only one element in the theory of coordination failures. Coordination failures may arise in the context of search models as a result of the organization of trade or the search technology applied in combination with asymmetric information, on the one hand, or as a result of the characteristics of markets (imperfect competition) and technology (increasing returns to scale), on the other hand. It is argued that the theory of coordination failures represents an elementary and static framework, which has to be extended in a number of directions to incorporate more characteristics of modern economies. Furthermore, the analyses discussed in this chapter may, for a large part, be characterized as partial equilibrium approaches. However, the impact of unsuccessful coordination is particularly important in the context of a macroeconomic approach with its focus on the interplay between decisions in separate markets. In the next chapters, we will attempt to extend our analysis in that direction and analyse the implications of asymmetric information in the commodity market together with the existence of real wage rigidity in the labour market.

Notes

1. The efficiency wage hypothesis was first advanced in the context of the less developed countries. It emphasized the link between wages, nutrition and illness (Leibenstein, 1957). This link made labour productivity depend on the real wage paid.

2. Note that the arguments that underlie the kinked demand curve are different from those originally put forward by Sweezy (1939). Sweezy analyzes firm behaviour in an oligopolistic market, whereas the theory above applies to atomistic markets with firms behaving as Nash–competitors.

3. The implications of alternative assumptions are considered by Stiglitz as well. For instance, with concave search costs there cannot be a single price equilibrium.

4. Van de Klundert (1987) is a review of the coordination failure literature.

5. This is also a major theme of Hoogduin and Snippe (1987, pp.430–431) and of Peeters (1987, p.447) in the microfoundations issue of *De Economist*.

5 Unemployment equilibria, efficiency wages and kinked demand curves

5.1 Introduction

The preceding chapter ended with the observation that the non-auction market approach has to be considered a useful starting point for subsequent analysis of macroeconomic concepts. In this chapter we will elaborate this position. An essentially static macroeconomic model will be developed, which is characterized by imperfect competition and the existence of rigidities in prices, on the one hand, and different levels of equilibrium output, on the other hand. In the context of this model, we will deal with the implications for demand management. The reason for this approach is twofold. On the one hand, the most popular modern explanation of price-inertia (the menu-cost/near-rationality approach) can be criticized on a number of points as has been concluded from the discussion of this approach in the preceding chapter. For that reason, we will follow the alternative explanation (see section 4.3.4), as suggested by, for instance, Stiglitz (1987), characterized by the existence of asymmetric information and positive search costs, which cause firm demand curves to display a kink. On the other hand, it can be argued that although the alleged effectiveness of economic policy has probably been the most important impetus for the development of 'traditional' (Keynesian) macroeconomic theory, it has received only moderate attention in the new Keynesian approach. Moreover, the results obtained in new Keynesian macroeconomics are rather ambiguous in this respect. For instance, the theory of macroeconomic coordination failures has shown that under some conditions there may be multiple equilibria, which can be Pareto ranked. However, the analysis does not yet permit to answer the question how to get from one equilibrium to another. Alternatively, theories of hysteresis and/or imperfect competition create scope for real aggregate demand to influence economic activity. However, this does not automatically imply that these models allow for successful demand management, since it is not clear how the government sector will be able to influence real aggregate demand.

The model to be developed, is a short-run model for a closed economy. It only applies to situations where the demand for labour constitutes the short side of the market. Two markets are distinguished, the commodity market and the labour market, two goods, a composite commodity, which is produced in a large number of varieties, and labour, and there is one non-produced good, which serves as a numeraire. Real wages are determined by firms in line with the efficiency wage theory . Commodity prices are set by firms with respect to a downward sloping demand curve. The representative household maximizes utility with respect to consumption, real households savings and effort. Firms buy labour in order to produce and sell varieties of the composite commodity. Each variety is produced by a large number of firms. Productive capacity is exogenous. Production is immediate and the commodities are perishable. Firms maximize profits. To analyze the scope for demand management, a government sector is introduced in the model which purchases commodities from firms and offers unemployment benefits to households. Government expenditures are financed through taxation (firm profits) and real aggregate savings. Finally, the supply of individual labour has been normalized at unity. In section 5.2, we will discuss the activities of the household sector, whereas in section 5.3 the behaviour of firms will be analyzed. Section 5.4 discusses the scope for policy in the context of real wage rigidities. Section 5.5 deals with that question in the context of nominal rigidities. Section 5.6 offers some final observations.

5.2 Household behaviour

The representative household maximizes utility with respect to the consumption of varieties (C_i) of a composite commodity (C), real households savings (S_r) and effort (e). Since households savings are completely taxed away, the utility of savings can be considered as a subjective valuation of government expenditures.[1] Furthermore, we assume that the utility function is strictly concave in consumption and savings and strictly separable in effort and spending. Under these assumptions, the utility (U) obtained from consumption and real savings is given in equation [2.1].[2]

$$U = C^{\alpha} S_r^{\,1-\alpha} \qquad [5.1]$$

with

$$C = \left[\sum_{i=1}^{n} n^{-1/\theta} C_i^{(\theta-1)/\theta} \right]^{\theta/(\theta-1)} \qquad [5.2]$$

$$\sum_{i=1}^{n} P_i C_i = PC \qquad [5.3]$$

$$0 < \alpha < 1 < \theta$$

n = the number of varieties
P_i = the price of variety C_i
P = the average price level

In order to derive the demand for consumption goods and real savings it is convenient to maximize [5.2] subject to [5.3] in the first place. This yields

$$C_i = \frac{C}{n}\left(\frac{P_i}{P}\right)^{-\theta} \qquad [5.4]$$

with

$$P = \left[\frac{1}{n}\sum_{i=1}^{n} P_i^{(1-\theta)}\right]^{1/(1-\theta)} \qquad [5.5]$$

In the second place, utility U (equation [5.1]) is maximized with respect to C and S_r subject to the following budget constraint.

$$X = C + S_r \qquad [5.6]$$

In this respect, X denotes household's real disposable income. It is straightforward to derive that

$$C = \alpha X \qquad [5.7]$$

and

$$S_r = (1-\alpha)X \qquad [5.8]$$

$$V = \sigma_1 X \qquad \sigma_1 = \alpha^{\alpha}(1-\alpha)^{(1-\alpha)} \qquad [5.9]$$

V = indirect utility function

Substitution of equation [5.7] into equation [5.4] gives the demand for variety C_i as a function of X.

$$C_i = \frac{\alpha X}{n}\left(\frac{P_i}{P}\right)^{-\theta} \qquad [5.10]$$

The next step is to determine the supply of labour effort. It is assumed that there is a positive relationship between the supply of effort and worker quality (productivity). The supply of effort represents the worker's investment in human capital. This investment is only beneficial to individuals who apply for a job. People who join the unemployment pool on average have lower worker quality. However, worker quality can only be improved at the expense of effort costs. The latter are reflected by $c(e)$, the disutility of effort. It is assumed that the representative worker may either be employed or unemployed. The expected utility U_1 of a person who applies for a job but has the risk of unemployment is given by equation [5.11].

$$U_1 = (1-u)\sigma_1 w + u\sigma_1 d - c(e) \qquad [5.11]$$

u = the rate of unemployment

$c(e)$ = disutility of effort ($c', c'' > 0$)
w = real wage income
d = real unemployment benefit

On the other hand, the utility U_2 of a person who does not apply for a job is given by equation [5.12].

$$U_2 = \sigma_1 d \qquad [5.12]$$

The supply of effort can be derived from the optimizing condition that at the margin, households will be indifferent between the supply of one additional unit of labour and the joy of one additional unit of leisure. Hence, the reservation wage satisfies $(1-u)\sigma_1 w + u\sigma_1 d - c(e) = \sigma_1 d$. Thus in equilibrium the optimal level of effort is determined by

$$e = e\big(\sigma_1(w - d)(1-u)\big) \qquad [5.13]$$

For the sake of simplicity, we will specify the effort supply function [5.13] as

$$e = \big(\sigma_1(w-d)(1-u)\big)^{\beta} \qquad 0<\beta<1 \qquad [5.14]$$

The supply of effort is positively dependent on the relative wage level offered by firms and negatively on the level of unemployment. The relationship between effort and unemployment reflects the argument that in a situation of unemployment where workers are randomly separated from their jobs and outsiders loose skills, a higher level of unemployment implies a lower level of productivity on the job (Price, 1988, pp. 159–160).[3]

5.3 The behaviour of firms

Firms (indexed by h) behave under conditions of imperfect competition. Both in the commodity market and in the labour market, they set prices. Firms buy labour l_{ih} in order to produce and sell varieties C_i of a particular commodity. In this respect it is assumed that each variety is produced by f firms, where f is a large number. Productive capacity is exogenous. Production q_{ih} is immediate and the commodities are perishable. The representative firm aims at maximizing profits (PRF_{ih}).

$$PRF_{ih} = P_{ih}\, q_{ih} - W_{ih}\, l_{ih} \qquad [5.15]$$

P_{ih} = the commodity prices of variety i set by firm h
W_{ih} = the nominal wage offered by firm h ($h = 1,..,f$)

Firms maximize profits with respect to both a production and demand constraint. Production is characterized by the following production function, where e_{ih} is determined in line with equation [5.14].

$$q_{ih} = q(e_{ih} l_{ih}) \qquad [5.16]$$

For the sake of simplicity, denote $\overset{*}{l}_{ih} = e_{ih} l_{ih}$. Substitution of this last relationship into [5.16] yields

$$q_{ih} = q(\overset{*}{l}_{ih}) \qquad [5.17]$$

We will take equation [5.17] to exhibit diminishing returns.

In the absence of storage possibilities, a firm, operating under conditions of imperfect competition, will always fulfill the demand observed for its product. Firms in sector i face the following demand curve.

$$q_{ih} = \left[(\alpha X/n + g_i)/f\right] \left[\frac{P_{ih}}{P}\right]^{-\theta} \qquad [5.18]$$

$$X = Lw + (N-L)d \qquad [5.19]$$

g_i = government expenditure with respect to commodities of variety i

Equation [5.18] expresses local commodity demand relative to its proportional share of aggregate demand as a downward sloping function of the firm's relative price. For the sake of simplicity it is assumed that expenditure behaviour of the government sector is similar to that of households. The general price level is taken as given. It is assumed that firms consider themselves small compared to the economy as a whole, which in this respect implies that changes in individual firm prices do not affect the general price level. Equation [5.18] can be inverted to obtain

$$P_{ih} = P\left(q_{ih}/\bar{q}\right)^{-1/\theta} \qquad [5.20]$$

$$\bar{q} = (\alpha X/n + g_i)/f \qquad [5.21]$$

Substitution of $\overset{*}{l}_{ih} = e_{ih}l_{ih}$ and equation [5.20] into equation [5.15] yields

$$PRF_{ih} = P\left\{\left(q_{ih}/\bar{q}\right)^{-1/\theta} q_{ih} - \frac{w_{ih}}{e_{ih}} \overset{*}{l}_{ih}\right\} \qquad [5.22]$$

$$w_{ih} = W_{ih}/P \qquad [5.23]$$

w_{ih} = the real wage offered by firm h

The decision problem of every individual firm is to maximize profits by choosing q_{ih} and w_{ih} subject to the production constraint, equation [5.17], and the specified form of the effort supply function, equation [5.14]. If we assume that firms behave as Cournot–Nash competitors the following two first–order conditions can be obtained. Firstly,

$$P_{ih} = P \frac{\theta}{\theta - 1} \frac{w_{ih}}{e_{ih}} \left[\frac{\partial q_{ih}}{\partial \overset{*}{l}_{ih}}\right]^{-1} \qquad [5.24]$$

Equation [5.24] spells out the condition that in imperfectly competitive markets, firms set prices by imposing a mark–up on nominal labour costs (in efficiency units) at the margin. The size of the mark–up depends on the (relative) price elasticity of demand, θ. In general, the price elasticity of demand will be dependent on the number of competitors in the economy, which implies that profit margin depends on the number of firms. The profit margin decreases if the number of firms increases. If the number of firms approaches infinity, the profit margin approaches zero. Secondly, we have

$$\frac{\partial e_{ih}}{\partial w_{ih}} \frac{w_{ih}}{e_{ih}} = 1 \qquad [5.25]$$

The real wage w_{ih} minimizes labour cost per efficiency unit. From equations [5.14] and [5.25] it can be derived that

$$w_{ih} = d/(1-\beta) = w \qquad [5.26]$$

Real wages in the efficiency wage sector of the economy are determined by a constant mark–up over the real unemployment benefit. The size of the mark–up is dependent on β and reflects the 'the productivity–enhancing effects of wage increases' (Summers, 1988, p.3). With diminishing returns the labour demand schedule (in efficiency units) will be downward sloping, as can be derived from equation [5.24]. As a result (remember that $0<\beta<1$), the equilibrium level of employment in an economy with an efficiency wage sector will be lower than in a competitive economy, where $w = d$.

From equation [5.18] it can be derived that equality of (firm) supply and demand in the commodity market implies $P_{ih} = P$. In that situation, [5.24] becomes

$$1 = \frac{\theta}{\theta-1} \frac{w_{ih}}{e_{ih}} \left(\frac{\partial q_{ih}}{\partial l^*_{ih}} \right)^{-1} \qquad [5.27]$$

The equilibrium demand for labour (in efficiency units) can be derived from equation [5.27]. For instance, in case of a Cobb–Douglas technology and by taking account of equations [5.26], [5.27] and [5.14], the representative firm's demand for labour will be

$$l^*_{ih} = \left\{ F \frac{\theta-1}{\theta} \left\{ \beta\sigma_1(1-u) \right\}^{\beta} \left\{ d/(1-\beta) \right\}^{-(1-\beta)} \right\}^{1/(1-\tau)} \qquad [5.28]$$

$$F = \tau A K_{ih}^{1-\tau} \qquad [5.29]$$

with

τ = the labour elasticity of production
K_{ih} = the fixed capital stock
A = total factor productivity

From equation [5.28] it follows that $\partial l^*_{ih}/\partial u < 0$. This dependency emerges in the model because of the negative relationship between productivity and unemployment [5.14]. In a situation of unemployment where workers are randomly separated from their jobs and outsiders loose skills, a higher level of unemployment implies a lower level of productivity on the job. As a result, an increase in the aggregate level of unemployment lowers the equilibrium demand for labour of the firm. However, since every firm acts accordingly, the aggregate level of employment will decrease as well, which in turn increases aggregate unemployment. The model displays a bootstrap property in this respect, or to put it differently a coordination failure (Cooper and John, 1988) which may open up the possibility for multiple equilibria or path-dependence (hysteresis) in the sense of Price (Price, 1988, p.159–160).

5.4 The effectiveness of policy

Equilibrium in the product market is determined by equation [5.30].

$$fnq_{ih} = \alpha X + \sum_{i=1}^{n} g_i \qquad [5.30]$$

In equation [5.30] nf denotes the number of firms in the economy and q_{ih} is determined in line with equations [5.17] and [5.28]. Since every firm supplies the quantity of a variety demanded and since firms are identical, real aggregate supply and demand will be equal. Furthermore, in equilibrium every firm charges the same price. As a result $Pfnq_{ih} = PQ = PRF + WL$, where Q denotes aggregate real output and PRF aggregate nominal profits. Since it is assumed that government expenditures and unemployment benefits are financed through firm profits and aggregate savings we have

$$PQ = PG + (N-L)D - PS_r + WL = PG + PC = PG + \alpha PX,$$

where G denotes aggregate real government expenditures and D the nominal unemployment benefit.

Equilibrium in the labour market is determined by the following condition.

$$fnl^{*}_{ih} = (1-u)Ne \qquad [5.31]$$

After substitution of equations [5.14], [5.26] and [5.28] into equation [5.31] and some rearrangements the equilibrium level of unemployment can be determined.

$$u = 1 - \left[\left(\frac{fn}{N}\right)^{1-\tau} F\,\frac{\theta-1}{\theta}\,(\sigma_1\beta)^{\beta\tau}\left(\frac{d}{1-\beta}\right)^{-(1-\beta\tau)}\right]^{1/(1-\beta\tau-\tau)} \qquad [5.32]$$

In order to get meaningful solutions we have to assume $(1+\beta)\tau<1$ (which is not very restrictive since $0<\tau,\beta<1$), otherwise $\partial u/\partial N<0$ and $\partial u/\partial w^{*}<0$. Furthermore, additional restrictions have to be imposed on the size of the parameters (A, β, τ and σ_1) and exogenous variables (K and N) in order to assure $0<u<1$. However, despite the fact that it has to be allowed for some degree of arbitrariness, we may conclude from equation [5.32] that the equilibrium level of unemployment is independent of aggregate demand and real aggregate output is determined in the labour market. The price elasticity of the aggregate supply curve equals zero. In order to illustrate the ineffectiveness of demand management in that situation, the impact of a nominal shock can be described. Money can be incorporated in the model by means of a 'transactions technology' (e.g. Ball and Romer, 1987a, 1987b), which implies that real aggregate demand equals the aggregate supply of real balances. On an economy-wide level this implies that $\alpha X + \sum_{i=1}^{n} g_i = M/P$ where

M denotes the aggregate supply of money needed to finance transactions. Since real aggregate demand equals the level of real income, which is determined in the labour market in line with equation [5.32], it immediately follows that a change in the level of the money supply can only imply a proportional change in the aggregate price level. Real aggregate demand is not affected by the level of money supply. The economy is dichotomized. An increase in the level of money supply will only result in an increase in the general price level.

To conclude, in a symmetric equilibrium all firms charge the same price, offer the same nominal wage, whereas production technology and demand elasticities are identical as well. Under the assumption that firms are not constrained in the labour market, aggregate employment can be derived from equation [5.31] and [5.28] as a function of the efficiency wage, given the technology applied in production and the (relative) price elasticity of demand. In the commodity market supply equals demand, whereas in the labour market unemployment may be observed, given the efficiency wage and the level of labour supply. The economy is characterized by real (relative) wage stickiness. Nominal prices and wages are flexible. An increase in the money supply (as an example of a demand shock) will only result in an increase in the general price level.

5.5 The effectiveness of policy with rigid prices

It can be concluded from the preceding analysis that the incorporation of real wage rigidities allows for a unique positive equilibrium rate of unemployment. Unemployment rates only change in as far as real wage levels are affected by exogenous events as for instance a preference shock, a productivity shock or a change in the level of the real unemployment benefit. There is no scope for demand management in this respect. In order to open up the possibility of a continuum of equilibria corresponding to one commodity price in the context of the model developed, nominal rigidities can be introduced. As has been discussed in the preceding chapter, nominal inertia have been rationalized through the assignment of a lump-sum cost to nominal price adjustment (menu costs), whereas the incorporation of menu costs/near rationality in macroeconomic models is due to e.g. Akerlof and Yellen (1985), Blanchard and Kiyotaki (1987) and Ball and Romer (1987a, 1979b). Although the explanation of nominal rigidities by means of this near-rational behaviour has interesting features, the assignment of lump-sum costs to nominal price adjustments remains rather arbitrary as has been put forward in section 4.3.2. As a result, the applicability of the approach for the analysis of unemployment equilibria is ambiguous.

For these reasons, Buiter (1987) and Van Ees (1989) have presented an alternative explanation to enable aggregate demand to have a potential influence on economic activity, which as will be argued in this paper allows for nominal changes to affect equilibrium output as well. Following Negishi (1975, 1979) and Stiglitz (1979, 1987), it is assumed that the firm's local demand curve is kinked. The rationalization of the kink has been discussed in section 4.3.3 and can be derived from the existence of asymmetric information in the commodity market together with the assumption of rapidly increasing marginal search costs. The reader is referred to the abovementioned section for a more elaborate discussion of the most important characteristics. In this chapter we will confine ourselves to the consequences of incorporating a kinked firm demand curve into a macroeconomic model. Let equation [5.33] describe an inverted kinked demand curve.

$$\frac{P_{ih}}{P} = \min\left\{ \left(q_{ih}/\overline{q}\right)^{-1/\theta_1}, \left(q_{ih}/\overline{q}\right)^{-1/\theta_2} \right\} \qquad [5.33]$$

with

$$1 < \theta_2 < \theta < \theta_1 \qquad [5.34]$$

The arguments underlying condition [5.34] are illustrated in figure 5.1.

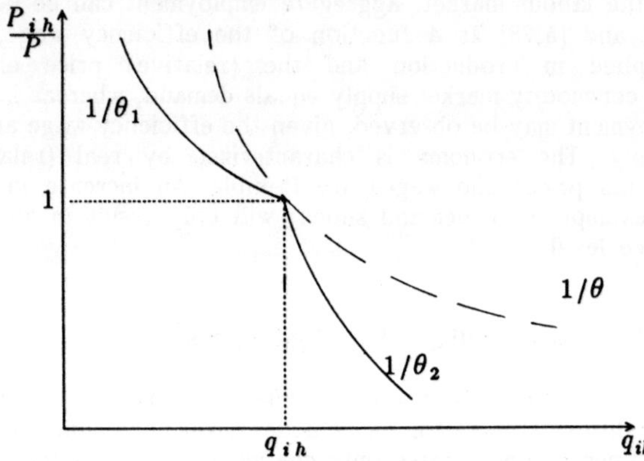

Figure 5.1

In the absence of asymmetries in information and search costs the inverted demand curve observed by the firm is represented by equation [5.20]. The associated price flexibility of demand equals $1/\theta$.

$$P_{ih} = P\left(q_{ih}/\overline{q}\right)^{-1/\theta} \qquad [5.20]$$

In the presence of asymmetries in information and search costs, the price flexibility of demand has to be lower if $q_{ih} < \overline{q}$, which implies $\theta < \theta_1$. On the other hand, if $q_{ih} > \overline{q}$, $\theta_2 < \theta$ since the firm will only attract relatively few new customers if it contemplates lowering its price.

Maximizing firm profits [5.15] by taking account of equation [5.33] and [5.17] yields two first-order conditions, equation [5.25] and

$$\frac{\theta_2}{\theta_2 - 1}\frac{w_{ih}}{e_{ih}}\left[\frac{\partial q_{ih}}{\partial l^*_{ih}}\right]^{-1} \geq \frac{P_{ih}}{P} \geq \frac{\theta_1}{\theta_1 - 1}\frac{w_{ih}}{e_{ih}}\left[\frac{\partial q_{ih}}{\partial l^*_{ih}}\right]^{-1} \qquad [5.35]$$

In expression [5.34] θ_1 denotes the left-hand side price elasticity of demand, whereas the right-hand side elasticity is denoted by θ_2. As $\theta_2 < \theta_1$, $\frac{\theta_2}{\theta_2 - 1} > \frac{\theta_1}{\theta_1 - 1}$. Furthermore, rigidity in relative prices implies $P_{ih} = P$ since the analysis started from a symmetric equilibrium. Hence, condition [5.35] will be fulfilled if

$$\frac{\theta_1}{\theta_1 - 1} \leq \frac{e_{ih}}{w_{ih}} \frac{\partial q_{ih}}{\partial l^*_{ih}} \leq \frac{\theta_2}{\theta_2 - 1} \qquad [5.36]$$

Condition [5.36] will always be fulfilled since in the initial equilibrium situation equation [5.27] applies and condition [5.34] holds. Hence, relative prices will be rigid and equal to unity.

As in the case of the preceding section, the commodity market clears ([5.30]). However, in a situation with rigid prices a commodity market equilibrium is determined by aggregate *demand*. As long as condition [5.35] holds any change in demand conditions will be followed by a similar change in economic activity. Any new level of output will be sustainable as an equilibrium. To put it differently, with inertia the economy displays a continuum of symmetric Nash equilibria characterized by different levels of output. This range of output levels can be described by $q_2 \leq q_{ih} \leq q_1$, where q_2 solves

$$\frac{P_{ih}}{P} = 1 = \frac{\theta_2}{\theta_2 - 1} \frac{w_{ih}}{e_{ih}} \left[\frac{\partial q_{ih}}{\partial l^*_{ih}}\right]^{-1}$$

and q_1 solves

$$\frac{P_{ih}}{P} = 1 = \frac{\theta_1}{\theta_1 - 1} \frac{w_{ih}}{e_{ih}} \left[\frac{\partial q_{ih}}{\partial l^*_{ih}}\right]^{-1}$$

In this respect, q_1 and q_2 denote profit maximizing levels of firm output, i.e. marginal costs equal marginal revenues. However, with a kinked demand curve as a result of search costs this condition cannot be fulfilled, which implies that the actual level of firm output cannot be determined by the marginal condition. As the equilibrium condition in the commodity market implies a one-to-one correspondence between aggregate real output and demand and because of complete symmetry between firms, the level of firm output is determined by the level of local firm demand as long as firm demand falls between q_2 and q_1. Furthermore, since $q_{ih} = q(l^*_{ih})$ the demand for labour of the representative firm is given by

$$l^*_{ih} = q^{-1}\left((\alpha X + \sum_{i=1}^{n} g_i)/nf\right) \qquad [5.37]$$

or since $l^*_{ih} = e_{ih} l_{ih}$

$$nf l_{ih} = \frac{nf}{e_{ih}} q^{-1}\left[(\alpha X + \sum_{i=1}^{n} g_i)/nf\right] \qquad [5.38]$$

As e_{ih} is determined by $w_{ih} = d/(1-\beta)$, the optimal level of the efficiency wage, equation [5.38] implies that with rigid commodity prices the aggregate demand for labour is completely determined by the aggregate demand for commodities. Every change in real aggregate demand will affect the rate of unemployment in the economy.

Next, we will consider the effectiveness of economic policy. Observe that with rigid commodity prices the economy can be represented by the following two equations.

$$Q = \alpha X + G \qquad [5.39]$$

$$Q = fnq_{ih}, \; G = \sum_{i=1}^{n} g_i, \; X = Lw + (N-L)d$$

and

$$L = \frac{nf}{e} q^{-1}\left[(\alpha X + G)/nf\right] \qquad [5.40]$$

Equation [5.39] denotes equilibrium in the commodity market, whereas equation [5.40] represents aggregate employment on the assumption that supply for labour exceeds demand. If one takes account of equations [5.14] and [5.26] it can be observed that equations [5.39] and [5.40] represent a system of two equations in two unknowns (Q and L) with two exogenous variables G and d (on the assumption that condition [5.35] is fulfilled). From total differentiation of equations [5.39] and [5.40] it can be derived that

$$\frac{dL}{dG} = \frac{\partial q}{\partial Q}^{-1} e^{-1}\left[1 - \frac{\partial q}{\partial Q}^{-1} \frac{\alpha\beta d}{1-\beta} e^{-1} + \beta\right]^{-1} \qquad [5.41]$$

$$\frac{dQ}{dG} = \frac{\alpha\beta d}{1-\beta}\left(\frac{dL}{dG}\right) + 1 \qquad [5.42]$$

Equation [5.41] represents the employment multiplier of real government expenditures, whereas equation [5.42] denotes the Keynesian income multiplier. These multipliers have positive values if the expression between square brackets in equation [5.41] is positive. It can be derived that this requirement will be fulfilled in case

$$d < \frac{1-\beta}{\beta}\left\{(1 - u)\sigma_1\right\}^{\beta/(1-\beta)}\left\{(1+\beta)^{-1}\alpha\frac{\partial q}{\partial Q}^{-1}\right\}^{-1/(1-\beta)} \qquad [5.43]$$

The reason we have to impose condition [5.43] is that an increase in government expenditure has two effects on the level of employment in the model. In the first place, a real demand stimulus has a direct positive impact on employment through increased production. However, in the second place, there is a negative indirect effect, since an increase in real demand tends to rise productivity through a decline in unemployment, which given the level of aggregate commodity demand causes the demand for labour to fall. The restriction [5.43] is needed to assure that the direct effect dominates the indirect effect. Observe that all the arguments on the right-hand side of condition [5.43] have a positive value. Condition [5.43] can be fulfilled by the arbitrary choice of the level of d, which is an exogenous variable in the context of the model. Hence, positive multipliers are possible, in a situation with rigid prices. In addition, it can be observed from equation [5.42] that in that case the Keynesian income multiplier has a value that exceeds unity.

It can be concluded that an increase in aggregate real demand tends to increase real equilibrium economic activity and employment. Unambiguously an increase in real government expenditure has a positive impact on the level of aggregate demand and output. However, a proper judgement of the effectiveness of fiscal policy also takes account of the way in which the government will finance an increase in expenditure. The debt–finance issue cannot be addressed within the context of this model since it is assumed that the government does not have to refund the loans that are obtained from the household sector. The model has to be made intertemporal in order to analyze all the effects of debt–financed policy. On the other hand, the effectiveness of monetary policy can be addressed, since any increase in real government expenditure can be financed by issuing money in order to fulfill the transactions technology we have assumed in section 4. It can be immediately concluded from the preceding analysis that as long as real rigidity (condition [5.35]) implies nominal rigidity in equilibrium monetary policy is effective. However, this implication is not straightforward. The assumption that all firms 'play Nash' is important in this respect. A Nash–competitor assumes that its activities do not affect the decisions of all other agents. Since the analysis presupposed the existence of a symmetric equilibrium with commodity price level P, every agent takes in his optimal price–output strategy the commodity price P of all other competitors as given. In that situation, a decision to leave prices unaltered implies that firms stick to the given commodity price P. In that case real rigidity implies nominal rigidity, although the actual level of P by itself is undetermined in the context of this model. Since the level of w is fixed by condition [5.25], it can be observed that in that case the level of the nominal wage is fixed. The argument that the efficiency wage theory only fixes relative wages is of no relevance in this model since the level of the efficiency wage is determined by a constant mark–up over the competitive benefit d. As a result, it can be concluded that monetary policy can be effective in a situation where commodity markets are characterized by imperfect information and small positive search costs. Observe furthermore that this conclusion does not hinge on the argument that agents are 'fooled' by the government sector, nor does it imply that the formation of expectations has been irrational.

5.6 Some final observations

In this chapter, we have developed a macroeconomic model characterized by imperfect competition. Rigidity in real wages is explained by the efficiency wage theory. Rigidity in real commodity prices may originate from the existence of positive search costs, which give rise to a kinked demand curve. In case the economy is characterized by real (relative) wage stickiness, flexible (relative) prices and flexible nominal wages, it has been concluded that real aggregate demand cannot be affected by demand management. In particular a change in the level of money supply does not influence the level of economic activity. The economy is dichotomized. An increase in the level of money supply will only result in an increase in the general price level. On the other hand, if the economy is characterized by real price and real wage rigidity as an optimal response to a change in demand conditions a different picture emerges. Aggregate demand shocks may exert a direct influence on the level of economic activity and given the value of aggregate labour supply, unemployment may arise in the economy after a contraction in commodity demand. In the context of the model developed in this paper, aggregate economic activity can be stimulated by an increase in real government expenditure. Debt–financed fiscal policy cannot be addressed properly in the context of this model since it is assumed that the government does not have to refund the loans that are obtained from the household sector. On the other hand, monetary policy and money-financed fiscal policy can be effective in a situation where firms are Nash-competitors and commodity markets are characterized by imperfect information and small positive search costs.

The approach followed in this chapter contains a number of suggestions for subsequent research. To analyze the impact of debt-financed fiscal policy, the analysis has to be made intertemporal. This extension also implies the introduction of an additional financial market, on the one hand and the explicit analysis of investment decisions, on the other hand. In addition, the analysis of the time path of the economy enables a more explicit study of the problem of the persistence of unemployment. In the next chapter we will address these issues in the context of a sequential approach.

Notes

1. Of course, the assumption that government expenditures are considered to be substitutes for private consumption is rather ambiguous. However, since this ambiguity does not apply to the analysis of the consequences of demand management for the performance of the economy as a whole with respect to output and employment, which is the object of analysis of this paper, we think that our approach is legitimate as a short cut.

2. In order to facilitate computations we have chosen simple specifications of household and firm behaviour to illustrate our argument. With the exception of the effort supply decision our model of household behaviour is similar to Blanchard-Kiyotaki (1987). The derivation of the demand for varieties of a composite commodity by means of a nested C.E.S. utility function has been developed by Dixit and Stiglitz (1977).

3. It could be argued that this argument should be analyzed in a dynamic context since workers only loose skills in a situation where they have actually joined the unemployment pool. For the sake of simplicity, we follow a static approach in this chapter, which implies that the unemployment variable in equation [5.14] only offers an indication of the *anticipated* productivity loss (see also Price (1988) p. 177). Note furthermore that the postulated relationship between effort and unemployment in this chapter is different from the relationship assumed in Shapiro and Stiglitz (1984). The explanation of this difference is that whereas Shapiro and Stiglitz deal with the consequences of unobservable effort (monitoring problems), we are concerned with observable effort and the consequences of differences in skills. Our approach is more in line with the insider-outsider theory of wage determination, which can be regarded as complementary to the efficiency wage approach (Lindbeck and Snower, 1987).

6 A macroeconomic model of adjustment

6.1 Introduction

In the preceding chapter, we have adapted a (comparative) static approach of the analysis of the implications of market imperfections. In the last section of chapter 5, the need for dynamics was emphasized for two reasons. In the first place, the implications of debt-financed fiscal policy can only be addressed properly by means of an intertemporal model. This extension also implies the introduction of a bond market, on the one hand and the intertemporal analysis of investment behaviour, on the other hand. In the second place, the analysis of the characteristics of the time path of the economy can be of interest by itself, particularly if the adjustment processes are rather prolonged. Moreover, in a situation where the long-run equilibrium cannot be determined because of analytical complexities, a numerical analysis of the time path is all that is left for the study of the characteristics of the economy. In addition, the sequential approach we apply in this chapter may have the advantage that it provides some preliminary insights in the process of trade, which precedes the establishment of an equilibrium situation, since the existence of this last situation is not assumed beforehand. As was mentioned in the introduction of this monograph, the theories discussed in the preceding chapters do not explicitly take the exchange process into account.

In this chapter we will develop a dynamic model with the following characteristics. The sequential-analytical approach we apply is similar to Snippe (1985). Time is divided in arbitrary small discrete periods. The agents' decisions in financial markets, the bond market, the money market and the market for short-term loans, on the one hand, and in the commodity market and the labour market, on the other hand, are intertwined and taken at the beginning of every unit period. All decisions are synchronized. Production takes one period and the commodities are stored. Sales are made out of stock. (Dis)Investments cause adjustments of productive capacity with a lag of one period. The determination of commodity prices is analogous to Hahn (1978) and incorporates the implications of asymmetric information (the perceived demand and supply curves are kinked), which, as we have argued in the preceding chapters, is an important characteristic of any process of trade. Hahn (1978) relaxes the fixprice assumption in non–Walrasian equilibrium models 'by allowing agents to have conjectures of how a given perceived ration may be relaxed by their willingness to offer a different price'(ibid p. 2). This concept not only allows the removal of the Walrasian auctioneer but at the same time avoids monopolistic competition. Perhaps it should be emphasized that the concept serves analytical purposes only. It has no empirical relevance but endogenizes a market characteristic. Excess commodity supply implies a monopolistic market, excess demand a monopsonistic market, whereas with market clearing, there exists an auction market.[1] Finally, it is assumed that agents cannot observe that other agents are rationed or at least do not take advantage of such a situation. Wage adjustments, on the other hand, are determined according to a Phillips curve, whereas the rate of interest clears the bond market. Commodity prices, the interest rate and wages are only adjusted at the junction of two periods. Expectations are autoregressive expectations. Despite the introduction of this last simplification and the arbitrary character of wage formation, the model cannot be solved analytically. The characteristics of the model are studied by means of a number of simulation experiments.

In this chapter we will develop the model with the above–mentioned characteristics. The results of the simulation experiments are reported in the next chapter. The organisation of this chapter is as follows. In section 2 we will consider briefly the incorporation of time in economic theory and we will explain our choice for a sequential analytical approach. In section 3 we will outline the transactions between the sectors of the model by means of a flow of funds approach. Section 4 deals with household behaviour, whereas section 5 discusses the behaviour of firms. Finally, in section 6, the characteristics of the financial sector and the government sector are described.

6.2 The introduction of time in the analysis

The structure of the macroeconomic model to be developed is directed toward the study of adjustment processes. An adjustment process can be defined as a search for behavioural rules or decisons that are consistent with the environment of the agent. In this respect, consistency implies that the agent can realize his objectives given this environment, whereas the environment of an agent encompasses everything that cannot be controlled but nevertheless affects the realization of the agent's objectives. If we drop the assumption that these adjustment processes do not take time, a number of analytical problems arise. In the first place, the concept of time needs a more precise definition. In the second place, it needs to be illustrated how that concept of time enters the analysis and how it affects other concepts such as for instance the notion of equilibrium. In this section, we briefly explain our choices in this respect.

As we have illustrated in chapter 2, in mainstream economic theory time refers to an analytical concept, not to calendar or historical time. The concept of time is closely related to the definition of period since every time-consuming process can be considered to occur in a sequence of instants or periods. Two definitions of a period can be distinguished in the literature. In the first definition, a period denotes a principle of isolated abstraction. We refer to this concept as a Marshallian period. It may be applied in order to reduce complex dynamic processes to more manageable proportions. In this context, a period indicates that during a period only a *limited* number of variables can change. Different periods refer to different sets of changing variables and hence to different adjustment processes. Every period is self-contained, i.e. the equilibrium following the adjustment process in a single period is completely determined by current parameters (Hicks, 1985, p. 25). In order to draw conclusions about the complete process of adjustment, the set of partial adjustment processes and the possible interactions between these processes have to be considered simultaneously (e.g. Kuipers, 1981). We think that this method of analysis has considerable appeal mainly because it is a relatively simple method. However, we do not think it is appropriate for a truly dynamic analysis, since the method neglects the irreversibility of economic processes. The same event can be a part of different adjustment processes since the latter may refer to different periods. Furthermore, the linkage between different periods is missing. In our opinion, both this linkage and the irreversibility of processes are essential characteristics of a dynamic theory.

In the second definition, a period refers to a situation of rest. During a period every change in the variables under analysis is excluded. For instance, a period may be defined as the span of time between two moments of market activities. During the period markets are closed, in between they are open. All activities are synchronized and undertaken at the beginning of a period. This second definition of a period builds upon a general assumption that every analysis is based on some elementary non-divisible principles. This concept of a period can be considered a straightforward application of a dynamic analysis. The period represents an entity. Within the period changes are impossible, since this would imply another definition of an elementary period.[2] A situation of rest is a natural starting point for every dynamic analysis.

However, the second definition of a period does not necessarily imply an analysis of adjustment processes. Also, if we consider a sequence of single self-contained periods, adjustment processes are only reduced to sequences of static equilibria. This extension in itself is not very useful (although the concept of irreversibility has been accounted for), since in a sequential analysis it is assumed that adjustment processes between two periods do not take time. The market process is not analyzed. Hence, there is no fundamental difference with a (comparative) static method. For an analysis to be dynamic the linkages between two sucessive periods have to be specified as well. In the context of the sequential-analytical approach there are two alternatives, the (temporary) equilibrium method developed by Hicks (1939) and the sequential method originally developed by Lindahl (1930). Both methods introduce expectations as the linkage between two periods. However, Lindahl explicitly introduces expectations as *independent* variables in the determination of a single period equilibrium. Expectations are determined by the history of the model, which implies that change has become intrinsic to the analysis. The single period is not self-contained. On the other hand, in the context of Hicks's temporary equilibrium method current-period expectations are influenced by current experience.

Expectations of the current period adjust according to what happens during the trading process on the 'Hicksian' Monday. In the flexprice temporary equilibrium model, the current equilibrium price and current equilibrium price expectations are reciprocally determined. This characteristic makes the method quasi-static, which reduces its complexity considerably. However, 'though changes in actual prices do affect expectations, and changes in expectations do affect actual prices, cause precedes effect. The lag may be short, but in principle it is always there. In truly dynamic analysis there must be lags' (Hicks, 1985, p. 70). Since it is our objective to develop such a dynamic analysis in this chapter, we will apply the concept of a sequential analysis as developed by Lindahl.

In the context of both methods of sequential analysis, flexible (market clearing) prices as well as rigid (non-market clearing) prices can be introduced. Either these prices are given or they are determined by the agents at the beginning of every elementary period. In a situation where agents determine prices under limited information about relevant variables and parameters, rationing might occur. Quantity rationing implies that agents cannot realize the transactions they have planned at the outset of the elementary period. In the context of fixprice disequilibrium theory this may lead to the establishment of non-Walrasian equilibria at the end of a single period. As we have argued in chapter 3, fixprice disequilibrium theory can be criticized since the establishment of non-Walrasian equilibria (and underlying rationing schemes) requires more information than is assumed to be present with respect to the determination of prices. However, in the context of this section it may be more important to observe that fixprice equilibria represent equilibria in flows. Initially, fixprice equilibria always coincide with a disequilibrium in stocks. A stock equilibrium represents a condition with respect to the balance sheet. It can be defined as a situation where desired stocks are equal to the actual stocks at a point in time, given plans and expectations about what will happen after that point in time. In the absence of a stock equilibrium, a situation of disequilibrium (inequality of demand and supply in a single period), on the one hand or a non-Walrasian equilibrium, on the other hand, is carried forward. Trading opportunities do not necessarily disappear because of the disequilibrium situation. It may well be that they are only postponed for a while. The distinction between a situation of disequilibrium and a non-Walrasian equilibrium is only of second order of importance in this respect. For this reason, we will focus on the adjustment processes toward a stock equilibrium and allow for disequilibria (inequality of demand and supply) at the end of a single period. Flow equilibria only assure the maintainance of a stock equilibrium if a stock equilibrium existed at the outset of a single period.

The sequential-analytical approach has the following implications for the model to be developed in this chapter. During the period only quantity adjustments can take place. Prices, stocks (wealth) and productive capacity can only be changed at the junction of two periods. Prices are set on the basis of information about actual transactions and prices in the previous period. Elementary periods are linked through changes in stocks and expectations. These changes reflect the consequences of actual transactions in the last period. The lagstructure that underlies the decisions with respect to employment, production and desired stock adjustment is related to the timestructure of the model. Production and employment decisions are taken in the same period. Production takes one period. At the end of the period all commodities are stored, which implies that production- and employment decisions are related to next-period sales. On the other hand, investments have an expenditure effect in the period in which the investment decision is taken. The effect on capacity will emerge at the moment the investment goods are available, which is at the beginning of the immediately following period. In the context of the investment decision, the expected future development of sales during the complete planning period is considered. In this respect, there is a lag of two periods since the production and installment of the investment goods, on the one hand and the production of goods for sale, on the other hand, takes two periods.

6.3 Transactions and other characteristics

The transactions of the sectors in the financial markets of the model can be presented in the following framework of the uses and the sources of funds (flows). Actual end-of-period stocks are listed between parentheses.

Table 6.1: Flow of funds account of actual transactions

	Households	Firms	Banks	Government	
BONDS	$\Delta BDH/R$	$-\Delta BSF/R$	$\Delta BDB/R$	$-\gamma_6 PSD$	0
	(BDH/R)	$(-BSF/R)$	(BDB/R)	$(-BSG/R)$	(0)
CREDIT		$-\Delta CRDF$	$\Delta CRSB$	$-(1-\gamma_6)PSD$	0
		$(-CRDF)$	$(CRSB)$	$(-CRDG)$	(0)
MONEY	ΔMDH	ΔMDF	$-\Delta M$		0
	(MDH)	(MDF)	$(-M)$	(0)	
	$-SH$	$-SF$	$-SB$	$-SG$	0
	$(-WH)$	$(-WF)$	$(-WB)$	$(-WG)$	(0)
	0	0	0	0	0

BDB = end-of-period stock of bonds held by banks
BDH = end-of-period stock of bonds held by households
BSF = end-of-period stock of bonds issued by firms

BSG = end-of-period stock of government bonds
$CRDF$ = end-of-period stock of credit demanded by firms
$CRDG$ = end-of-period stock of bank-loans to the government
$CRSB$ = end-of-period stock of bank-loans
MDH = households' end-of-period stock of money balances
MDF = firms' end-of-period stock of money balances
M = end-of-period stock of money balances supplied by banks
PSD = public sector deficit
R = the end-of-period interest rate on bonds
SH, SF, SB, SG = current-period flow of savings of households, firms, banks and the government, respectively
WH, WF, WB, WG = total wealth of households, firms, banks, and the government, respectively

In the flow of funds framework the first three rows refer to the transactions in a particular asset in each period. The last row represents the net accumulation of wealth of each sector and represents the savings-equals-investment (flow) identity of a closed economy ($S - I \equiv PSD$). Columns represent balance sheets (in parentheses) of the sectors of the model at the end of each period. Rows as well as columns sum to zero, reflecting that sales equal purchases in the markets, on the one hand, and liabilities equal assets, on the other hand.

From the flow of funds framework, it can be concluded that

$$PSD \equiv \Delta CRDG + \Delta PRLG \qquad [6.1]$$

$PRLG$ = private sector loans to the government sector (bonds)

A fixed proportion of the current-period government budget deficit is financed by the issue of short-term loans.

$$(1-\gamma_6)PSD \equiv \Delta CRDG \qquad [6.2]$$

From the balance sheet of the banking system, we derive

$$\Delta M \equiv \Delta BDB/R + \Delta CRSB - SB \qquad [6.3]$$

On the other hand, the equality of the end-of-period supply and demand of nominal balances is given by equation [6.4].

$$M_{-1} + \Delta M \equiv MDH + MDF \qquad [6.4]$$

M_{-1} = the beginning-of-period stock of nominal balances

The end-of-period level of bond-financed government debt equals

$$BSG/R \equiv BSG_{-1}/R + \gamma_6 PSD \qquad [6.5]$$

The equality of the end-of-period supply and demand in the bonds market and the market for credit is given by equations [6.6] and [6.7], respectively.

$$BDH + BDB \equiv BSG + BSF \qquad [6.6]$$

$$CRSB \equiv CRDF + CRDG \qquad [6.7]$$

Finally, the last row gives the overall equilibrium condition with respect to wealth in the different sectors.

$$WH + WF + WB + WG \equiv 0 \qquad [6.8]$$

In the model four atomistic markets are explicitly distinguished, the commodity market, the labour market, the bond market and the market for credit. Because of Walras' law the money market is not considered. The market for credit and the labour market are characterized by sticky prices. The market for bonds is a flexprice market. In the commodity market prices are determined endogeneously, but these price setting procedures do not necessarily induce market clearing.

Commodities, labour and financial assets are homogeneous. Bonds are consoles, which implies that each bond pays one money unit a period in perpetuity. There is no risk of default so that old and new bonds can be considered equivalent. Consequently, both old and new bonds are traded in the same market. Furthermore, there is no difference between corporate and government bonds. Finally, the market for credit is demand determined, and the interest rate on credit is determined as a fixed mark-up on the interest rate on bonds. As in the bond market, there is no difference between government and corporate short-term loans. It is assumed that short-term credits mature after one period and that the interest rate on credits is determined as a fixed negative mark up on the long-term bond rate.

6.4 Household behaviour

6.4.1 *Introduction*

Households aim at maximizing utility. At the beginning of a period they decide on intended levels of consumption and wealth. The preferred composition of end-of-period wealth is determined as well. Rational behaviour implies that the abovementioned decisions are intertwined and taken simultaneously. Households' activities are constrained by the aggregate of current-period disposable income and beginning-of-period wealth (the budget constraint). Current-period commodity prices, wages and asset prices affect this constraint. Households assume these prices to be given, unless they have not been able to realize intended commodity transactions in the previous-period. Under these circumstances, households try to improve the fulfilment of their intentions by adjusting both commodity prices and quantity demanded. Current-period prices are determined according to a kinked conjectural supply curve, in order to reflect imperfect information dissemination in the commodity market on the side of firms. Decisions on current-period commodity prices are then part and parcel of households' utility maximization problem. Furthermore, households may face constraints with respect to their transactions, that result from discrepancies between supply and demand in markets other than the one under consideration. However, these spillovers only effect *next*-period supply and demand. Constraints are not considered *ex ante*. Individuals do not formulate perceptions about current-period rationing schemes beforehand. In this section the households' utility maximization problem is formalized. In this respect, we compare households' decisions in situations of preceding-period demand rationing, on the one hand, with the decisions in situations in which there is no demand rationing, on the other hand.

6.4.2 *The households' decision problem*

The households' decision problem is summarized below. The problem is to maximize current-period utility

$$U = \alpha_1 ln\ C^e(0,0) + \alpha_2 ln \frac{MDH^e(0)}{b_1 P_h^e(0,1)} + \alpha_3 ln \frac{BDH(0)}{R(0,0) b_1 P_h^e(0,1)}$$

$$0 < \alpha_i < 1,\ i = 1,2,3 \qquad [6.9]$$

subject to the following budget constraint

$$MDH(-1) + \frac{BDH(-1)}{R(0,0)} + \{W(0,0)L(0,0) + BDH(-1) + DIV(-1)$$

$$+ \alpha_4 BDB(-1) + \alpha_5\alpha_6 R(-1,-1)[CRDF(-1) + CRDG(-1)]\}(1-\alpha_7) =$$

$$P(0,0)C^e(0,0) + \frac{BDH(0)}{R(0,0)} + MDH^e(0) \qquad [6.10]$$

where

$$\sum_{i=1}^{3} \alpha_i = 1 \qquad [6.11]$$

with,

U	=	total utility in period 0
$C^e(0,0)$	=	households' current-period consumption plans at the beginning-of-period 0
$L(0,0)$	=	the level of employment in period 0
$MDH^e(0)$	=	households' beginning-of-period 0 desire of the end-of-period *t* stock of money balances
$BDH(0)$	=	households' beginning-of-period 0 demand for an end-of-period 0 number of bonds
$P_h^e(0,1)$	=	households' beginning-of-period 0 expectation of the level of commodity prices in period 1
$MDH(-1)$	=	households' end-of-period -1 stock of money balances
$BDH(-1)$	=	households' end-of-period -1 number of bonds
$R(0,0)$	=	period 0 level of the rate of interest on bonds
$W(0,0)$	=	period 0 level of the nominal wage rate
α_4	=	the share of bank earnings on bonds transferred to households
α_5	=	the share of bank earnings on credit transferred to households
α_6	=	fixed mark-up rate on the bond interest rate, which determines the interest rate on credit
α_7	=	income tax rate
$P(0,0)$	=	period 0 level of commodity prices
$DIV(-1)$	=	realized firm profits in period -1
$BDB(-1)$	=	banks' end-of-period -1 number of bonds
$CRDF(-1)$	=	end-of-period -1 stock of credit demanded by firms

$CRDG(-1)$	=	end-of-period 1 stock of credit demanded by the government sector
b_1	=	a one-period discount factor

Since the variables of the model are related to different moments and periods we have adopted a notation that takes account of this characteristic. $Z(t)$ denotes the level of a variable Z at the end of period t. On the other hand, $Z(t,t)$ denotes the (expected) end-of-period t value of Z at the beginning of period t. Similarly, $Z(t,t+1)$ denotes the (expected) end-of-period $t+1$ value of Z at the beginning of period t. A superscript e denotes the desired or expected level of the variable under consideration. From equation [6.10] it can be observed that households have three sources of current-period income. In the first place, they receive wage income, in the second place, they receive all firm profits and in the third place, they receive their share of the revenues of the banking system (α_4 of bond earnings and α_5 of earnings on credits). It is assumed that the remaining revenues are accumulated by the banking sector. The government collects a part of these retained earnings as taxes (section 6.6.1). For the sake of simplicity, we have chosen not to model the equity market explicitly in this respect. Furthermore, it is assumed that 'dividends' are paid with a delay of one period.

In a situation with quantity constraints, intended and realized values may be different. As the bond market is a competitive market, households will always realize their demand for bonds. The actual level of money balances may be different from the intended level as households may not be able to realize their plans in the commodity market. The difference between intended and realized transactions in the commodity market reflects the quantity constraints observed in this market. From equation [6.9] it can be observed that leisure does not yield utility. Furthermore, spending and portfolio decisions are intertwined and taken simultaneously. The rationale for this assumption and its implications have been discussed by Tobin, Buiter, Snippe and Sterken, among others (e.g. Tobin, 1982, Buiter, 1980, Snippe, 1985, Sterken, 1988). To include asset variables in the utility function is a matter of dispute. With regard to money variables this dispute originates from Patinkin (1956). At best, the inclusion of financial assets and money in the utility function is accepted as a short cut since this approach allows for a consistent and simultaneous derivation of the demand for financial assets (including money balances). However, it should be observed that the demand for assets is assumed and not explained in this way (Fischer, 1987). We may regard the liquidity services provided by money as a possible reason for including cash balances in the utility function. It can be argued that the choice for money above interest-bearing assets represents a preference for flexibility. A preference for transferring wealth (both interest-bearing assets and money) and income to spending can be explained from the existence of time preference and/or precautionary motives. Since a decision to transfer wealth implies the transfer of spending opportunities to the future, we consider the real value of wealth with respect to future prices. To derive the real value of wealth in the current period a discount factor has been added.

Period t commodity prices are set by either firms or households, depending on the quantity constraints encountered in the commodity market in the previous period. Just like firms, households set prices on the assumption of a kinked perceived supply curve. In this respect, households assume the following kinked supply curve in the commodity market.

$$P(0,0) = A^e(0,0)C^e(0,0) + B(0,0) \quad [6.12]$$

$$A^e(0,0) > 0$$

$$A^e(0,0) = \begin{cases} a_h^e(0,0) & \text{if } C^e(0,0) < C(-1,-1)(1+g) \\ a_h^{1e}(0,0) & \text{if } C^e(0,0) > C(-1,-1)(1+g) \end{cases} \quad [6.13]$$

with

$a_h^e(0,0)$	= households' beginning-of-period 0 estimation of the period 0 value of parameter a, below the kink in the perceived supply curve
$a_h^{1e}(0,0)$	= households' beginning-of-period 0 estimation of the period t value of parameter a, above the kink in the perceived supply curve
$C(-1,-1)$	= realized consumption in the preceding period
g	= exogenous rate of growth of the (working) population

Initial levels of $a_h^e(0,0)$ and $a_h^{1e}(0,0)$ are set arbitrarily. These coefficients are adjusted each period for expected inflation and population growth. In this way the time pattern of commodity prices according to [6.12] is in line with the normal development of commodity prices in a situation where market clearing in the commodity market is expected $\left((P(0,0) = P(-1,-1)(1+\pi^e(0,0))\right)$. The following adjustment functions are put forward:

$$a_h^e(0,0) = a_h^e(-1,-1)\left\{\frac{1+\pi^e(0,0)}{1+g}\right\} \quad [6.14]$$

$$a_h^{1e}(0,0) = a_h^{1e}(-1,-1)\left\{\frac{1+\pi^e(0,0)}{1+g}\right\} \quad [6.15]$$

$$0 < a_h^e(0,0) < a_h^{1e}(0,0)$$

$$\pi^e(0,0) = \pi^e(-1,-1) + \alpha_8\left(\frac{P(-1,-1) - P(-2,-2)}{P(-2,-2)} - \pi^e(-1,-1)\right) \quad [6.16]$$

$$0 < \alpha_8 < 1$$

where

$$\pi(t-1,t-1) \equiv \frac{P(t-1,t-1) - P(t-2,t-2)}{P(t-2,t-2)} \quad \text{all } t \quad [6.17]$$

$\pi^e(0,0)$	= households' beginning-of-period 0 estimation of the current- period rate of inflation.

As mentioned already, expectations are adaptive expectations ([6.16]). Finally, parameter $B(0,0)$ is determined by equation [6.18].

$$B(0,0) = P(-1,-1)(1+\pi^e(0,0)) - A^e(0,0)C(-1,-1)(1+g) \qquad [6.18]$$

6.4.3 *Household behaviour in the absence of demand constraints in previous periods*

In situations of preceding-period excess supply and equality of demand and supply, the short-side of the market equals demand. Consequently, all participants on the demand side of the commodity market realize their intentions. The actual current-period commodity price is taken as given. In that situation, the demand for commodities, money and bonds can be obtained by maximization of [6.9] subject to [6.10] where prices are taken as exogenous. Households' current-period demand for commodities is then determined by:

$$C^e(0,0) = \alpha_1 \frac{AU}{P(0,0)} \qquad [6.19]$$

$$\begin{aligned} AU = {} & MDH(-1) + \frac{BDH(-1)}{R(0,0)} + \{W(0,0)L(0,0) + BDH(-1) + \\ & DIV(-1) + \alpha_4 BDB(-1) + \alpha_5\alpha_6 R(-1,-1)[CRDF(-1) \\ & + CRDG(-1)]\}(1-\alpha_7) \end{aligned} \qquad [6.20]$$

The current-period commodity price $P(0,0)$ is taken as a parameter in equation [6.19]. Equation [6.19] shows that in the absence of any quantity constraints, households' commodity demand is related to beginning-of-period real wealth and real labour income. Equation [6.19] implies a real wealth effect: a positive change in the real value of beginning-of-period money holdings has a positive impact on households' demand for consumption goods. In the absence of constraints in the commodity market, the demands for bonds and money are given by equation [6.21] and [6.22], respectively.

$$\frac{BDH(0)}{R(0,0)} = \alpha_3 AU \qquad [6.21]$$

$$MDH^e(0) = \alpha_2 AU \qquad [6.22]$$

The coefficients of equations [6.21] and [6.22] have the expected sign. A higher current- period rate of interest implies a higher current-period demand for bonds. Higher levels of beginning-of-period wealth and current income have similar effects. Equation [6.22] represents households' desired end-of-period stock of money balances. The level of money balances positively depends on beginning-of-period wealth and current income.

Households' actual transactions depend on the quantity restrictions in the several markets. Since financial markets are cleared by prices, the intended end-of-period stock of bonds will always be equal to the actual stock. In the commodity market households can be rationed in their intended purchases. Actual or realized current-period consumption is given by equation [6.23].

Furthermore, for the sake of simplicity, it is assumed that both firms and the government always realize their intentions in the commodity market.

$$C(0,0) = min\left\{C^e(0,0),\ INV(-1) - I(0,0) - G(0,0)\right\} \qquad [6.23]$$

where

$C(0,0)$ = realized consumption in period 0

$INV(-1)$ = the beginning-of-period 0 stock of commodities

$I(0,0)$ = realized (=intended) investments in period 0

$G(0,0)$ = realized (=intended) government expenditures in period 0

The actual end-of-period stock of money balances in period 0 ($MDH(0)$) reflects the transactions in the other markets of the model.

$$MDH(0) = MDH(-1) + \frac{BDH(-1)}{R(0,0)} + \Big\{W(0,0)L(0,0) + BDH(-1) + DIV(-1) + \alpha_4 BDB(-1) + \alpha_5\alpha_6 R(-1,-1)\big[CRDF(-1) + CRDG(-1)\big]\Big\}(1-\alpha_7) - P(0,0)C(0,0) - \frac{BDH(0)}{R(0,0)} \qquad [6.24]$$

From [6.24] it can be derived that

$$WH(0) = MDH(-1) + \frac{BDH(-1)}{R(0,0)} + \Big\{W(0,0)L(0,0) + BDH(-1) + DIV(-1) + \alpha_4 BDB(-1) + \alpha_5\alpha_6 R(-1,-1)\big[CRDF(-1) + CRDG(-1)\big]\Big\}(1-\alpha_7) - P(0,0)C(0,0) \qquad [6.25]$$

$WH(0)$ = the end-of-period level of household wealth

To conclude, observe that the decision problem presented in this section illustrates households' perception *ex ante* that in the absence of constraints in the commodity market in the preceding period, households perceive this market as a competitive system characterized by perfectly flexible prices. Furthermore, households perceive an end-of-period equilibrium in stocks in a situation where actual end-of-period stocks of financial assets are equal to intended end-of-period stocks. In the next section we will derive the optimal decisions *ex ante* of the households in situations where they have actually experienced quantity constraints in the commodity market *ex post*, i.e. at the end of the preceding period.

6.4.4 *Household behaviour in a situation of excess commodity demand in the preceding period*

In a situation of preceding-period excess commodity demand, households have faced a quantity constraint in the commodity market. This situation implies that households have not been able to trade whatever they wish at the going price. To relax the observed restriction on commodity transactions, households can adjust current-period prices as well as quantity demanded. Given the simultaneity in decision making, this implies that the decision on prices is incorporated into households' maximization procedure. Households behave as if they are monopsonist in the commodity market in a situation of preceding-period excess commodity demand. Furthermore, the perceived supply curve displays a kink to reflect the impact of search costs on the side of the selling agents. In order to consider the implications of price determination by households, the budget relationship [6.10] has to be adapted (equation [6.26]).

$$MDH(-1) + \frac{BDH(-1)}{R(0,0)} + \Big\{W(0,0)L(0,0) + BDH(-1) + DIV(-1)$$

$$\alpha_4 BDB(-1) + \alpha_5\alpha_6 R(-1,-1)\big(CRDF(-1) + CRDG(-1)\big)\Big\}(1-\alpha_7) =$$

$$\Big\{A^e(0,0)C^e(0,0) + B(0,0)\Big\}C^e(0,0) + \frac{BDH(0)}{R(0,0)} + MDH^e(0) \qquad [6.26]$$

Equation [6.26] has been obtained by the substitution of the inverted perceived supply curve [6.12] into equation [6.10]. Maximizing utility (equation [6.9]) subject to equation [6.26] yields the following equation for the demand for consumption goods.

$$C^e(0,0) = \frac{-B(0,0) \pm \Big\{B(0,0)^2 + 4(2-\alpha_1)\alpha_1 A^e(0,0)AU\Big\}^{1/2}}{2(2-\alpha_1)A^e(0,0)} \qquad [6.27]$$

With respect to [6.27] it can be observed that only positive solutions are permitted, which implies that, as the denominator is positive ($0 < \alpha_1 < 1$ and $A^e(0) > 0$), only positive roots are allowed. Hence, from [6.27] a unique level of consumption can be obtained as a function of disposable income and beginning-of-period wealth. The adjusted demand for money balances (equation [6.28]) can also be derived from the maximization procedure underlying equation [6.27].

$$MDH^e(0) = \alpha_2\Big\{AU + A^e(0,0)\big(C^e(0,0)\big)^2\Big\} \qquad [6.28]$$

Finally, the adjusted demand for bonds is given in equation [6.29].

$$\frac{BDH(0)}{R(0,0)} = \frac{\alpha_3 MDH^e(0)}{\alpha_2} \qquad [6.29]$$

From equation [6.13] it can be derived that the solutions (equations [6.27], [6.28] and [6.29]) of the households' maximization problem that includes the adapted budget relationship (equation [6.26]) are defined over an interval, which is positioned either to the left or to the right of $C(-1,-1)(1+g)$. Which position of the interval applies, depends on the branch of the kinked perceived supply curve that has been incorporated into the decision problem, i.e. the $a_h^e(0,0)$–branch or the $a_h^{1e}(0,0)$–branch. Hence, admissible sets of solutions to the decision problem in question are defined by a level of $C^e(0,0)$, which has to fall within the boundaries of the relevant interval. If the $a_h^e(0,0)$–branch is considered, $C^e(0,0) < C(-1,-1)(1+g)$. If the $a_h^{1e}(0,0)$–branch is considered, $C^e(0,0) > C(-1,-1)(1+g)$. In a situation where none of the two sets of solutions fulfills these requirements, households choose the quantity consumed and the commodity price of the preceding period adjusted for expectations and population growth. Hence, prices are not adjusted in response to observed quantity constraints, and quantity adjustments are assumed to clear the commodity market.

$$C^e(0,0) = C(-1,-1)(1+g) \qquad [6.30]$$

$$P(0,0) = P(-1,-1)(1+\pi^e(0,0)) \qquad [6.31]$$

In this situation, the demand for money balances as well as the demand for bonds are adjusted in line with the expected quantity adjustments in the commodity market. Since current–period consumption is determined by equation [6.30], utility is now maximized with respect to money balances and bonds subject to the budget equation [6.32].

$$MDH(-1) + \frac{BDH(-1)}{R(0,0)} + \Big\{W(0,0)L(0) + BDH(-1) + DIV(-1)$$

$$\alpha_4 BDB(-1) + \alpha_5\alpha_6 R(-1,-1)\big(CRDF(-1) + CRDG(-1)\big)\Big\}(1-\alpha_7) =$$

$$P(-1,-1)(1+\pi^e(0,0))C(-1,-1)(1+g) + \frac{BDH(0)}{R(0,0)} + MDH^e(0) \quad [6.32]$$

The demand for money and the demand for bonds are given by equations [6.33] and [6.34].

$$MDH^e(0) = \alpha_2/(\alpha_2+\alpha_3)\big(AU - P(-1,-1)(1+\pi^e(0,0))C(-1,-1)(1+g)\big) \qquad [6.33]$$

$$BDH(0) = \alpha_3/(\alpha_2+\alpha_3)R(0,0)\big(AU - P(-1,-1)(1+\pi^e(0,0))C(-1,-1)(1+g)\big) \qquad [6.34]$$

6.5 Firm behaviour

6.5.1 *Introduction*

Firms aim at maximizing profits and plan simultaneously at the beginning of every period current–period production, demand for labour, current–period sales, investments (including desired stock–piling), and how to finance these activities. Production takes one period, which implies that current–period commodity demand has to be met by decreasing inventories. For that reason production, sales and stock decisions reflect expectations of both current- and next-period demand and supply conditions. Firms may purchase commodities to change productive capacity and technology. Investment decisions are taken with respect to long-term expectations of the pattern of supply and demand in the different markets over time and are directed toward full utilization of productive capacity. Firms' intended activities are financed by issuing bonds, by drawing on money balances inherited from the past and by current-period receipts. If firms face unexpected liquidity shortages banks provide short-term credit to relieve this constraint in the current period.

6.5.2 *Firms' expectations concerning the demand for goods*

At the beginning of a period firms form expectations with respect to the demand for commodities. In a situation where the beginning-of-period commodity stock exceeded the observed commodity demand in the preceding period, firms are able to determine the current-period commodity price. Since producers have incomplete information about the actual relationship between prices and commodity demand, they take the supply decision with respect to a conjectural demand curve.

Period t commodity prices are set by firms given the quantity constraints observed in the commodity market in the previous period. Firms set prices on the assumption of a kinked perceived demand curve. In this respect, firms perceive the following demand conditions in the commodity market. Equation [6.35] gives firms' perception of demand on the assumption that a price increase is considered.

$$P(0,0) = -a_f^e(0,0)Y_f^e(0,0) + b_f(0,0) \qquad [6.35]$$

$$b_f(0,0) = P(-1,-1)(1+\pi^e(0,0)) + a_f^e(0,0)Y(-1,-1)(1+g) \qquad [6.36]$$

$$a_f^e(0,0),\ b_f(0,0);\ Y_f^e(0,0) < Y(-1,-1)(1+g)$$

$a_f^e(0,0)$ = firms' beginning-of-period 0 estimation of the period 0 value of parameter a, above the kink in the perceived demand curve

$Y_f^e(0,0)$ = producers' beginning-of-period perception of current-period commodity demand

$Y(-1,-1)$ = realized sales in the preceding period

Expected inflation is already defined in equation [6.16]. Equation [6.37] specifies the expected current-period relationship between price and commodity demand if a price cut is considered.

$$P(0,0) = -a_f^{1e}(0,0)Y_f^e(0,0) + b_f^1(0,0) \qquad [6.37]$$

$$b_f^1(0,0) = P(-1,-1)(1+\pi^e(0,0)) + a_f^{1e}(0,0)Y(-1,-1)(1+g) \qquad [6.38]$$

$$a_f^{1e}(0,0),\ b_f^1(0,0) > 0;\ Y_f^e(0,0) > Y(-1,-1)(1+g)$$

$a_f^{1e}(0,0)$ = firms' beginning-of-period 0 estimation of the period 0 value of parameter a, below the kink in the perceived demand curve

With respect to the calculation of parameters $a_f^e(0,0)$ and $a_f^{1e}(0,0)$, the following relationships apply.

$$a_f^e(0,0) = a_f^e(-1,-1)\left\{\frac{1+\pi^e(0,0)}{1+g}\right\} \qquad [6.39]$$

$$a_f^{1e}(0,0) = a_f^{1e}(-1,-1)\left\{\frac{1+\pi^e(0,0)}{1+g}\right\} \qquad [6.40]$$

On the other hand, in a siuation where firms are not constrained in the commodity market, they take decisions in the current period on the perception of given current–period prices since they do not feel the need to change prices, nor do they observe the opportunity to do so.

Taken together, the above implies the following kinked perceived current–period demand curve

$$P(0,0) = \beta_1\left[-a_f^e(0,0)Y_f^e(0,0) + b_f(0,0)\right] + \beta_2\left[-a_f^{1e}(0,0)Y_f^e(0,0) + b_f^1(0,0)\right] + \beta_3 P(0,0) \qquad [6.41]$$

In situations where the available commodity stock is smaller than or equal to commodity demand in the preceding period $\beta_3 = 1$ and $\beta_1 = \beta_2 = 0$. Hence prices are treated parametrically. In the opposite situation either $\beta_3 = 0$, $\beta_1 = 1$, $\beta_2 = 0$ if $P(0,0) > P(-1,-1)(1+\pi^e(0,0))$, or $\beta_3 = 0, \beta_1 = 0$, $\beta_2 = 1$ if $P(0,0) < P(-1,-1)(1+\pi^e(0,0))$.

Since production takes one period, firms consider current– and next–period demand conditions in the commodity market simultaneously. With respect to the decisions on production and sales, producers apply a two–period planning horizon, which implies that firms determine expectations of next–period commodity price at the beginning of the current period. In this respect, firms' perceive quantity constraints only as temporary phenomena, which are assumed to be corrected by the price–setting procedure in the current period. Prices are set in the conviction that they match current–period demand and supply and firms expect to have the right perception of commodity demand. Consequently, it is firms' perception that the possibility of price setting disappears after the current period. After the current period, firms expect prices to be given. Firms' market position in the current period only offers a temporary opportunity to gain a monopoly profit. With respect to expected next–period prices the following adjustment function is assumed.

$$P^e_f(0,1) = \beta_4 P^e(-1,0)\left[1+ \pi^e(-1,-1) + \beta_5(Y_d(-1,-1)-INV(-2))/INV(-2)\right] + (1-\beta_4)P^e(-2,-1)\left[1+ \pi^e(-2,-2) + \beta_5(Y_d(-2,-2)-INV(-3))/INV(-3)\right] \quad [6.42]$$

$$0 < \beta_4,\beta_5 < 1$$

with

$P^e_f(t,t+1)$ = firms' beginning-of-period t expectation of period $t+1$ commodity price.
$INV(t-1)$ = beginning-of-period t level of inventories
$Y(t,t)$ = period t level of aggregate demand

6.5.3 *Constraints on production and sales*

Current-period production is characterized by the following Cobb-Douglas production function

$$Q(0,0) = AL(0,0)^{\beta_6}K(-1)^{(1-\beta_6)} \quad [6.43]$$

$$0 < \beta_6 < 1$$

with

$Q(0,0)$ = planned production in period 0
$L(0,0)$ = employment in period 0
$K(-1)$ = the fixed beginning-of-period stock of capital, which is equal to the capital stock at the end of the preceding period
A = total factor productivity

Equation [6.43] reflects the assumption that the beginning-of-period stock of capital is fixed and fully utilized every period. If the labour market in the current period is characterized by excess demand, then current-period production will be constrained by the available supply of labour.

$$Q(0,0) \leq A\left[N(-1)(1+g)\right]^{\beta_6}K(-1)^{(1-\beta_6)} \quad [6.44]$$

$N(t-1)(1+g)$ = the working population at the beginning of t

Current-period production costs consist of wage payments and capital costs. Depreciation costs depend on the size of the fixed beginning-of-period stock of capital. In this respect, a constant rate of depreciation is assumed. For further details, see section 6.5.5 where the investment decision is discussed. Current-period labour costs are equal to the product of the current-period money wage rate $W(0,0)$ and the current-period level of employment.

Current-period sales can be constrained by commodity demand, on the one hand, and by beginning-of-period inventories, on the other hand. In addition, price expectations may stimulate firms to transfer a part of beginning-of-period stock of commodities to the next period. Firms do not plan to hold stocks longer than the planning period (of two unit-periods), which implies that the intended stock at the beginning of the next period will be exactly equal to the expected level of commodity demand in the next period.

$$Y_f^e(0,0) = INV(-1) - inv(0,0) \qquad [6.45]$$

$inv(0,0)$ = part of the beginning-of-current-period stock, that firms plan to transfer to the next period.

$$INV(0) = inv(0,0) + Q(0,0) \qquad [6.46]$$

$$Y_f^e(0,1) = INV(0) \qquad [6.47]$$

$Y_f^e(t,t+1)$ = the expected level of commodity demand in the next period at the beginning of t

Finally, it is assumed that firms can only transfer a part of the beginning-of-period stock to the next period. Furthermore, it is impossible that $inv(0,0)$ falls below zero. The combination of these two assumptions gives condition [6.48]

$$0 \le inv(0,0) \le \beta_7 INV(-1) \qquad [6.48]$$
$$0 \le \beta_7 < 1$$

6.5.4 *Producers' current-period decisions on employment and commodity supply*

Firms aim at maximizing expected cash-flow over a two-period planning horizon. All payments are settled at the beginning of the period. The expected cash flow is given in equation [6.49].

$$PRF(0,0) = P(0,0)Y_f^e(0,0) + P_f^e(0,1)Y_f^e(0,1)b_1 - W(0,0)L(0,0) \qquad [6.49]$$

b_1 = a one-period discount factor

For computational purposes we write [6.41] as:

$$P(0,0) = A_1 Y_f^e(0,0) + A_2 \qquad [6.41a]$$

with

$$A_1 = -\beta_1 a_f^e(0,0) - \beta_2 a_f^{1e}(0,0)$$

$$A_2 = \beta_1 b_f(0,0) + \beta_2 b_f^1(0,0) + \beta_3 P(0,0)$$

and [6.43] as

$$Q(0,0) = A_3 L(0,0)^{\beta_6} \qquad [6.43a]$$

$$A_3 = AK(-1)^{(1-\beta_6)}$$

Substitution of [6.41a], [6.45], [6.46] and [6.47] in [6.49] gives

$$PRF = \left\{A_1 \cdot (INV(-1) - inv(0,0)) + A_2\right\}\left(INV(-1) - inv(0,0)\right)$$

$$+ P_f^e(0,1)\left\{Q(0,0) + inv(0,0)\right\}b_1 - W(0,0)L(0,0) \qquad [6.50]$$

Maximizing *PRF* subject to [6.43a] yields the following first-order conditions.

$$\frac{\partial PRF}{\partial inv(0,0)} = -2A_1 INV(-1) + 2A_1 inv(0,0) - A_2 + b_1 P_f^e(0,1) = 0 \qquad [6.51]$$

and

$$\frac{\partial PRF}{\partial L(0,0)} = b_1\beta_6 P_f^e(0,1)A_3 L(0,0)^{\beta_6 - 1} - W(0,0) = 0 \qquad [6.52]$$

Denoting *det H* as the determinant of the Hessian matrix of second-order derivatives, we have

$$detH = \begin{vmatrix} 2A_1 & 0 \\ 0 & b_1(\beta_6 - 1)\beta_6 P_f^e(0,1)A_3 L(0,0)^{(\beta_6 - 2)} \end{vmatrix}$$

which gives the principal minors He_1 and He_2 of *det H* that specify the associated second-order conditions for a maximum.

$$He_1 = 2A_1 < 0 \qquad [6.53]$$

$$He_2 = 2A_1\left\{b_1(\beta_6 - 1)\beta_6 P_f^e(0,1)A_3 L(0,0)^{(\beta_6 - 2)}\right\} > 0 \qquad [6.54]$$

The specification of A_1 ([6.41a]) immediately implies that only in case the firm sets the commodity price ($\beta_2 \vee \beta_1 = 1$ and $\beta_3 = 0$) second-order conditions are fulfilled. If producers take prices as given, both He_1 and He_2 are zero ($A_1 = 0$). In that situation [6.51] indicates that optimal profits are independent of $inv(0,0)$. As a result, the optimal transfer of commodities cannot be determined from equation [6.51]. From a theoretical point of view this conclusion is not ambiguous, since in a competitive market firms assume that they can sell any quantity of commodities at the given price. There are no reasons to consider the transfer of commodities to future periods to be profitable. However, there is one exception. If exogenous developments cause the discounted expected commodity price in the next period to exceed the current-period commodity price, firms plan to transfer commodities to the next period as much as possible. On the other hand, if the discounted expected commodity price in the next period is lower than the current-period commodity price, firms do not consider any transfer at all. In case the two variables are equal in size, firms are indifferent whether or not to transfer commodities to the next period. Equation [6.51] captures all three opportunities, which will be clear after substitution of $A_1 = 0$ and $A_2 = P(0,0)$ ([6.41a]) into [6.51].

$$\frac{\partial PRF}{\partial inv(0,0)} = - P(0,0) + b_1 P_f^e(0,1) = 0 \qquad [6.51a]$$

Equation [6.51a] implies the following decisions, with respect to the transfers of commodities to the next period in a situation where firms take prices as given.

A. The expected discounted next-period price exceeds the current-period price.

$$b_1 P_f^e(0,1) > P(0,0), \text{ i.e. } \frac{P_f^e(0,1) - P(0,0)}{P(0,0)} > R(0,0)$$

In that situation the transfer of commodities has a positive effect on expected profits, since equation [6.51a] has a positive value. The best possible policy for firms is to transfer, as much as possible, commodities to the next period. Thus, recalling [6.48], $inv(0,0) = \beta_7 INV(-1)$.

B. The expected discounted next-period price is lower than the current-period price.

$$b_1 P_f^e(0,1) < P(0,0), \text{ i.e. } \frac{P_f^e(0,1) - P(0,0)}{P(0,0)} < R(0,0)$$

This is the opposite case of A: $inv(0,0) = 0$.

C. The expected next-period price equals the current-period price.

$$b_1 P_f^e(0,1) = P(0,0), \text{ i.e. } \frac{P_f^e(0,1) - P(0,0)}{P(0,0)} = R(0,0)$$

In this situation firms are indifferent to the transfer of commodities to the next period. We will interpret this situation as one in which firms do not expect changes in the conditions in the commodity market. Hence, $INV(0) = INV(-1)(1+g)$, which implies $inv(0,0) = INV(-1)(1+g) - Q(0,0)$.

In situations where firms determine the commodity price, the optimal transfer of commodities can be calculated by solving [6.51]

$$inv(0,0) = INV(-1) + \left\{ \frac{A_2 - b_1 P_f^e(0,1)}{2A_1} \right\} \qquad [6.55]$$

If $inv(0,0)$ is constrained by the upper limit given in [6.48], it is optimal to set $inv(0,0)$ equal to this constraint, since [6.51] is monotonic in $inv(0,0)$. Thus, in that situation the best possible transfer is given by

$$inv(0,0) = \beta_7 INV(-1) \qquad [6.56]$$

The optimal demand for labour, $L^*(0,0)$, is derived from equation [6.52].

$$L^*(0,0) = \left\{W(0,0)/(b_1 P_f^e(0,1)\beta_6 A_3)\right\}^{\frac{1}{(\beta_6 - 1)}} \quad [6.57]$$

with

$$L(0,0) = min\left\{L^*(0,0),\ N(-1)(1+g)\right\} \quad [6.58]$$

Because of the kink in the perceived demand curve, the level of $inv(0,0)$ depends on the branch of the perceived demand curve under consideration, which is reflected in the values of A_1 and A_2.

First, consider the upper branch (equation [6.35]) of the perceived demand curve ($\beta_1 = 1$, $\beta_2 = \beta_3 = 0$). The associated restriction on current–period commodity prices is:

$$P(0,0) > P(-1,-1)(1+\pi^e(0,0))$$

which implies

$$\left\{INV(-1) - inv_e(0,0)\right\} < Y(-1,-1)(1+g)$$

$inv_e(0,0)$ can be derived by substitution of the relevant expressions of A_1 and A_2 as well as of $b_f(0,0)$ in equation [6.55].

$$inv_e(0,0) = INV(-1) - 0.5P(-1,-1)(1+\pi^e(0,0))/a_f^e(0,0) - 0.5Y(-1,-1)(1+g) + 0.5b_1P_f^e(0,1)/a_f^e(0,0) \quad [6.59]$$

Replacing in [6.59] $a_f^e(0,0)$ by $a_f^{1e}(0,0)$ yields $inv_{1e}(0,0)$, which represents the optimal transfer of commodities to the next period in case the lower branch (equation [6.37]) of the perceived demand curve is considered ($\beta_2 = 1$, $\beta_1 = \beta_3 = 0$). The associated restriction on current–period prices is given by

$$P(0,0) < P(-1,-1)(1+\pi^e(0,0))$$

which implies

$$\left\{INV(-1) - inv_{1e}(0,0)\right\} > Y(-1,-1)(1+g)$$

$inv_{1e}(0,0)$ is given by [6.60]

$$inv_{1e}(0,0) = INV(-1) - 0.5P(-1,-1)(1+\pi^e(0,0))/a_f^{1e}(0,0) - 0.5Y(-1,-1)(1+g) + 0.5b_1P_f^e(0,1)/a_f^{1e}(0,0) \quad [6.60]$$

The optimal solution $\left\{inv(0,0),\ L(0,0)\right\}$ maximizes profits [6.49] and is chosen from the possible solutions $\{(inv_e(0,0),\ L(0,0)),\ (inv_{1e}(0,0),\ L(0,0))\}$ and meets the restrictions imposed by the branch of the kinked demand curve under consideration. If the solutions distinguished by $inv_e(0,0)$, and $inv_{1e}(0,0)$ do not meet this last requirement, then the location of the kink in the perceived demand curve will be the optimal solution. Thus, in that situation

$$inv(0,0) = INV(-1) - Y(-1,-1)(1+g) \qquad [6.61]$$

and

$$P(0,0) = P(-1,-1)(1+\pi^e(0,0)) \qquad [6.62]$$

6.5.5 *Firms' investment behaviour*

Firms change productive capacity in order to meet the expected growth of effective commodity demand in the long run. In the long run, firms are assumed to perceive the economy as a competitive system. Observe that only in a situation of a supply constraint in the commodity market, firms perceive the commodity market as if it were characterized by imperfect competition. Furthermore, firms' current–period activities are directed toward the termination of this situation after one unit–period, through price and quantity adjustments. On the assumption that firms' perception of demand is correct, their activities are successful. Hence, in the long run the commodity market is expected to clear. A unique equilibrium price is established, since all available information is processed. The commodity price in the long run represents a datum for the individual firm. Expected commodity prices are treated parametrically and firms minimize production costs subject to a technology constraint only. Furthermore, firms' investment decisions are taken on the assumption of full substitution between factors and are directed toward complete utilization of available capacity. Expectations about nominal wages in the long run are adaptive, which implies that nominal wage formation in the short run (= the unit–period) causes only a partial adjustment of expected nominal wages in the long run. The reason for this behaviour is that, at least for some part, short–run fluctuations in nominal wages are expected to cancel out over a succession of unit–periods. Furthermore, it is assumed that investment decisions are taken with the intention to match the demand for and the production of commodities in the long run. Firms do not plan to hold inventories in the long run. In addition, they take account of production lags. A current–period investment decision changes capacity at the beginning of the next period, which implies that inventories may change at the beginning of the period thereafter. With respect to their investment decisions, firms anticipate a flow of sales receipts starting two periods from now, on the one hand, and a flow of production costs from the next period onwards, on the other hand.

The above implies the use of different discount factors in order to calculate the present value of sales receipts, production costs and costs of finance that result from a given investment project. Firms' current–period investments can be derived from the minimization of the firms' discounted production costs subject to a production constraint. The minimization problem underlying the firms' investment decision is given in equation [6.63].

$$min \sum_{t=0}^{\infty} b_1^{\,t}\Big\{b_1 W_f^e(t,t+1)L(t,t+1) + P(t,t)\Big\{K(t) - (1 - \beta_8)K(t-1)\Big\}\Big\} \qquad [6.63]$$

subject to

$$Y(t,t+2) = F(L(t,t+1),\ K(t)) \qquad [6.64]$$

$$I(t,t) = K(t) - (1 - \beta_8)K(t-1) \qquad [6.65]$$

$$b_1 = \left\{\frac{1}{1 + R(0,0)}\right\} \qquad [6.66]$$

$Y(t,t+2)$ = the beginning-of-period t expectation of sales in period $t+2$
$L(t,t+1)$ = the beginning-of-period t expectation of employment in period $t+1$
b_1 = a discount factor
$I(t,t)$ = current-period gross investments
β_8 = rate of depreciation

In the maximization procedure above, it is assumed that firms have an infinite planning horizon. The interest rate on bonds is considered to be the appropriate discount rate. The following first-order conditions can be derived.

$$b_1^{\,t+1}W_f^e(t,t+1) - \lambda F_L = 0 \qquad [6.67]$$

$$b_1^{\,t}P(t,t) - b_1^{\,t+1}\Big\{P(t+1,t+1)(1 - \beta_8)\Big\} - \lambda F_K = 0 \qquad [6.68]$$

$$Y(t,t+2) - F(L(t,t+1),\ K(t)) = 0 \qquad [6.69]$$

where

F_L = the physical marginal productivity of labour in period $t+1$

F_K = the physical marginal productivity of capital in period $t+1$

λ = the Lagrange parameter

If it is assumed that $P_f^e(t,t+i+1) = P_f^e(t,t+i)(1+ \pi^e(t,t+i))$, on the one hand, and that the assumption of static inflationary expectations holds in the long run, $(\pi^e(t+i,t+i) = \pi^e(t,t))$ and $P(t+i,t+j) = P_f^e(t,t+j)$; on the other hand, equation [6.70] can be derived from equation [6.68], on the assumption that $\beta_8\pi^e(t,t) \approx 0$.

$$P_f^e(t,t+1)\Big\{R(t,t) + \beta_8 - \pi^e(t,t)\Big\} = \lambda F_K b_1^{\,-(t+1)} \qquad [6.70]$$

From equations [6.67] and [6.70] it can be derived that

$$\frac{F_K}{F_L} = \left\{\frac{P_f^e(t,t+1)}{W_f^e(t,t+1)}\right\}\left\{R(t,t) + \beta_8 - \pi^e(t,t)\right\} \qquad [6.71]$$

If we assume a Cobb–Douglas technology, on the one hand, and if we take account of the assumption that investments are directed toward full utilization of all available capacity, on the other hand, the intended stock of capital ($K^*(t)$) can be determined from equation [6.72].

$$K^*(t) = \frac{(1-\beta_6)N(t+1)W_f^e(t,t+1)}{\beta_6 P_f^e(t,t+1)(R(t,t) - \pi^e(t,t) + \beta_8)} \qquad [6.72]$$

where

$$N(t+1) = N(t)(1+g)$$

It is assumed that firms' investment demand is never constrained in the commodity market. Furthermore, firms take account of delivery constraints, which implies the following equation for current–period gross investments ($I(t,t)$).

$$I(t,t) = \beta_9(K^*(t) - K(t-1)) + \beta_8 K(t-1) \qquad [6.73]$$

$$0 < \beta_9 < 1$$

Firms finance expenditures by drawing on accumulated cash balances, by supplying bonds and by using current sales receipts. This implies the following budget identity in the current period.

$$P(0,0)I(0,0) + W(0,0)L^*(0,0) + BSF(-1) + DIV(-1,-1) + CRDF(-1)$$

$$(1 + \alpha_6 R(-1,-1)) - P(0,0)Y_f^e(0,0) - MDF(-1) - \frac{BSF(0) - BSF(-1)}{R(0,0)}$$

$$= 0 \qquad [6.74]$$

$$\alpha_6 > 1$$

Dividend payments are equal to

$$DIV(0,0) = P(0,0)Y_f(0,0) - W(0,0)L(0,0) - BSF(-1) - \beta_8 P(0,0)K(-1)$$
$$- \alpha_6 R(-1,-1)CRDF(-1) \qquad [6.75]$$

From [6.74] the beginning–of–period supply of bonds can be derived

$$BSF(0) = R(0,0)\Big\{P(0,0)I(0,0) + W(0,0)L^*(0,0) + BSF(-1)$$

$$+ DIV(-1,-1) + CRDF(-1)(1 + \alpha_6 R(-1,-1)) - P(0,0)Y_f^e(0,0)$$

$$- MDF(-1)\Big\} + BSF(-1) \qquad [6.76]$$

Equations [6.74] and [6.76] imply that firms do not plan to hold money balances at the end of the period. The level of actual end-of-period money balances depends on the realized level of current-period sales and labour costs. In a situation where actual sales exceed expected sales, end-of-period money balances will be affected positively. An encountered quantity constraint in the labour market has a similar impact. In opposite situations, firms may encounter liquidity shortages. In order to relieve these shortages, banks supply short-term loans. The end-of-period level of short-term loans is given in equation [6.77].

$$CRDF(0) = max\Big\{0,\ P(0,0)I(0,0) + W(0,0)L(0,0) + BSF(-1) + DIV(-1,-1) + CRDF(-1)(1 + \alpha_6 R(-1,-1)) - P(0,0)Y_f(0,0) - MDF(-1) - \frac{BSF(0) - BSF(-1)}{R(0,0)}\Big\} \qquad [6.77]$$

Finally, from equations [6.76] and [6.77] it can be derived that

$$WF(0) = MDF(-1) - \frac{BSF(-1)}{R(0,0)} - CRDF(-1) + \Big\{P(0,0)Y_f(0,0) - \Big\{P(0,0)I(0,0) + W(0,0)L(0,0) + BSF(-1) + DIV(-1,-1) + CRDF(-1)\alpha_6 R(-1,-1)\Big\}\Big\} \qquad [6.78]$$

It can be observed that $WF(0)$ does not represent the end-of-period level of wealth held by firms in the usual meaning of wealth. From table 6.1 it can be derived that the firms' balance sheet is constituted only of financial assets, liabilities and total 'wealth' of firms. In particular, the capital stock is not incorporated in our definition of firm 'wealth.' Furthermore, as firms transfer all profits to the household sector, there is no accumulation of earnings in the firm sector. As a result, $WF(0)$ is equal to the difference between *financial* assets (MDF) and liabilities (BSF/R and $CRDF$) and reflects the current-period value of the capital stock.

6.6 The behaviour of banks and the government sector

6.6.1 *The government sector*

It is assumed that real government expenditures are independently determined by the government sector. A part of these expenditures (γ_1) is proportional to the size of the working population, another part is used for stabilization policy. Government expenditures depend negatively on the expected rate of inflation and positively on the discrepancy between the actual rate of unemployment and the 'natural' rate of unemployment, i.e. the unemployment rate which is perceived as the equilibrium rate of unemployment. In this respect, the parameters γ_2 and γ_3 are policy parameters and reflect government preferences for a stable price level, on the one hand and a stable unemployment rate, on the other hand.

$$G(0,0) = max\left(0, \gamma_1 - \gamma_2\pi^e(0,0) + \gamma_3(U(-1,-1) - U_n)\right)N(0) \qquad [6.79]$$

$$\gamma_1, \gamma_2, \gamma_3 > 0$$

$G(0,0)$ = real government expenditures in period 0
U_n = the 'natural' rate of unemployment
$U(t,t)$ = the actual rate of unemployment in period t.

Government expenditures have to be financed by a proportional income tax. In a situation where taxes fall short of expenditures, the creation of bonds as well as short-term loans provide sources of additional finance. Current-period tax payments are given in equation [6.80].

$$T(0,0) = \alpha_7\Big\{W(0,0)L(0,0) + BDH(-1) + \alpha_4 BDB(-1) + DIV(-1) +$$

$$\alpha_5\alpha_6 R(-1,-1)\left(CRDF(-1) + CRDG(-1)\right)\Big\} \qquad [6.80]$$

$T(0,0)$ = total current-period tax payments.

The current-period goverment budget deficit equals the difference between government expenditures and receipts.

$$PSD(0,0) = P(0,0)G(0,0) + \alpha_6 R(-1,-1)CRDG(-1) + BSG(-1) - T(0,0)$$

$$- \gamma_4 BDB(-1) - \gamma_5\alpha_6 R(-1,-1)\left(CRDF(-1) + CRDG(-1)\right) \qquad [6.81]$$

$$\gamma_4, \gamma_5 > 0$$

with

$PSD(0,0)$ = the current-period government deficit
$BSG(-1)$ = the stock of bonds issued by the government at the end of the preceding period
$CRDG(-1)$ = the stock of short-term loans issued by the government at the end of the preceding period

In order to finance the current-period deficit, bonds and short-term loans to the banking system are issued in a arbitrarily fixed proportion. This proportion represents a policy parameter.

$$BSG(0) = max\left(0, \gamma_6 R(0,0)PSD(0,0) + BSG(-1)\right) \qquad [6.82]$$

$$CRDG(0) = max\left(0, (1-\gamma_6)PSD(0,0) + CRDG(-1)\right) \qquad [6.83]$$

$$0 \leq \gamma_6 \leq 1$$

Finally,

$$WG(0) = WG(-1) + SG(0,0) \qquad [6.84]$$

$$SG(0,0) = -BSG(0)/R(0,0) - CRDG(0) - min\left(0,\ WG(-1)\right) - min\left(0,\ PSD(0,0) - (BSG(0) - BSG(-1))/R(0,0) - (CRDG(0) - CRDG(-1))\right) \quad [6.85]$$

The specification of equation [6.85] can be explained from the existence of maximum conditions in equations [6.82] and [6.83], which reflect that the government sector cannot be a net–supplier of credit and a net–demander of bonds. In case of a budget deficit [6.82], [6.83] and [6.85] imply $SG(0,0) = -BSG(0)/R(0,0) - CRDG(0) - WG(-1)$ $(WG(-1) \leq 0)$. In case of a budget surplus and $BSG(0)/R(0,0) = CRDG(0) = WG(-1) = 0$, $SG(0,0) = PSD(0,0)$ $(PSD(0,0) < 0)$. In intermediate situations characterized by a budget surplus and positive short and long–term debts it is assumed that these debts are paid off in the first place. The remaining surplus is then added to goverment wealth.

6.6.2 *The banking system*

The purpose of the banking sector in this model is simply to provide short– and long–term loans to the government as well as to the private sector. This section only offers a rather limited attempt to rationalize the behaviour of banks. We consider a more rigorous foundation of the activities of the banking system to fall beyond the scope of this analysis. From the flow of funds account of section 6.3 it can be derived that short– and long–term loans are provided to the government sector and to the private sector. The consolidated balance sheet of the complete banking system gives the following picture.

Banks' balance sheet

assets	liabilities
CRDF	*WB*
BDB/R	*M*
CRDG	

From the balance sheet the following equation for the current–period supply of money can be derived.

$$M(0) = CRDF(0) + BDB(0)/R(0,0) + CRDG(0) - WB(0) \quad [6.86]$$

Furthermore, from equation [6.8] we derive

$$WB(0) = -\left\{WH(0) + WF(0) + WG(0)\right\} \quad [6.87]$$

We will now discuss the behavioural relationships of banks. As mentioned, the supply of short–term loans to firms and the government sector are demand–determined. With respect to the demand for bonds the following stock adjustment relationship is put forward.

$$BDB(0) = \gamma_7 \big(R(0,0) - R(-1,-1)\big) / R(-1,-1) - \gamma_8 \Big\{BDB(-1) / \big(R(-1,-1)WB(-1)\big)\Big\} + BDB(-1) \qquad [6.88]$$

$$\gamma_7, \gamma_8 > 0$$

The current-period demand for bonds by banks depends on changes in the rate of interest positively, on the one hand, and on the share of bonds in total wealth negatively, on the other hand. Equation [6.88] reflects that only *changes* in the rate of interest cause adjustments in banks' portfolios. With respect to short-term bank loans we have assumed in section 6.3 that supply is demand-determined, i.e. $CRSB(0) = CRDF(0) + CRDG(0)$. Finally, it is assumed that bank activities do not involve any costs. As a result, interest payments to banks are equal to bank profits. These profits are subjected to a proportional income tax (tax rates are γ_4 and γ_5). After-tax profits are paid to households as dividend payments for some part (α_4 and α_5) and added to bank wealth for the remaining part.

6.7 Transactions in the commodity and labour market

Before we can start with analyzing the characteristics of the model developed in this chapter, we have to reconsider the behaviour in the commodity and labour market in order to determine the current-period transactions in these markets. In the commodity market the current-period price is set endogeneously. However, these price setting procedures do not always induce market clearing. Commodity supply is provided for by firms

$$Y_f^e(0,0) = INV(-1) - inv(0,0) \qquad [6.45]$$

Households, firms and the government sector demand commodities

$$Y_d(0,0) = C^e(0,0) + G(0,0) + I(0,0) \qquad [6.89]$$

Actual current transactions in the commodity market are equal to the minimum of the beginning-of-period commodity stock and demand.

$$Y(0,0) = min\Big\{INV(-1),\ C^e(0,0) + G(0,0) + I(0,0)\Big\} \qquad [6.90]$$

Remember in this respect that it is assumed that the government sector as well as firms are not constrained in their commodity demand, which implies that in case of a current-period excess demand situation, the burden of adjustment falls on the demand for consumption purposes by households.

The labour market is a fixprice market. In this respect, we will not offer a rigorous choice-theoretic foundation of wage formation. For the sake of simplicity, current period nominal wages are determined according to equation [6.91].

$$W(0,0) = W(-1,-1)\Big\{1 + \pi^e(0,0) + \gamma_9 min\big(0,\ U_n - U(-1,-1)\big) +$$

$$\gamma_{10} max\left(0,\ U_n\ -\ U(-1,-1)\right) \qquad [6.91]$$

$$\gamma_9,\ \gamma_{10}\ >\ 0$$

$$U(-1,-1)\ =\ \left(N(-1)\ -\ L(-1,-1)\right)/N(-1) \qquad [6.92]$$

Equation [6.91] is the convential expectations–augmented Phillips curve and indicates that nominal wages are adjusted positively for expected inflation and negatively for unemployment in the preceding period. With respect to the formation of expected nominal wages the following adaptive adjustment mechanism is assumed.

$$W^e_f(0,1)\ =\ \gamma_{11}\left\{W^e_f(-1,0)\ +\ \gamma_{12}\left(W(0,0)\ -\ W^e_f(-1,0)\right)\right\}\ +\ (1-\gamma_{11})$$

$$\left\{W^e_f(-2,-1)\ +\ \gamma_{12}\left(W(-1,-1)\ -\ W^e_f(-2,-1)\right)\right\} \qquad [6.93]$$

$$0\ <\ \gamma_{11},\ \gamma_{12}\ <\ 1$$

Labour is demanded by firms and supplied by households. Current–period transactions in the labour market are equal to minimum of supply and demand

$$L(0,0)\ =\ min\left\{L^*(0,0),\ N(-1)(1+g)\right\} \qquad [6.58]$$

With the description of labour market transactions, the development of the model has been completed. In the next chapter we will analyse the characteristics of the model by means of simulation experiments.

Notes

1. Groenveld (1982) takes exactly the opposite approach. This distinction refers to distribution of market power as a result of a situation of non–market clearing, *e.g.*, consumers set prices in a situation of excess supply since they can then *ceteris paribus* enforce a lower price. Although Groenveld's method has some appeal it is in our opinion ambiguous that agents choose to change their situation when they have realized their optimal plans as price taking agents. The application of the *ceteris paribus* clause is not straightforward in this respect.

2. The distinction between continuous and discrete time is of no relevance in this respect since continuous time may be represented by infinitely small periods.

7 A macroeconomic model of adjustment: some illustrative processes

7.1 Introduction

The analysis of economic processes, which can be generated with the macroeconomic model we have developed in the preceding chapter[1] will be the subject to deal with in chapter 7. As has already been emphasized, the complexity of the model does not allow for an analytical approach. Instead we have performed a number of dynamic simulations, the results of which will be reported here. However, before we start the discussion of the simulation results it may be useful to summarize some important characteristics of the model and to relate them to the purpose of this study.

In the introduction to this monograph, we have defined the purpose of our study as an attempt to provide some insights into the characteristics of economic processes in a set-up where the existence of perfect coordination is not assumed beforehand. Furthermore, the implications of heterogeneity among agents are considered in as far as they may affect the formation of (commodity) prices. The first element of this object of research has been incorporated in the model by adopting a sequential-analytical approach. Since time is divided into arbitrary small unit-periods and since *current-period* expectations precede and are independent of actual events in the current unit-period, we take account of the irreversibility of economic processes and at the same time develop a framework for a more explicit analysis of the activities that move economic processes. Agents' current-period expectations concerning the current-period demand and supply constraints in the commodity market can be frustrated in the context of the model. As a result, agents revise their expectations at the beginning of the next unit-period before they decide on their activities in that period. The point of interest dealt with in this chapter is to what extent these revisions permit conclusions with respect to the performance of the economic system as a whole, on the one hand, and how sensitive these results are for changes in parameter values, on the other hand. The second element of our object of research deals with the implications of heterogeneity among agents. For the sake of simplicity we confine our analysis to the impact of heterogeneity among agents on the determination of commodity prices. To that purpose kinked perceived demand and supply curves have been introduced in the commodity market. In the literature (see chapters 4 and 5), kinked demand curves have served as an analytical device that enabled the existence of commodity price rigidity. In this chapter we will analyse the implications of kinked demand and supply curves in a more dynamic environment. Furthermore, we have endogenized the degree of competition in the commodity market in line with Hahn (1978). The degree of competition depends on the quantity constraint observed in the commodity market in the preceding unit-period. The commodity market in a unit-period can be characterized by perfect, monopolistic or monopsonistic competition.

Another characteristic of the model is the existence of production lags. The lags imply that sales can only be made out of stock. In the literature (see chapter 4) storage possibilities have been regarded as an additional source of price rigidity, on the one hand and as a buffer between demand and production, on the other hand. We will consider the role of inventories in the model within the context of these theoretical observations.

Since the model includes a government sector it is no more than natural to discuss the implications of the existence of this sector. From section 6.6.1 a number of different policy devices can be derived. In the first place, equation [6.79] allows for policy activism as well as for more non-activist expenditure policies. The first policy regime is obtained if $\gamma_{2,3} > 0$, the second regime can be captured by $\gamma_{2,3} = 0$. In the second place, the economic implications of different tax policies can be illustrated through changes in the household income tax rate α_7 or through changes in the corporate income tax rates γ_4 and γ_5. Since firm profits are completely transferred to households, the corporate income tax applies to banks only. In this chapter we will run simulations which provide some insights into the economic consequences of different policies within the context of the model.

In this chapter we will analyze the characteristics of the model by means of numerical experiments. It should be emphasized that this procedure has some drawbacks, which suggests that it may be useful to precede the analysis of the next sections by some observations about the scope and relevance of the material presented there. The most important argument against our approach is that it does not permit any observations about the establishment or the characteristics of some terminal (steady) state in the context of the model. The ultimate implication of our rejection of the temporary equilibrium method is that we cannot determine an equilibrium position or time path at all. In the context of this chapter, this argument implies that where we have chosen, as we have, to run simulations for a sequence of 100 unit-periods, we cannot generalize our observations about the performance of the economic system beyond the limits of the simulation period. Furthermore, these observations are always conditional on the set of parameter values used. Hence, we consider the simulation experiments reported in this chapter only as illustrations of possible time patterns that can be generated within the context of the model. We will not attempt to generalize these results. On the other hand, as has been argued in section 6.2, we do not regard the temporary equilibrium assumption as a useful starting device for the analysis of dynamic processes, since it assumes what it has to explain, the establishment of an equilibrium position. Seen from that perspective, the approach we have followed here has to be preferred.

The organization of this chapter will be as follows. Simulation experiments will be presented in sections 7.2, 7.3 and 7.4. After some general observations about the simulation method (section 7.2.1), the first simulation discussed in section 7.2.2 will serve as a bench-mark projection. Alternative simulations will be discussed with reference to this bench-mark case. The results of alternative projections are presented in section 7.3 and 7.4. The first two alternative experiments deal with implications of different tax policies, the third with government expenditures and the fourth experiment with expectations formation. Section 7.5 concludes this chapter with some final observations.

7.2 The bench-mark simulation

7.2.1 *Introduction*

The simulation experiments have been performed by means of CESIM. CESIM is a computer package for simulation of linear and non-linear dynamic models. It has been developed by Siep Kronenberg of the CCSO-research group of the University of Groningen (Department of Economics). Cesim derives from a full-fledged (non-)linear dynamic system a small non-recursive set of key variables. An iterative technique designed for that purpose is used to solve this set. Values for the other variables of the model are then determined recursively.

The simulation period consists of 100 unit-periods. CESIM needs initial values of the lagged endogenous variables which implies in the context of the model that endogenous simulations have been carried out from the fourth unit-period onwards. We will offer a graphical treatment of the characteristics of each simulation run. Unfortunately, the number of variables in the model is too large to present a diagram for each variable. For that reason, we have chosen to discuss only the most typical developments in a subset of variables of the model. The analyses of the simulation experiments will be directed toward the observations made in the introduction to this chapter, which summarize the purpose of this research. In order to analyze the implications of asymmetric information for the determination of commodity prices, the developments in this last variable ($P(t,t)$), the rate of inflation ($\pi^e(t,t)$ and $\pi(t,t)$) and expected future prices ($P^e_f(t,t+1)$ will be analyzed. Inventory adjustments, the co-existence of rigid prices and the implications for production patterns can be discussed by means of a comparison of the developments in the variables $INV(t)$, $P(t,t)$ and $Q(t,t)$. Economic developments in the absence of a coordination device with respect to commodity market transactions can be analyzed by focusing on the overall performance of the model. This overall performance is reflected in the developments of several categories of variables. In the first place, we may consider the discrepancies between expected and realized values of different variables. Particularly, the differences between expected and realized current-period consumption ($C^e(t,t)$ and $C(t,t)$), expected and actual end-of-period money balances of households ($MDH^e(t)$ and $MDH(t)$) and firms ($MDF^e(t)$ and $MDF(t)$), expected and actual end-of-period inventories and aggregate demand ($INV^e(t)$, $INV(t)$ and $Y(t,t)$), expected and realized sales ($Y^e_f(t,t)$ and $Y(t,t)$), expected and actual production as well as productive capacity ($Q^e(t,t)$, $Q(t,t)$ and $Q_{max}(t,t)$ and expected and actual inflation ($\pi^e(t,t)$ and $\pi(t,t)$) will be considered. In the second place, the developments in actual stocks and flows can be of interest by itself. This applies, for instance, to the developments in production, inventories, wealth components ($WH(t)$, $WF(t)$, $WB(t)$ and $WG(t)$), credit ($CRDF(t)$) and unemployment ($U(t,t)$). In the third place, the overall picture of the model is completed by the developments in the price determination procedure in the commodity market. Periods of price setting by households (firms) denote excess commodity demand (supply). In this respect, we will characterize the regime in the commodity market by the dummy variable $NR(t.t)$ (non-ration). $NR(t,t)$ will be zero in a situation of excess commodity demand and unity in a situation of excess commodity supply. A separate dummy variable ($NR1(t,t)$) has been used in the simulation experiments to denote a situation of equal commodity demand and supply. However, the simulations show that this last situation is never attained. For that reason, no diagrams of $NR1(t,t)$ have been included in this chapter. In the next section we will start the description of the simulation results.

7.2.2 *A bench-mark projection*

In this section we will present a rather detailed discussion of the first simulation experiment, which serves as a bench-mark for the discussion of the alternative projections. The analyses of the latter projections will be relatively brief.

A. Parameter values

With respect to the bench-mark projection the following arbitrary set of parameter values has been chosen. In parentheses we have listed the equations of the model where a parameter is incorporated for the first time.

A1. Household behaviour

$\alpha_1 = 0.193177$	(6.9)
$\alpha_2 = 0.0891$	(6.9)
$\alpha_3 = 0.717723$	(6.9)
$\alpha_4 = 0.60$	(6.10)
$\alpha_5 = 0.60$	(6.10)
$\alpha_6 = 1.1$	(6.10)
$\alpha_7 = 0.34$	(6.10)
$\alpha_8 = 0.20$	(6.16)

A2. Firm behaviour

$\beta_1 = 0 \vee 1$	(6.41)
$\beta_2 = 0 \vee 1$	(6.41)
$\beta_3 = 0 \vee 1$	(6.41)
$\beta_4 = 0.50$	(6.42)
$\beta_5 = 0.10$	(6.42)
$\beta_6 = 0.75$	(6.43)
$\beta_7 = 0.70$	(6.48)
$\beta_8 = 0.07676$	(6.63)
$\beta_9 = 0.20$	(6.73)
$A = 0.90$	(6.43)

A3. The behaviour of banks and the government sector

$\gamma_1 = 0.29$	(6.79)
$\gamma_2 = 3.00$	(6.79)
$\gamma_3 = 0.33$	(6.79)
$\gamma_4 = 0.20$	(6.81)

$\gamma_5 = 0.20$ (6.81)
$\gamma_6 = 0.80$ (6.5)
$\gamma_7 = 9300$ (6.88)
$\gamma_8 = 1.68$ (6.88)

A4. Wage adjustment parameters and exogenous variables

$\gamma_9 = 0.25$ (6.91)
$\gamma_{10} = 1.1$ (6.91)
$\gamma_{11} = 0.5$ (6.93)
$\gamma_{12} = 0.1$ (6.93)
$g = 0.00$ (6.13)
$U_n = 0.03$ (6.79)

B. Simulation results

We will start the discussion with the behaviour of the economy as a whole. This discussion focuses on the characteristics in the separate markets. The implications of asymmetric information and the role of commodity stocks will also be analyzed in this context. The discrepancies between expected and realized values of the variables will be dealt with afterwards.

Figure 7.1 depicts the situation in the commodity market as it can be derived from the time path of the variable $NR(t,t)$. Remember that $NR(t,t) = 0$ denotes excess demand in the preceding unit-period, whereas $NR(t,t) = 1$ indicates preceding-period excess supply in the commodity market. From figure 7.1 a rather regular pattern of regime switches emerges. With the exception of period 70–82 the simulation run is characterized by unit-periods of persistent excess supply and demand in the commodity market. At the outset of the simulation experiment there is one unit-period of excess supply. Except unit-period 10, unit-periods 3–12 are characterized by excess commodity demand. A rather prolonged period of excess commodity supply (19 unit-periods) follows. From unit-period 31 until unit-period 50 a situation of excess commodity demand prevails. Period 52–70 is characterized by excess supply followed by 13 unit-periods of frequent regime switches in the commodity market. A situation of excess commodity demand emerges in period 83–98, whereas unit-period 99 is characterized by excess commodity supply and unit-period 100 by excess commodity demand. There is no indication that the economy will settle down in one of the two regimes. Starting initially from a situation of excess commodity supply (exogenously determined) and full employment in the third unit-period, production decreases by 35% in the fourth unit-period (figure 7.2) because a zero unemployment rate causes the real wage rate to rise by 3.3%. As a result, unemployment in the fourth unit-period jumps to 37% of the working population (figure 7.3), which depresses aggregate expected consumption (–1%) (figure 7.15) by a fall in labour income. However, the decrease of consumption demand is outnumbered by a boost in investments (figure 7.11), which is caused by a low predetermined level of the expected commodity price in the third unit-period. This expectation reflects both optimism with respect to future sales as well as a higher future real wage level. Both elements have a positive impact on investment demand. As a result, aggregate demand in unit-period 4 is larger than the commodity stock (figure 7.4), which starts off a period of excess commodity demand in the fifth unit-period. The fall in production implies that inventories in unit-period 5 fall by 35%. On the demand side, it can be derived from equation [6.79] that a rising unemployment rate enforces the government sector to increase expenditures in unit-period 5 (+42%). Furthermore, the level of investments remains relatively high, whereas a zero rate of unemployment in unit-period

5 caused by a lower real wage rate and a higher capital stock, implies an increase in consumption demand. As a result, the situation of excess commodity demand persists and becomes worse, which is illustrated by a sharp fall in actual consumption. Remember in this respect that we have assumed that demand restrictions in the commodity market only affect the demand for consumption goods. In short (we will return to these characteristics in due course) this persistence can be explained by the following developments. On the supply side of the commodity market, productive capacity is fully utilized (period 5–8, figure 7.2 Q and $Qmax$ coincide). On the demand side rising real wages, a higher bonds portfolio (figure 7.8) and a tight labour market stimulate aggregate commodity demand. This situation comes to an end in unit-period 10 because of a gradual decline in investments (figure 7.11), caused by a falling expected long-run real wage level. As the long-run level of the nominal wage ([6.93]) adjusts only adaptively to fluctuations in the level of the actual nominal wage, the expected long-run real wage decreases. Furthermore, the level of government expenditures falls because of inflation and a tight labour market ([6.79]). As a result, the economy enters a persistent period of excess commodity supply (period 11–30).

From figure 7.4 it can be derived that this situation of excess commodity supply aggravates during period 12–22 and improves in the following period (23–30). Eventually a regime switch results in unit-period 31. A more or less similar time-pattern can be distinguished in the rate of unemployment (figure 7.3). From figure 7.5 it can be concluded that in the first part of the period of excess commodity supply (until unit-period 18) commodity prices continue to rise notwithstanding the situation of excess commodity supply. The commodity market is characterized by 'real' price rigidity in period 10–14. As the expected rate of inflation is positive, commodity prices rise with expected inflation in this situation. From unit-period 15 to 30, firms operate on the right-hand side of the kinked demand curve. Hence, they plan to lower the 'real' commodity price. Since expected inflation continues to be positive until unit-period 22, initially, commodity prices continue to increase, the increase in prices now being smaller than expected inflation as firms try to improve the excess supply situation by means of 'real' price adjustments. From unit-periods 18 to 30, the firms' commodity price falls. Expected inflation becomes negative in unit-period 23 because expectations are adjusted adaptively. The rate of unemployment increases not because of a dual decision hypothesis on the side of firms, but results from the developments in expected commodity prices and nominal wages, which depress the demand for labour ([6.57]). Because of downward nominal wage stickiness, the expected next-period commodity price is more responsive to a situation of excess commodity supply than the nominal wage to excess labour supply. As a result real labour costs rise and the employment situation deteriorates in period 10–21. The improvement of the employment situation in period 21–30 is caused by the following developments. In the first place aggregate demand increases because a growing level of real wealth increases the demand for consumption goods and because a rising unemployment rate and a falling rate of expected inflation have a positive impact on the level of government expenditures. In the second place, a higher level of aggregate demand *ceteris paribus* implies a smaller positive discrepancy between the beginning-of-period commodity stock and aggregate demand, which in turn tends to slow down the decrease of expected commodity prices. On the other hand, nominal wages fall because of expected deflation and high rates of unemployment. As a result, real labour costs fall and employment increases in period 21–30. Since the positive aggregate demand effect is stronger than the improvement of production levels, the economy enters a regime of excess commodity demand in unit–period 31.

After unit–period 30 a relatively prolonged period of excess commodity demand emerges, which ends in unit–period 49. First of all, it can be observed, for instance, from diagrams 7.2, 7.3 and 7.4 that the simulation period is characterized by a more smoothly time pattern of most economic variables after unit–period 30. Furthermore, from figure 7.4 it can be derived that the excess demand situation is primarily caused by the developments on the demand side in the commodity market. On average, production as well as inventory levels are constant as can be observed from figures 7.2 and 7.4, respectively. On the other hand, the demand for consumption goods (*Ce* in figure 7.15) and investments (figure 7.11) initially increase and subsequently fall (after unit–period 41 for *Ce* and 44 for *I*), which explains the time pattern of aggregate demand. The time pattern of consumption demand can be explained from the developments in nominal household wealth and income (variable *AU* [6.20]) and commodity prices. In the first part of the period of excess commodity demand, *AU* increases since household wealth increases (figure 7.9) because households accumulate money balances in a situation where they cannot realize their intentions in the commodity market (figure 7.14). An increasing level of *AU* has a positive impact on the demand for consumption goods ([6.27]). Furthermore, commodity prices fall which, given the numerical level of the relevant variables and parameters, also has a positive effect on consumption demand as can be derived from equation [6.27]. The decrease in commodity prices in a situation of excess commodity demand can be ascribed to expected inflation. Because of adaptive expectations the latter variable continues to have a negative value until unit–period 43. As a result, the depressing impact of expected deflation on commodity prices initially dominates the positive impact of the excess demand situation in the commodity market. To put it differently, households perceive a relative increase in commodity prices in the context of a deflationary environment as sufficient to relieve the quantity restrictions observed in the commodity market. Since all households act accordingly, relative positions do not change, which requires a subsequent increase of ('real') prices. This adaptive process initially achieves a slow–down of deflation and finally the emergence of inflation (in unit–period 41). Expected inflation becomes positive in unit–period 44. A similar process in opposite direction can be observed at the beginning of a period of excess commodity supply (for instance in period 52 – 57). Hence, the observed sluggishness of price adjustment, in this case as a result of expectations formation, initially has a procyclical impact on the scarcity proportions in the commodity market. After unit–period 40, commodity prices start to increase, which has both a negative direct as well as an indirect impact on the level of consumption demand since higher prices depress the level of excess money balances, which in turn decreases the level of nominal household wealth.

The time pattern of investment can be explained from the developments in expected nominal wages ($W^e_f(t,t+1)$, *Wef* in figure 7.7) and expected commodity prices ($P^e_f(t,t+1)$, *Pef* in figure 7.5). From an inspection of the time pattern of these two variables in the two diagrams it can be concluded that expected real wages initially rise and subsequently fall which explains the development of investment demand in this period of excess commodity demand. Government expenditures fall during this period, which can be ascribed to the time pattern of expected inflation. From equation [6.79] it can be observed that expected inflation and government expenditures are negatively related. On average, the impact of the unemployment rate on the level of government is only slightly positive and too small to compensate the negative impact of expected inflation. The rather capricious time pattern of the unemployment in a period of excess demand (figure 7.3), which can also be observed in the time pattern of actual production, inventories and actual consumption, results from the asymmetrical interaction of nominal wages and unemployment. Periods of (nearly) complete utilization of production factors cause relatively large increases in nominal wages durung the next unit-period. As a result, this next unit-period is characterized by a relatively low level of labour demand and subsequently a higher unemployment rate.

In unit-period 52 a second prolonged period of excess commodity supply begins which lasts until unit-period 70. Only in two respects are the two periods of excess supply different. First, it can be observed that the adjustments in the labour market (figures 7.3 and 7.7) and the commodity market (figures 7.2, 7.4 and 7.5) display a smoother time pattern in the second period of excess commodity supply. Secondly, firms do not plan to keep commodity prices rigid (corrected for inflation) as they did during the first 3 unit-periods of the first period of excess commodity supply. This difference in behaviour can be explained from the larger positive difference between actual and expected commodity prices (figure 7.5). The relationship between this differential and the rigidity of real commodity prices will be considered in more detail below. With respect to the other characteristics of the time patterns of the variables displayed in the diagram, one is referred to the analysis above of the developments in the first period of excess supply.

In unit-period 70 a period of frequent regime switches in the commodity market starts, succeeded by a period of excess commodity demand beginning in unit-period 83. The period of regime switches is characterized by price rigidity (corrected for expected inflation). Both households and firms operate on the kink of the perceived supply and demand curves. Expected inflation ($\pi^e(t,t)$, *INF* in figure 7.10) equals actual inflation ($\pi(t,t)$, *INFa* in figure 7.10). The observed frequency of regime switches is caused by discontinous jumps in the level of consumption demand, which can be explained in the following way. It can be derived from equations [6.19] and [6.27] that given a constant level of nominal household wealth and incomc (the variable *AU*), commodity prices and the chosen values of the relevant parameters, the demand for consumption goods will be higher in situations where households take prices as given than in situations where they act as monopsonists. This characteristic corresponds to the familiar theoretical notion that in case of perfect competition, transaction levels are higher than in case of imperfect competition. In a situation of excess commodity demand, households spend a smaller part (and since *AU* is increasing, a decreasing part as well, which is implied by the negative second-order derivative) of beginning-of-period wealth and current-period income to consumption. In the event of excess commodity demand households *a priori* choose to confine their claims on commodities because they use the information about the situation of excess demand that has been transmitted through the market. Since the level of the commodity stock is nearly equal to the level of aggregate demand any (also relatively small) upward shift in aggregate consumption demand immediately implies a regime switch, which explains that a unit-period of excess commodity supply is immediately followed by a unit-period of excess demand. A period of excess demand ends because of the asymmetrical interaction between nominal wages and the unemployment rate. A very low unemployment rate implies a relatively high nominal wage in the next unit-period. As a result, the demand for labour falls in the next unit-period which depresses both aggregate demand and production. Furthermore, aggregate consumption demand is relatively small in case of excess commodity demand, as has been explained above. This also implies that the overall depressing impact on demand dominates that on supply. Hence, a regime switch results. The period of frequent regime switches is followed by a period of excess commodity demand because of the following underlying tendencies. In the first place, the nominal level of commodity prices falls because expected inflation is negative. As has been explained, falling commodity prices have both a direct and an indirect positive impact on the level of consumption demand. In the second place, as the unemployment rate is constant on the average, the level of government expenditures is positively affected by expected deflation. In the third place, a government deficit throughout this period (figure 7.12) has a positive impact on the level of household wealth through an increased bond portfolio, although it can be observed from figures 7.8 and 7.9 that this effect is almost zero. Taken these developments together explains the beginning of a new area of excess demand in unit-period 83. This period, which ends in unit-period 99, has similar characteristics as the first prolonged period of excess commodity demand. For that reason a discussion of these characteristics is superfluous.

From figures 7.2, 7.4 and 7.5 the consequences of the existence of commodity stocks for the time patterns of production and prices in the short run can be derived. In the literature (see section 4.3.1 of chapter 4) it has been emphasized that the possibility to store commodities may constitute an additional explanation of particularly downward price stickiness. Furthermore, commodity stocks may serve as a buffer between production and demand in order to prevent developments on the demand side of the economy from having a large impact on the time pattern of production and employment in the short run. From an inspection of figures 7.2, 7.4 and 7.5 we may conclude that the model behaves in accordance with these observations. In the first place, a situation of excess commodity supply is characterized by relatively large fluctuations in the size of the actual stock of commodities. For instance, in period 10-17 aggregate demand decreases by about 6.5%. Production in this period only falls by 1.3% and approaches rather smoothly the level of aggregate demand during the next 5 periods. From unit-period 22 aggregate demand increases again as a result of falling commodity prices. In this period the increase in aggregate demand exceeds the increase in production. Meanwhile, inventories are adjusted to absorb the developments in demand. Relative commodity prices are initially rigid and start to fall only in case a situation of excess commodity supply is perceived as persistent and depresses expected commodity prices. Hence, commodity stocks serve as a buffer in the model. In the second place, the development in commodity prices only indirectly depends on the time patterns of demand and production. The negative difference between aggregate demand and the level of the commodity stock decreases the value of the expected commodity price. As has been mentioned already, the developments in the expected commodity price cause prices to be rigid. Eventually a decrease in the actual current-period price (corrected for expected inflation) results. Hence, our simulation results are not at variance with the hypothesis that the existence of commodity stocks supports the downward stickiness of commodity prices.

The developments in commodity prices are also affected by asymmetric information, as this characteristic shows up in the kinked commodity demand and supply curves of the model. Because of asymmetric information the price elasticity of the perceived demand curve is larger in case of a price increase than in case of a price decrease. As a result, it is optimal to adapt preceding-period commodity prices only for expected inflation if condition [7.1] is fulfilled.

$$
\begin{aligned}
&-2a_f^e(t,t)Y_f^e(t,t) \;+\; a_f^e(t,t)Y(t-1,t-1)(1+g) + \; P(t-1,t-1)(1+\pi^e(t,t)) \\
&> \\
&P_f^e(t,t+1)b_1 \\
&> \\
&-2a^{1e}_f(t,t)Y_f^e(t,t) \;+\; a^{1e}_f(t,t)Y(t-1,t-1)(1+g) + \; P(t-1,t-1)(1+\pi^e(t,t))
\end{aligned}
\quad [7.1]
$$

Condition [7.1] is obtained by rewriting equation [6.51]. Since the development in expected prices is only indirectly dependent on the development of actual prices, i.e. via expected inflation and aggregate demand, this condition does not necessarily have to be fulfilled at the start of a period of excess supply. Firms perceive an increase of actual prices in the past as an increase of future prices. As a result, the beginning of a period of excess commodity supply may even be characterized by increasing relative prices if the period of excess supply is preceded by a relatively long period of excess commodity demand, which has had a prolonged positive impact on expected prices. In that situation the first part of condition [7.1] is met with an equality sign. It is optimal to increase prices given that firms expect to sell a current-period excess supply at higher prices in the near future. However, the periods of excess commodity demand of the bench-mark simulation are too short and/or the negative discrepancy between the beginning-of-period commodity stock and current-period commodity demand is too small to observe this characteristic, which implies that the expected commodity price does not exceed the current price during a period of excess demand in this simulation experiment (figure 7.5). As a result, the current-period commodity price is rigid (corrected for inflation) only during the first period of persistent excess commodity supply (period 11–14) and during the period of frequent regime switches (70–81) during which period actual and expected commodity prices approach each other again (figure 7.5). As expected prices fall because of a persistent excess commodity supply, the current-period price eventually decreases since now the second part of condition [7.1] is met with equality. Firms are willing to sell a larger part of the current commodity stock immediately against a lower current-period price since they expect a subsequent fall in commodity prices in future periods. From figure 7.5 it can be concluded that with the exception of the first period of excess commodity supply, the current-period commodity price is set in a period of persistent excess commodity supply on the perception of a lower and falling level of the expected commodity price. Hence, current-period prices fall notwithstanding the existence of asymmetric information. Since pessimistic price expectations also depress current-period production and since a decrease in actual prices accomplishes a demand stimulus, both impulses cause the economy to move toward a new period of excess commodity demand.

In a situation of excess demand in the preceding unit-period the condition for rigid prices is derived from the households' decision problem, since the commodity market has turned into a buyers' market. Maximizing the utility function [6.9] subject to the budget equation [6.26] yields condition [7.2] for price rigidity as a first-order condition with respect to consumption.

$$\lambda\left(2a_h^e(t,t)C^e(t,t) \;+\; P(t-1,t-1)(1+\pi^e(t,t)) \;-\; a_h^e(t,t)C(t-1,t-1)(1+g)\right)$$

$$< \alpha_1/C^e(t,t) < \lambda\big[2a_h^{1e}(t,t)C^e(t,t) + P(t-1,t-1)(1+\pi^e(t,t)) - a_h^{1e}(t,t)C(t-1,t-1)(1+g)\big] \qquad [7.2]$$

In condition [7.2] λ denotes the Lagrange parameter, which equals $\alpha_2/MDH^e(t,t)$ as can be derived from maximizing the utility function with respect to nominal balances. From equations [6.27] and [6.28] it follows that nominal balances are positively dependent on the level of disposable income and beginning-of-period wealth (*AU*). A high level of *AU* has a depressing impact on the Lagrange parameter λ, which causes the last part of condition [7.2] to be ultimately met with an equality sign. This explains continuously rising prices in a situation of excess demand. The fact that decisions about commodity prices are intertwined with and taken simultaneously with households' decisions in all markets causes prices to rise instead of being rigid (corrected for expected inflation).

The developments in production and production factors are summarized in figures 7.2, 7.3 and 7.11. During periods of excess demand in the commodity market, the labour market is relatively tight, although a tendency toward a stable unemployment rate of about 3% at the end of the simulation period can be observed . Unit-periods of (more than) full employment are only experienced at the beginning of the simulation period (5-8). This period is characterized by disproportionately large increases in nominal wages, which can be explained from the curvature of the Phillips curve. During the period (5-8) it can be derived that real wages increase in a situation of persistent excess commodity demand. However, from equation [6.57] it can be derived that the demand for labour is affected by $W(t,t)/b_1P_f^e(t,t+1)$, i.e. the nominal current-period wage divided by the discounted expected commodity price. Figures 7.5 and 7.6 suggest that this proportion is nearly constant during the entire simulation period. For instance, in unit-period 25 this proportion is equal to 0.813 and in unit-period 100 to 0.805. The unemployment rate equals 7.2 in unit-period 25 and 3.1 in unit-period 100. It can be derived from equation [6.57] that fluctuations in the capital stock (the stock of capital is incorporated in variable A_3 ([6.43*a*])) cause proportional shifts in the level of unemployment. In this example this implies that 1%-point of the difference in unemployment can be ascribed to non-price factors, i.e to a change in the level of the capital stock (investments). The remaining 3.1%-point change is caused by a ±1% change in the aforementioned ratio of the nominal wage and the discounted expected commodity price, which implies a fairly elastic labour demand curve. We may conclude that fluctuations in the unemployment rate can be ascribed, to a large extent, to (small) fluctuations in the proportion $W(t,t)/b_1P_f^e(t,t+1)$ and to a smaller extent, to fluctuations in investments, i.e. to changes in the stock of capital. The fact that the labour market does not clear in the short run is due to the properties of nominal wage formation ([6.91]).

The production factor capital (figure 7.11) behaves differently. From the application of a Cobb-Douglas technology ([6.43]) it follows that the utilization of capital will always be complete. Furthermore, we have assumed that firms' investment plans will never be restricted in the commodity market, which implies that also in situations of excess commodity demand the expected stock of capital goods will always be equal to the actual stock of capital (with a delay of one unit-period because of the production lag). In addition, we have argued in section 6.5.5 that investment decisions are taken with the intention to match demand and supply in the long run. In the long run, firms perceive the economy as a competitive system. Prices are exogenous to the individual firms and supply equals demand, which explains why quantity constraints do not affect investment decisions other than through expected real wages and the real user costs of capital. As the nominal interest rate (figure 7.13) is nearly constant over the entire simulation period, investments are driven by expected real wages and inflation. The developments in the former variable are the primary cause of fluctuations in the level of investment as can be derived from figures 7.5, 7.7 and 7.11. With the exception of period 17 – 44 during which the pattern of expected inflation initially causes a decline and subsequently an improvement of investments (this last change is also enforced by an increase of the expected real wage rate (period 17 – 36)), expected inflation does not have a significant impact on the time pattern of investments. In the second part of the simulation period the fluctuations in the expected real wage rate are rather small as well, which explains the invariance of investment expenditures in this period. It can be observed that investments develop rather independently from the economic situation in the short run. Of course this characteristic of the model is disputable and illustrates to some extent that the desire to simplify the model has been accompanied by the introduction of *ad hoceries*.

The developments in the financial markets are summarized in figures 7.8, 7.9, 7.12 and 7.13. From figure 7.9 it can be derived that government wealth initially fluctuates around an average level of 0. At the end of the simulation period there is a tendency toward an increasingly negative level of government wealth. The development in government wealth mimics the time pattern of the public sector deficit in figure 7.12. It can be concluded that periods of excess commodity demand are characterized by a declining public sector deficit or a budget surplus. This pattern emerges as a result of higher income tax payments, on the one hand, and a relatively low level of government expenditures in inflationary periods, on the other hand. In a situation of excess commodity supply this pattern is reversed. In the second part of the simulation period the large fluctuations in the deficit disappear and there is a tendency toward a stable, positive level of the deficit.

The developments in the bond market (figure 7.8) are more or less reflected by the movements in wealth and wealth composition. Since bonds holdings are by far the largest component of financial wealth, fluctuations in the latter variable follow rather trivially from movements in the former variable. Observe in this respect that in figure 7.8 only the number of bonds is depicted. The developments in the bond market may be of some interest since this market is the only market in the model that is explicitly cleared by prices in every unit-period. The bond market is characterized by a moderate growth of bonds supply. This growth is due to the financial developments in the government sector. Medium-term fluctuations in the supply of bonds correspond to regime switches. During a period of excess commodity demand the growth in the supply of government bonds is relatively low or negative, as the budget deficit is relatively small (the surplus is relatively big) as a result of higher tax receipts and lower government expenditures. On the other hand, the growth in the supply of bonds by firms in a period of excess demand accelerates somewhat because of a boost in investment demand. On the demand side of the bond market the demand for bonds by households is stable in the long run whereas medium-term fluctuations reflect the pattern of regimes switches. This development in the household bond portfolio implies that the growth in the supply of bonds has to be compensated by an increasing demand for bonds by banks. Both developments reflect the diverging time-pattern of wealth accumulation as is illustrated in figure 7.9. Finally, the rate of interest appears to be rather stable. With respect to the developments in the bond market the following observations can be made. For the sake of simplicity, we have chosen to derive the supply of bonds by firms from the firms' budget identity (equations [6.76] and [6.74]), and not by means of a portfolio approach. Our choice implies that a fall in profit and thus a decline in corporate wealth has to be compensated by increasing debt. This process may be unstable since increasing interest payments put further pressure on future profits of the firm. Observe that our representation of the behaviour of the government in the bond market has similar (un)stability characteristics. However, the stable pattern in the bond market in the simulation experiment has been obtained by the *ad hoc* choice of a relatively high interest elasticity of the demand for bonds by banks. In the absence of a portfolio model of the financial sector this approach is a reasonable short-cut. The simplification seems legitimate since our primary interest concerns the development in the real sector of the model and not the developments in financial markets.

Finally, we will consider the developments in expected and realized values of one and the same variable. Expected and actual inflation is illustrated in figure 7.10. Households' expectation of nominal balances and actual nominal balances are depicted in figure 7.14, whereas expected and realized consumption is shown in figure 7.15. For the sake of completeness we may add that the unemployment rate reflects the discrepancy between households' expectation of the utilization of labour and the actual utilization of labour, since households do not attach utility to leisure. Firms' expected and actual nominal balances are graphed in figure 7.16, whereas firms' expectations about nominal wages and commodity prices are depicted in figures 7.7 and 7.5, respectively.

Comparison of expected and realized values leads to the following conclusions. In the first place, it can be observed that our choice to model expected inflation as an adaptive system cannot be rejected by pointing at the actual pattern of inflation. On average, expectations of inflation are correct, although expectations lag behind actual developments. There is no sign of systematic under- or overestimation of actual developments in inflation. A similar conclusion can be derived from figure 7.7 with respect to the modelling of the expected long-run wage rate. From figure 7.5 it can be observed that the time patterns of actual and expected commodity prices diverge during the first unit-periods of a period of excess commodity supply. This development can be explained by the fact that in that situation commodity prices continue to increase because of positive expected inflation since firms choose either to keep actual commodity prices rigid (corrected for expected inflation) or to adjust the commodity prices only a little downward, whereas expected commodity prices are already negatively affected by the existence of excess supply in the commodity market (with a delay of one unit-period). This asymmetrical adjustment pattern results in a systematically wrong prediction of the actual developments in the commodity price. In the second place, the discrepancies between households' actual and expected nominal balances, on the one hand, and households' actual and expected current-period consumption, on the other hand, can be explained by the following argument. In a period of excess commodity demand, households are constrained in the commodity market which immediately explains the positive difference between actual and expected consumption. In this situation where households cannot realize all their purchases, they accumulate nominal balances ([6.24]). Hence, the discrepancy between actual and expected money holdings depends on the situation experienced in the commodity market. In the absence of demand constraints in the commodity market households realize their intentions with respect to consumption as well as with respect to the composition of wealth. Finally, in a situation of excess commodity demand actual sales exceed expected sales, which causes the accumulation of actual money balances of firms. A supply constraint in the labour market has a similar impact. In a situation of excess commodity supply, actual sales fall below expected sales. As a result, firms experience liquidity shortages, which are relieved by the supply of bank credit.

Herewith we conclude our analysis by means of the first simulation experiment which will serve as a bench-mark for the following simulations. It should be emphasized once more that this analysis only illustrates one possible time pattern. In general, the model is very sensitive to parameter changes. Small changes may very soon create explosive time patterns. To some extent this also explains why the observed fluctuations in a few variables (particularly the rate of interest) are rather small.

figure 7.1

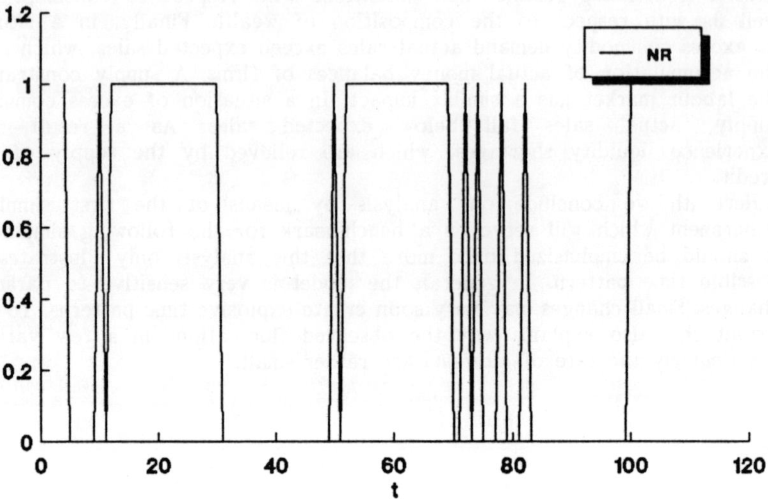

figure 7.2

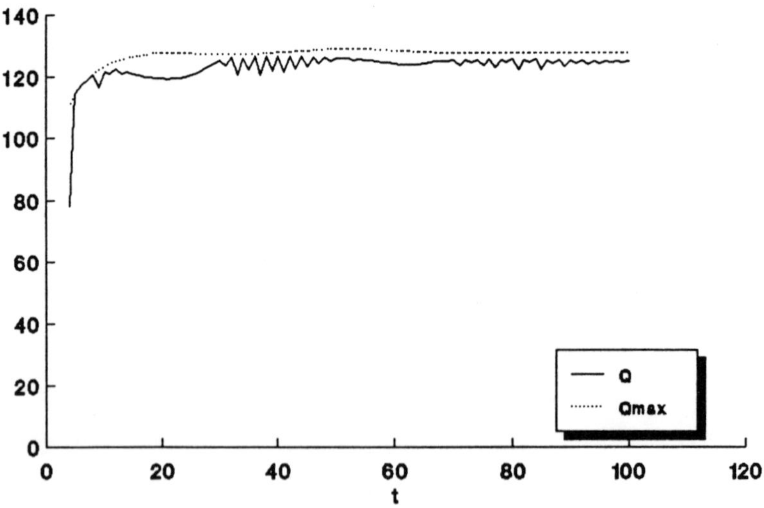

figure 7.3

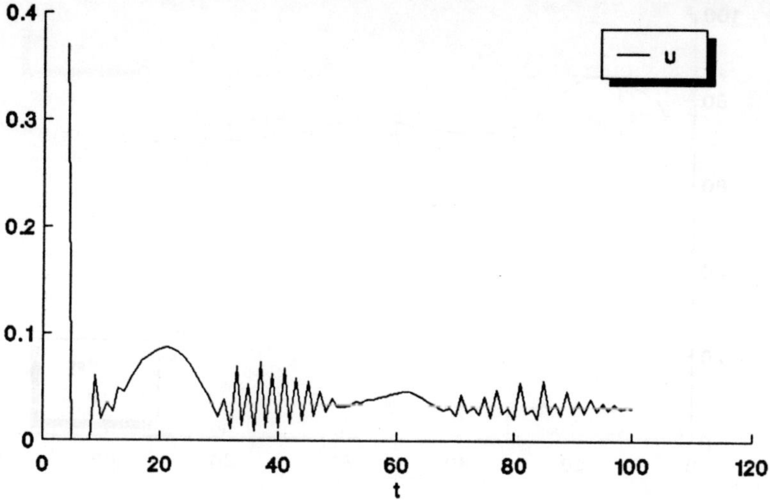

figure 7.4

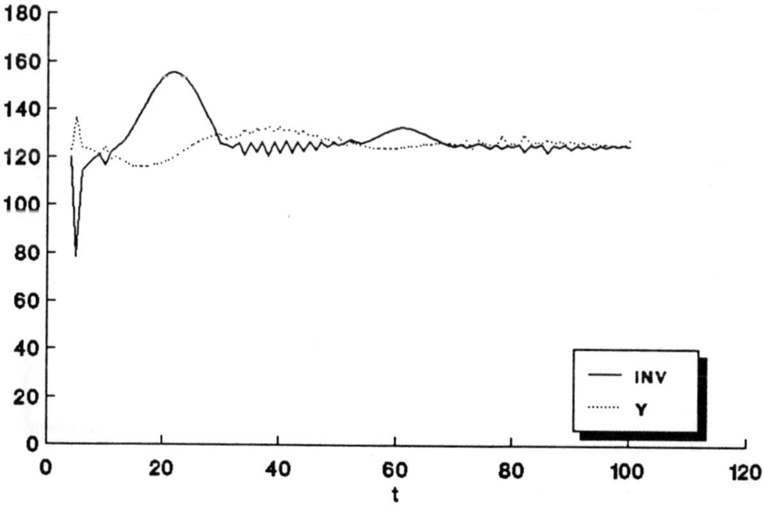

figure 7.5

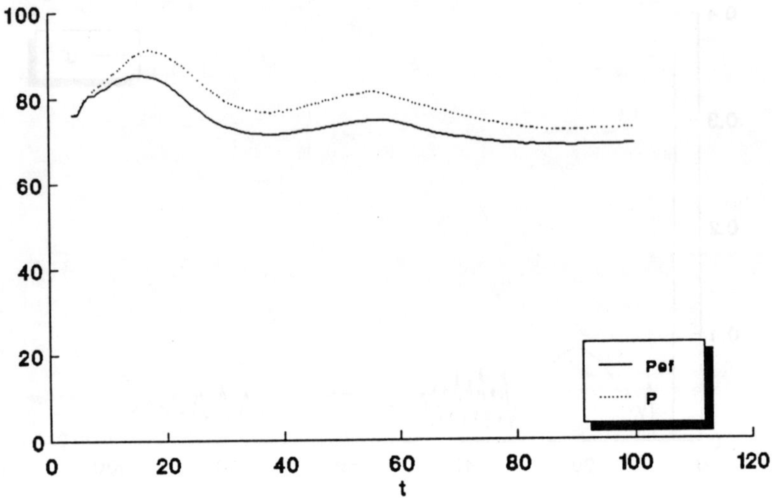

figure 7.6

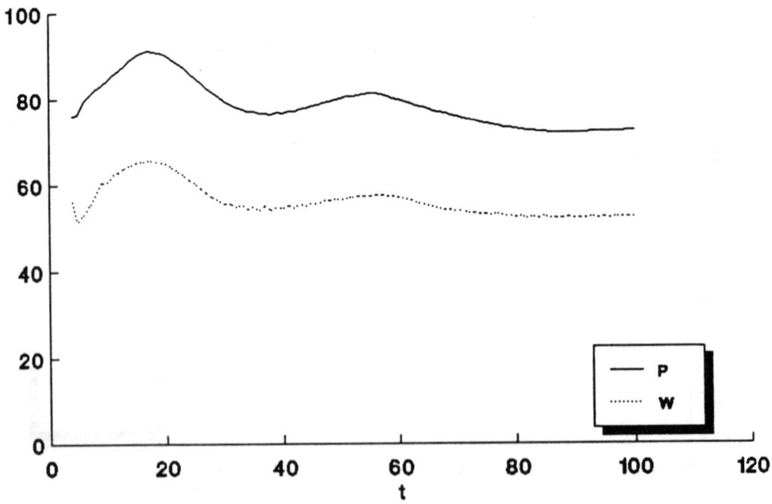

figure 7.7

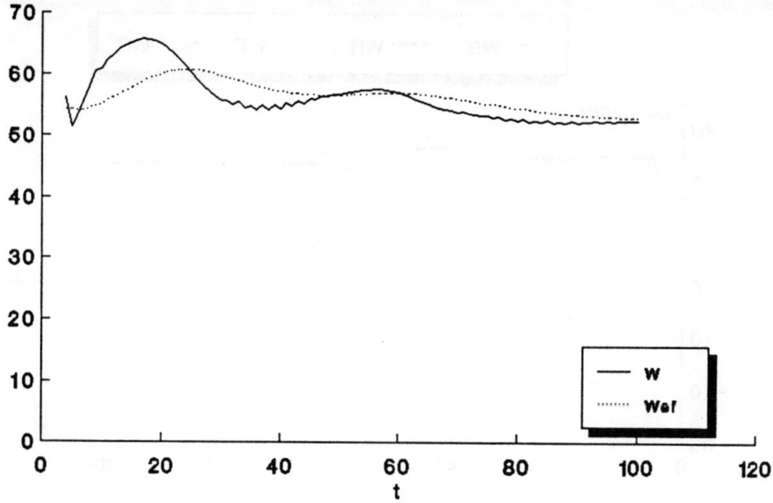

figure 7.8

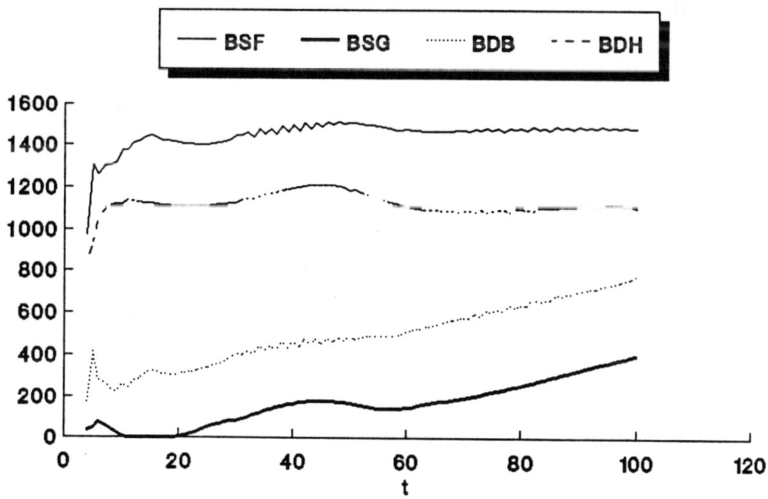

figure 7.9

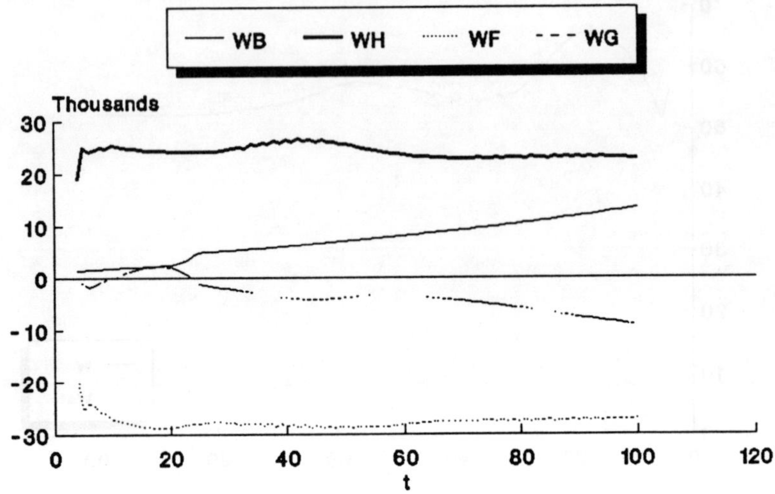

figure 7.10

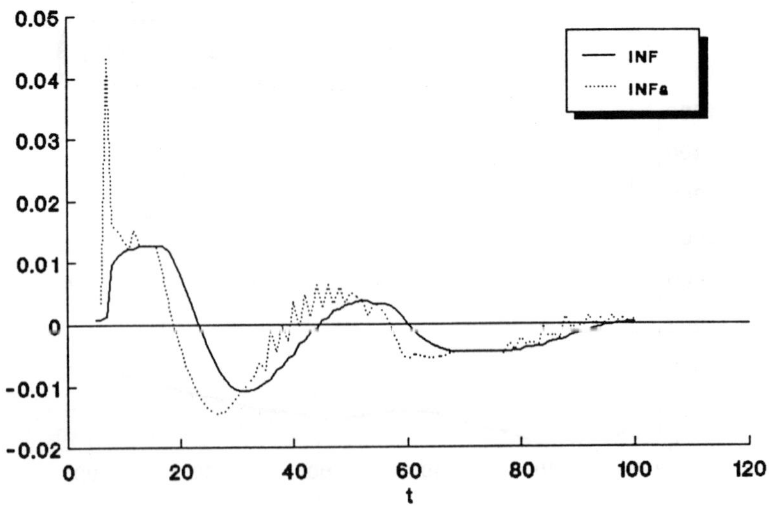

figure 7.11

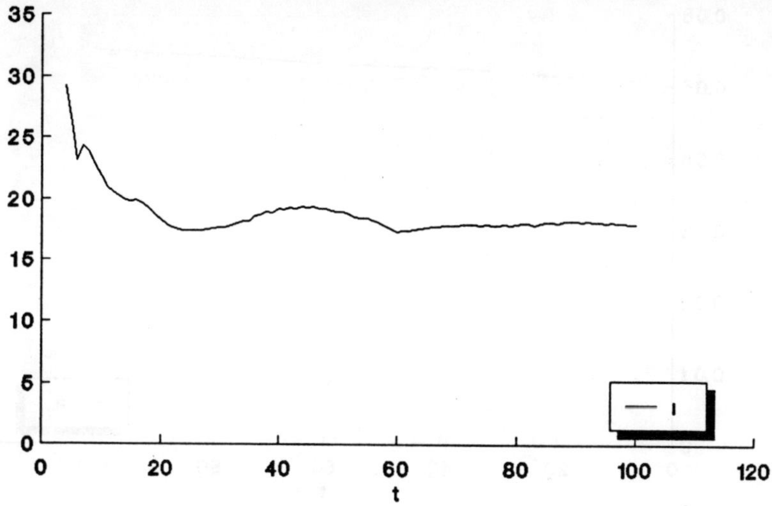

figure 7.12

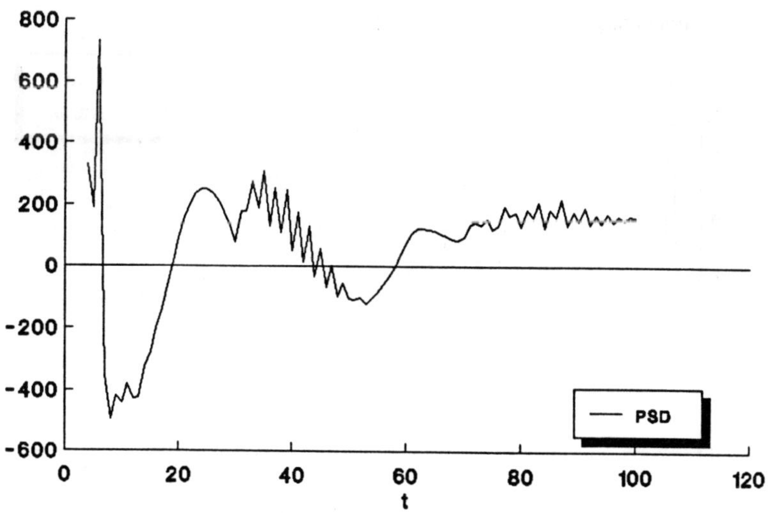

figure 7.13

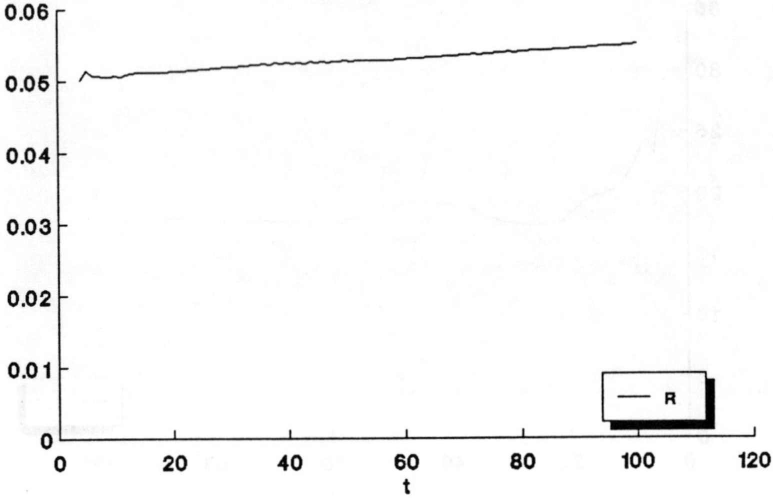

figure 7.14

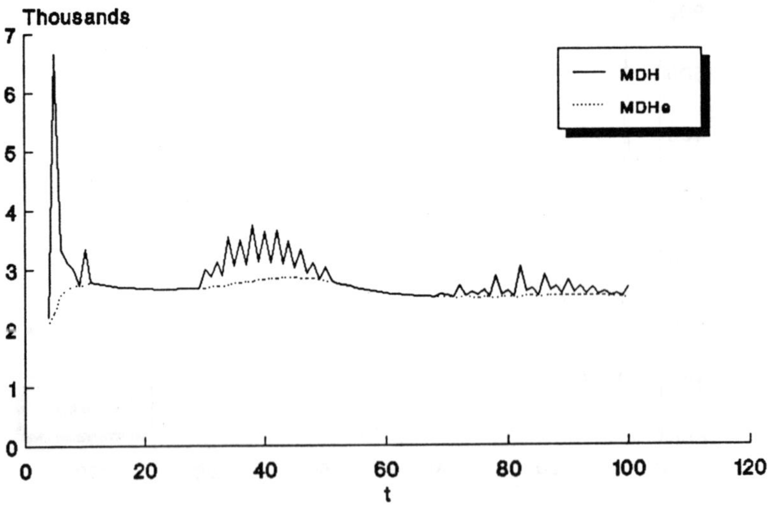

figure 7.15

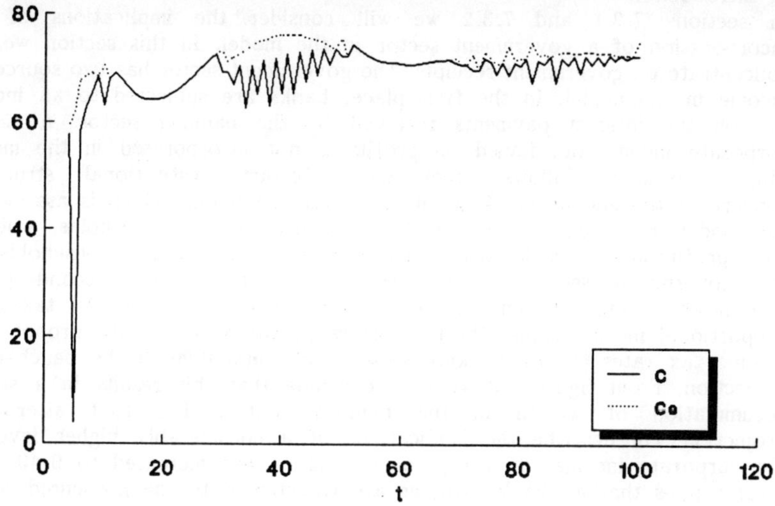

figure 7.16

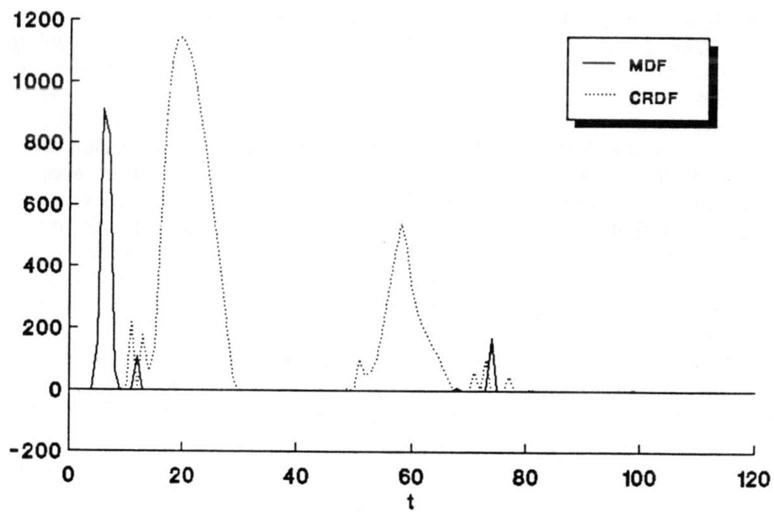

7.3 The impact of different tax policies and expenditure policy

7.3.1 *Tax policies*

A. Introduction

In sections 7.3.1 and 7.3.2 we will consider the implications of the incorporation of a government sector in the model. In this section we will concentrate on government receipts. The government sector has two sources of income in the model. In the first place, banks are subjected to an income tax on the interest payments received by the banking sector. A similar corporate income tax levied on profits is not incorporated in the model. This asymmetry follows from the arbitrary institutional structure, concerning the allocation of profits of firms and banks, which is assumed in the model. Firm profits are completely transferred to households, whereas bank profits are accumulated for some part and transferred to households and the government sector for the remaining part. In the second place, households' income, labour and non-labour income, is taxed. All taxes are proportional income taxes. The parameters γ_4 and γ_5 define the proportional income tax rates of the banking sector and equal 0.20 in the bench-mark projection. From figure 7.9 we may conclude that this results in a steady accumulation of wealth in the banking sector. The first alternative projection will describe the implications of a considerably higher level of the corporate income tax rate, i.e. γ_4 and γ_5 are increased to 0.40. This level implies that all bank earnings are transferred to the household sector (60%) and the government sector (40%). The second alternative projection will deal with the implications of a change in the level of the household income tax rate. In the bench-mark projection this rate (α_7) equals 0.34. Two alternative simulations have been carried out in this respect, one with $\alpha_7 = 0.28$, the other with $\alpha_7 = 0.40$, in order to analyze the implications of both a decrease and an increase in the income tax rate.

B. A higher corporate income tax rate for bank profits

Figure 7.17 depicts the regime switches in a situation where γ_4 and γ_5 are set equal to 0.40. The figure 1 is added to the symbols of the depicted variables in order to denote the first *alternative* simulation. After one unit–period of excess supply the economy is characterized by excess commodity demand until unit–period 12. A relatively long period of excess supply follows (period 12–31). After unit–period 31 the economy is characterized, as in the bench–mark projection by a period of excess demand until unit–period 50. In period 52–73 the commodity market is characterized by excess supply again. Finally, period 74–100 shows an ongoing pattern of frequent regime switches. As can be derived from a comparison of figures 7.17 and 7.1, the time pattern of regime switches of the alternative projection resembles, to a large extent, the pattern of the bench–mark projection. A different time pattern emerges after unit–period 70. In contrast with the bench–mark projection in which a period of frequent regime switches is followed by a period of excess commodity demand (83–99), the alternative simulation is characterized by a period of ongoing regime switches until the end of the simulation period. Moreover, the frequency of the switches has increased as well. A unit–period of excess commodity supply is immediately followed by a unit–period of excess commodity demand and vice versa. Hence, in comparison with the bench–mark simulation an increase in the banks' corporate income tax rate causes the economy to move a little into the direction of a situation of excess commodity supply at the end of the simulation period. This observation can be illustrated with the help of figure 7.18. In figure 7.18*a* we have depicted the difference between aggregate demand ($Y(t,t)$) in the alternative projection and in the bench-mark projection as a proportion of aggregate demand in the bench mark case. In figure 7.18*b* the proportional difference between the actual commodity stocks ($INV(t)$) is shown. On average, the effect on aggregate demand of an increase in the banks' income tax rate is rather moderate. Relatively large deviations from bench-mark aggregate demand levels emerge in the last 25 unit-periods. As has been explained in the preceding section, the time pattern of aggregate demand is caused by discretionary jumps in the demand for consumption goods in a period of regime switches. During the last 25 unit-periods a unit-period of excess commodity supply of this alternative simulation shows a high level of demand compared with demand in the bench-mark projection. In figure 7.18*a* such a unit-period of excess commodity supply shows a positive value of $(Y1-Y)/Y$ during the last 25 unit-periods. During periods of excess demand, the demand for consumption goods is relatively low (in comparison with the bench-mark projection) because the level of households wealth is generally lower than in the bench-mark simulation, as is indicated in figure 7.19 (remember that bonds holdings are the largest component of household wealth). As a result, a period of excess commodity demand corresponds to a a negative value of $(Y1-Y)/Y$ during the last 25 unit-periods. This is shown by a dip in figure 7.18*a*. On average, aggregate *consumption* demand is lower than in the bench-mark simulation, which reflects the fact that the impact of a lower level of household wealth is larger than the impact of a lower price level (figure 7.22). However, the lower rate of inflation, or better the higher rate of deflation, has a positive impact on government expenditures, which to some extent compensates the depressing impact of lower consumption demand on aggregate demand. In figure 7.18*b* the relative changes in inventories are depicted. It can be observed that the fluctuations in inventories are for a large part just the reverse of the shifts in aggregate demand. From figure 7.23 it can be concluded that with the exception of the last 25 unit-periods, a higher bank income tax rate does not affect the demand for labour. Furthermore, also in the last part of the simulation period the average difference between the unemployment rates in the alternative and in the bench-mark simulation equals approximately zero as can be derived from figure 7.23. Since investments are hardly affected as well, it can be concluded that the level of production will on average be the same as in the bench-mark simulation. Hence, the time pattern of commodity stocks will correspond to the time pattern of aggregate demand.

In figures 7.19, 7.20 and 7.21 the developments in the bond market have been depicted. From figure 7.19 it can be derived that a higher corporate income tax rate implies a lower level of the demand for bonds by banks. Since a higher tax rate implies higher government receipts, it is not surprising that the number of bonds supplied by the government decreases as well, as is illustrated in figure 7.20. The supply of bonds by firms does not change significantly (figure 7.19). The small increase at the end of the simulation period can be ascribed to the diverging pattern of wages and commodity prices (remember that we have derived the supply bonds from the firms' budget identity). As a result, the total supply of bonds falls with the decrease of the supply of government bonds. From figure 7.21 it can be observed that the absence in the second half of the simulation period of the government sector in the bond market results in a small decrease in the rate of interest, which implies that this depressing impact on the interest rate is only partly compensated by the decrease in the demand for bonds by households and banks. The observed fluctuations in the difference between the supply of government bonds in this alternative simulation in comparison with bonds supply in the bench-mark simulation in figure 7.20 are partly explained by the condition that the government sector cannot operate as a net-buyer in the bond market. Since the supply of government bonds in the alternative simulation equals 0 in unit-periods 10-18 and 51-100, the fluctuations shown in figure 7.20 reflect fluctuations (with an opposite sign) in the supply of government bonds in the bench-mark simulation. However, also in the bench-mark simulation the supply of government bonds equals zero until unit-period 18, which explains why the full effect of the lower supply of government bonds in the alternative simulation only becomes visible after unit-period 18. From unit-period 18 until unit-period 51 the supply of government bonds is positive and decreasing on average. A zero supply of government bonds is reached in period 51. After unit-period 51 the total supply of bonds is equal to the supply of bonds by firms and hence nearly constant. The time pattern in the total supply of bonds explains to a large extent the fluctuations in the rate of interest. In period 18-51 a relatively large decrease of the rate of interest can be observed as total bond supply is falling. Since the demand for bonds by banks is rather interest-elastic, banks' demand for bonds is falling as well. Households' demand for bonds falls only gradually, mainly because the level of household wealth is declining, on the one hand, because nominal wages and profits are falling (relative to the bench-mark simulation figure 7.22), and on the other hand, because households receive lower income transfers from banks because of a lower level of financial transactions by banks. In period 51 the total supply of bonds becomes constant on average. As the fall of household demand for bonds proceeds, the rate of interest increases somewhat which initiates a small increase in the demand for bonds by banks, which is necessary to clear the bond market. At the end of the simulation period the demand for bonds by banks is stable on average; the demand for bonds by households still falls because of the arguments spelled out above; the supply of bonds by firms is slowly increasing and the supply of government bonds equals zero. As a result, interest rates have to rise in order to clear the bond market, which explains the results depicted in diagram 7.21.

The developments in commodity prices, expected prices and wages are initially not much different from the time patterns in the bench-mark projection (figure 7.22). However, after unit-period 50 a different time pattern emerges, which corresponds to the falling level of consumption demand as a result of a lower level of household wealth. Since the rate of inflation affects expected commodity prices and nominal wages similarly, the time pattern of these variables is not much different from the time pattern of actual commodity prices. As in the bench-mark simulation a period of frequent regime switches is characterized by rigid prices (corrected for expected inflation), which implies that in this alternative simulation prices are 'rigid' for the last 25 unit-periods. However, since expected inflation is negative because the period of frequent regime switches follows after a period of excess commodity supply, only 'real' prices are rigid whereas the nominal price level falls. This rigidity, and hence the absence of a period of excess commodity demand at the end of the simulation period as can be observed in the bench-mark simulation (figure 7.1), explains the relatively sharp decrease in commodity prices at the end of the alternative simulation (figure 7.22). Since wages and expected commodity prices are not affected like actual commodity prices by a situation of excess commodity demand, this pattern cannot be traced in these variables. From figure 7.23 it can be observed that the unemployment rate is not affected very much by an increase in the bank income tax rate. On average there is a large similarity with the results of the bench-mark projection. Together with the observed invariance of aggregate demand (figure 7.18*a*) and the time pattern of commodity prices as shown in figure 7.22, this result illustrates that despite the imperfections in the commodity market and the labour market, price (and wage) adjustments still absorb a considerable part of the changes that are invoked on the economy. In the short run (or better from unit-period to unit-period) there may be quantity adjustments (particularly in commodity stocks but also in production, aggregate demand and employment), in the medium run price adjustments have a stabilizing impact. With respect to commodity prices, wages and inventories, we observe that in this simulation, as in the first simulation, commodity prices increase in a period of excess demand although they may initially fall as a result of expected inflation. In the first period of excess commodity supply, commodity prices initially are rigid (corrected for expected inflation). A similar observation can be made for a period of frequent regime switches. Commodity stocks initially increase to absorb the primary effects of a declining pattern of aggregate demand. Afterwards production levels adjust rather smoothly and stocks fall. All these observations have been explained in detail in the preceding part of this section. Hence it is not necessary to provide more detail here.

Since this second simulation is distinguished from the bench-mark case by an increase in the corporate income tax levied on bank profits, it is not surprising that the main impact of this increase shows up in the financial sector, in particular in the behaviour of banks and the government sector. Figure 7.24*b* depicts the absolute difference in government wealth, which, of course, reflects the absolute difference in the public sector deficit (figure 7.25). The overall impression is that in comparison with the bench-mark, the increase of the corporate income tax rate has resulted in an improved wealth position of the government sector, in smaller budget deficits and in larger budget surpluses. These developments in the government sector have been attained at the expense of a considerably lower level of bank wealth and, hence, a lower demand for bonds by banks during the entire simulation period (figure 7.19).

To conclude, it can be observed that a change in the corporate bank income tax rate essentially affects the financial sector of the economy. The influence on the real sector of the economy is rather modest. The general impression of this simulation equals the picture of the bench-mark projection. Our observations in the preceding section about the relative impact of prices, wages and the rate of interest on the level of aggregate demand, production and employment are confirmed by the results of this alternative simulation. In the next section, we will analyze to what extent these quantity adjustments can be initiated by changes in the household income tax rate.

figure 7.17

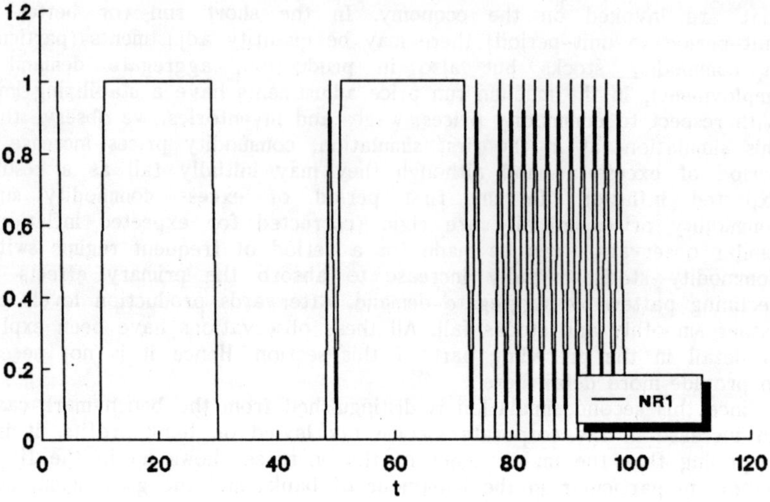

figure 7.18a

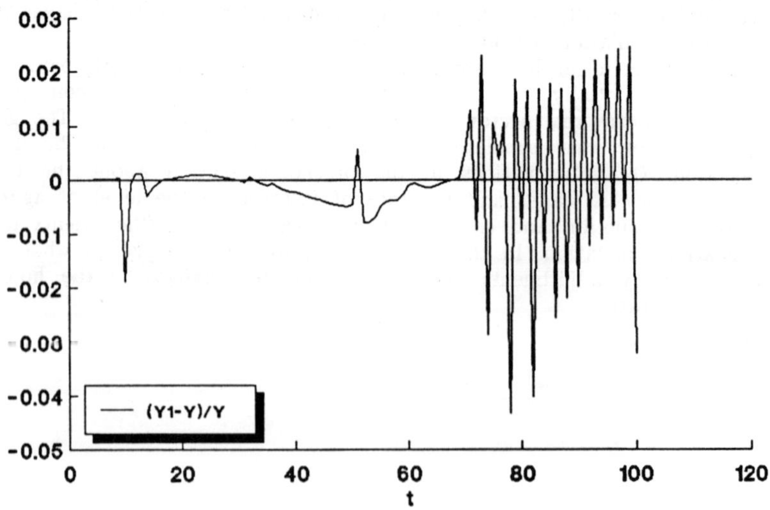

figure 7.18b

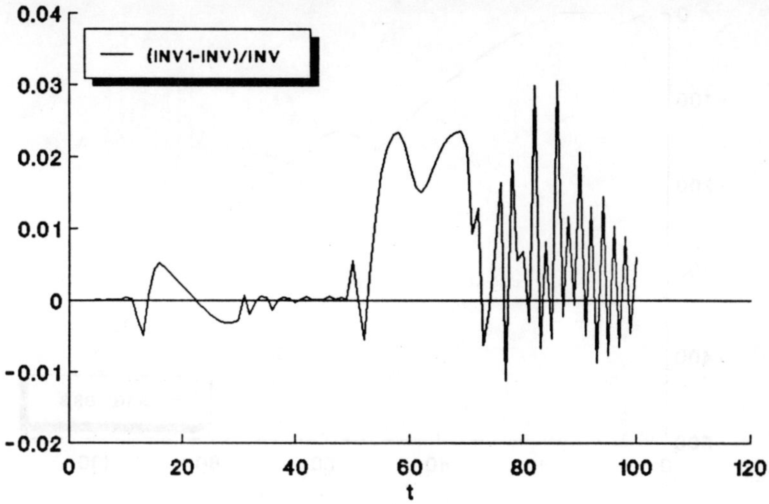

figure 7.19

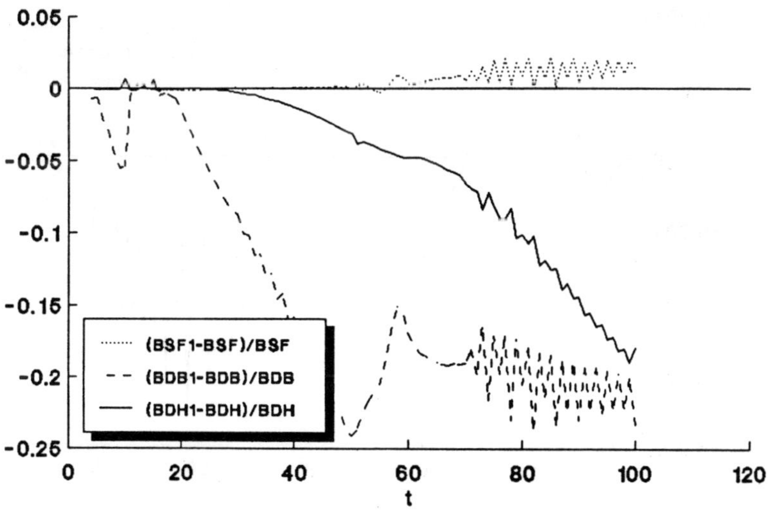

figure 7.20

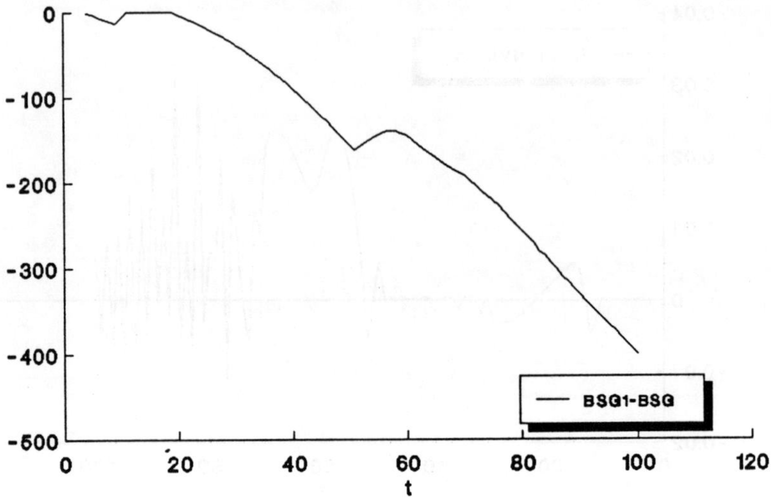

figure 7.21

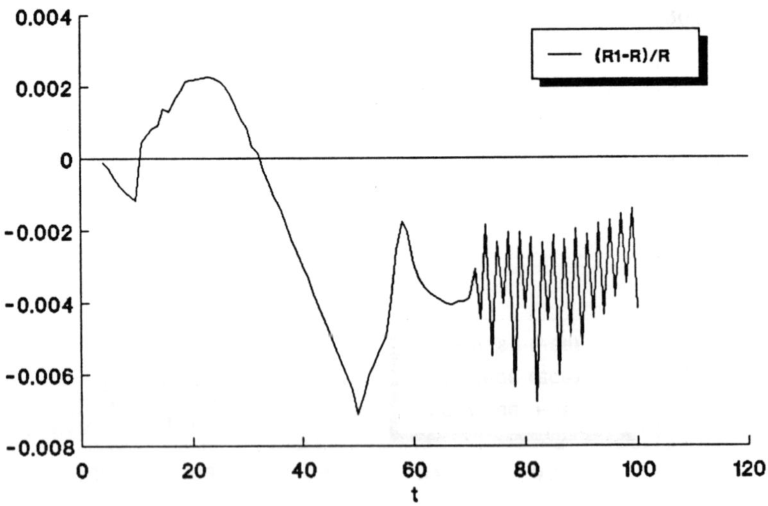

figure 7.22

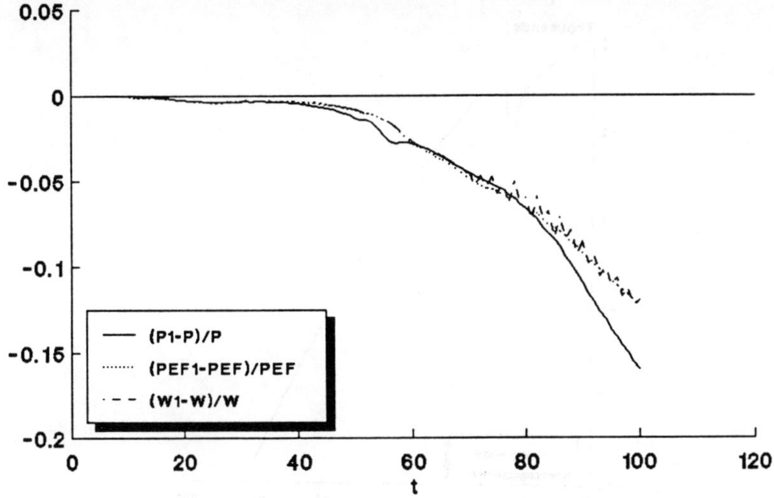

figure 7.23

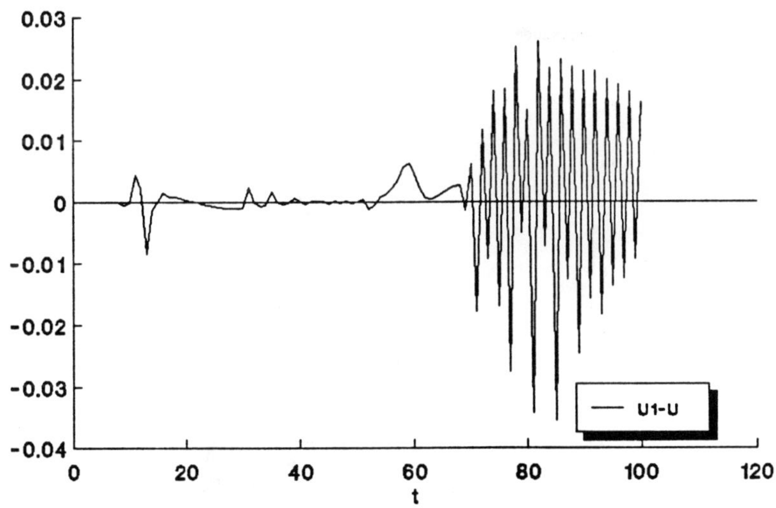

figure 7.24a

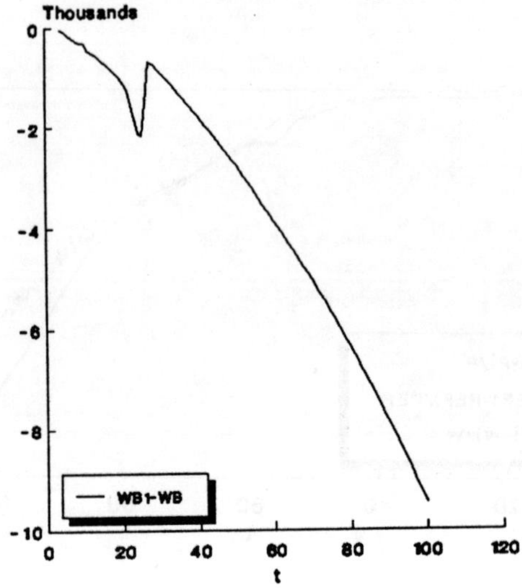

figure 7.24b

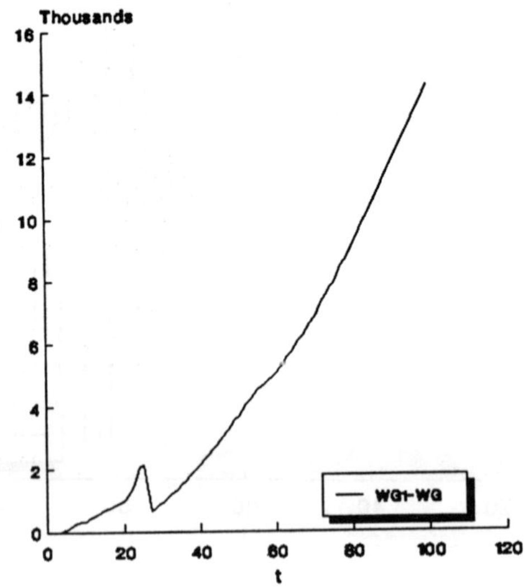

figure 7.25

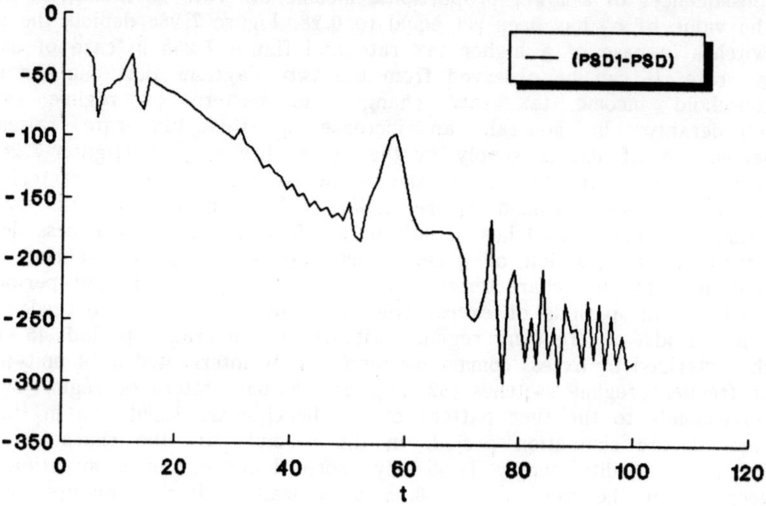

C. Changing the household income tax rate

This alternative projection consists of two simulation runs. The first simulation, distinguished by the adjective *2a* in the symbols, describes the implications of an increase in the income tax rate to 0.40. The second simulation, distinguished by the adjective *2b* in the symbols, describes the consequences of a lower proportional income tax rate on household income. The value of α_7 has been set equal to 0.28. Figure 7.26*a* depicts the regime switches in case of a higher tax rate and figure 7.26*b* in case of a lower tax rate. It can be observed from the two diagrams that changes in the household income tax rate change the pattern of regime switches considerably. In general, an increase in this tax rate raises the persistence of excess supply in the commodity market (figure 7.26*a*). A decrease in the tax rate raises the number of unit-periods characterized by excess commodity demand (figure 7.26*b*). With a higher income tax rate, the commodity market switches in unit-period 5 to a regime of excess demand, returns to a situation of excess commodity supply in unit-period 9 and continues to be characterized by this situation until unit-period 30. Thirteen unit-periods of excess commodity demand follow, succeeded by 4 unit-periods of frequent regime switches. On average, period 45 – 100 is characterized by excess commodity supply, only interrupted by 4 unit-periods of frequent regime switches (82 – 86). The global pattern of regime switches corresponds to the time pattern of the bench-mark simulation in the first part of the simulation period. In the second part the characteristic of excess commodity supply is clearly more dominant. In a situation of a decrease in the tax rate to 0.28 a radically different picture emerges, because of the positive impact on disposable income. The time-pattern of regime switches globally resembles the pattern of the bench-mark simulation on the understanding that the first period of excess commodity demand is 7 unit-periods longer than in the bench-mark experiment. After unit-period 29 the commodity market is characterized by excess demand. Furthermore, the simulation results do not indicate that it is very likely that a return to any other regime in the commodity market will take place.

In figure 7.27 the developments in the commodity price are depicted for the two different tax regimes and the bench-mark projection. It can be derived that an increase in the tax rate to 0.40 has a deflationary impact. Compared with the bench-mark simulation, commodity prices are lower during the entire simulation period. Because in the bench-mark simulation a period of excess commodity demand at the end of the simulation period creates upward pressure on the level of the commodity price, the negative difference between actual commodity prices in the alternative and in the bench-mark simulation especially shows up at the end of the simulation period. Commodity prices are rigid (corrected for expected inflation) at the beginning of the first prolonged period of excess commodity supply (9 – 13) and in the two periods of frequent regime switches (46 – 49, 82 – 86). Furthermore, 'real' commodity prices are rigid during the first 10 unit-periods of the second period of persistent excess commodity supply and during the last prolonged period of excess commodity supply (87 – 100). Despite this 'real' rigidity the nominal level of commodity prices decreases as a result of a negative expected inflation. In this respect, 'real' rigidity only implies that expected and actual rates of inflation are constant and equal. As has been argued in section 7.2.2, the primary cause of this rigidity in commodity prices is the level of expected commodity prices. A relatively high level of the expected future commodity price may cause ('real') commodity prices to be rigid or to increase even in a situation in excess commodity supply. In a situation where commodity prices persistently fall and hence expected inflation is negative for a prolonged period, the accompanying decrease in expected commodity prices is smaller because of the adaptive nature of expected commodity price formation ([6.42]), provided that the negative impact of the positive discrepancy between the actual commodity stock and aggregate demand is not too large. In that situation expected future commodity prices rise relative to current commodity prices. Since this development also provides a stimulus for production (real expected wages fall), such a situation cannot be stable as the discrepancy between stocks and aggregate demand grows. In line with this observation, our simulation results indicate that at the end of the simulation period (90 – 100) the fall in expected commodity prices exceeds the fall in actual prices, which implies that the depressing impact of a situation of excess commodity supply becomes dominant. Hence, we may conclude that downward 'real' commodity price rigidity in a situation of excess commodity supply cannot be persistent. However, as the result of this alternative simulation indicates, adjustment processes can be rather prolonged.

Compared with the bench–mark simulation, a tax rate of 0.28 implies a rather inflationary pattern of commodity prices. The simulation results in case of a lower household income tax rate are characterized by the absence of ('real') commodity price rigidity. From figure 7.27 it can be concluded that a decrease in the tax rate creates a period of accelerating inflation, although the acceleration speed is rather small. In the situation of a higher tax rate, deflation prevails. A further inspection of figure 7.27 reveals that also in this projection there is an asymmetry in the development of commodity prices. In periods of excess demand prices continue to rise. In a period of excess supply, commodity prices are initially rigid (corrected for expected inflation) and start to fall afterwards because the persistence of a situation of excess commodity supply depresses expected future commodity prices, which enforces the downward pressure on current commodity prices resulting from inflation. The downward flexibility of prices appears to be lower than the upward flexibility.

In figure 7.28*a* the time pattern of the difference in aggregate demand levels as a proportion of the level of aggregate demand in the bench–mark simulation is depicted in a situation of a higher household income tax rate. It can be observed that the level of aggregate demand in this alternative simulation fluctuates around the bench–mark level of aggregate demand. In the last 10 unit–periods aggregate demand in this simulation as a proportion of aggregate demand in the bench–mark simulation declines rather sharply. A more accurate analysis of the simulation results permits the following observations. In the first place, the level of aggregate consumption demand is significantly lower in the entire simulation period, which can be denoted as the direct impact of a higher income tax rate. On average, the decline in consumption demand amounts to a minimum of about 4% in unit–period 37 until about 48% in unit–period 100. This decline in consumption indicates that the depressing impact on consumption demand of lower after–tax labour and non–labour income as well as the erosion of household wealth through lower bond and money holdings exceeds the positive impact of lower commodity prices on consumption demand. In the second place, it can be observed that to some extent the composition of aggregate demand has changed. The level of government expenditures is structurally higher than in the bench–mark simulation, a result which can be explained from a lower level of inflation and an on average higher rate of unemployment (figure 7.30). Furthermore, the level of investment demand has increased as well, which can be explained from the fact that expected nominal wages have decreased less than expected commodity prices because of the adaptive nature of expected wage formation ([6.93]) and as a result of the asymmetrical pattern of wage adjustments in response to sharp fluctuations in the rate of unemployment (figure 7.30). The time pattern of real expected wages more than compensates the depressing impact of higher real user costs, which increase because of a higher rate of deflation. Moreover, the developments in expected commodity prices are responsible for the fluctuations in the deviations between the aggregate demand levels in the two simulations. The alternative simulation is characterized by a rather steady process of deflation which in turn implies a steady fall of the expected commodity price. However, the expected commodity price in the bench-mark simulation shows a rather fluctuating time-pattern (figure 7.5), which given the development in expected nominal wages (figure 7.7) causes some fluctuations in the investment pattern of the bench-mark simulation. These fluctuations, together with structurally higher levels of government expenditures and investments in the alternative simulation, which partly compensate the lower level of consumption expenditures, cause the deviations between the two aggregate demand levels as illustrated in figure 7.28*a*.

In figure 7.28*b* the time pattern of the difference in aggregate demand levels as a proportion of the level of aggregate demand in the bench-mark simulation is depicted in case of a lower income tax rate. After the explanation of the time pattern in a situation of a higher tax rate, the discussion of figure 7.28*b* can be rather brief. Aggregate consumption demand is increasingly higher than in the bench-mark situation and the level of government expenditures is structurally lower because of the increasing price level. The level of investments in this alternative simulation is, however, structurally higher than the investment level in the bench-mark simulation. Real expected wages in a situation of a lower tax rate are lower than in the bench-mark situation because of the adaptive nature of expected wage formation ([6.93]). However, the (negative) difference in this case is not as big as the (positive) difference in the case of a higher tax rate because now wage adjustments in response to fluctuations from unit-period to unit-period in the unemployment rate are more smoothly than with a higher income tax rate as can be observed from figure 7.30. As has already been explained, a negative difference between the actual unemployment rate and the 'natural' unemployment rate implies a considerably larger *increase* in nominal wages in the next unit-period than a positive difference of equal size between the two unemployment rates implies a *decrease* in nominal wages in the next unit-period. As a result, large fluctuations in the actual rate of unemployment around the 'natural' rate create an upward bias in the development of the nominal wage level. Since this simulation is characterized by relatively small fluctuations in the rate of unemployment, the development of actual nominal wages and (because of adaptive expectations) expected nominal wages is more in line with the development in expected prices. As a result, the decline in real expected wages is not as strong as the increase in this variable in case of a higher tax rate. Consequently, the depressing impact on investment is relatively small. Furthermore, real user costs of capital have decreased because of stronger inflation. With a lower income tax rate this last positive effect on investment exceeds the negative impact of a decline in real expected wages. Hence, the level of investments increases, although this increase is smaller than in a situation of a higher tax rate. As in the preceding paragraph, it can be observed that the short-run fluctuations which show up in diagram 7.29*b* are, to a large extent, caused by short-run fluctuations in aggregate investment demand in the bench-mark simulation. Finally, the structural increase in the unemployment rate at the end of the simulation period is due to the fact that although the nominal wage moves more in line with the expected commodity price, on average the ratio of the nominal wage and the expected price shows a tendency to increase. As a result, the average demand for labour gradually falls and the average rate of unemployment increases.

The differences in the developments in production and the use of production factors can be derived from figures 7.29 and 7.30. Figure 7.29 displays the difference in inventory levels as a proportion of the inventory level in the bench-mark simulation. Figure 7.30 depicts the deviations from the unemployment rate in the bench-mark projection, both for a higher, as well as a lower tax rate. The rather whimsical patterns depicted in the diagrams can be understood, to a large extent, by considering the fluctuations of the unemployment rate in the bench-mark case in periods of excess demand (figures 7.4 and 7.3, respectively). With respect to the bench-mark simulation it has already been observed that fluctuations in the level of commodity stocks correspond, to a large extent, to fluctuations in aggregate demand. This can also be derived from a comparison of the time-patterns displayed in figures 7.28 and 7.29: a peak in the level of aggregate demand corresponds to a dip in inventory levels. This illustrates the role of commodity stocks as a buffer mechanism. In case of a lower tax rate, the level of production and employment is positively affected by a higher stock of capital due to a generally higher level of investment. The decrease in actual nominal wages is smaller, however, than the fall in expected commodity prices, which *ceteris paribus* depresses the demand for labour. Capital is substituted for labour in the production process. Furthermore, in situations where the economy is operating at full or at nearly full capacity levels, nominal wages are pushed upward in the succeeding unit-period which explains the relatively sharp fluctuations in the rate of unemployment. Hence, the fluctuations in the difference between the unemployment rate ($U2a$) and the unemployment rate of the bench-mark simulation (U) correspond to fluctuations in the difference between the two levels of investment, on the one hand, and to the asymmetrical pattern of wage adjustments, on the other hand. On average, a higher tax rate implies a slightly higher level of production and higher inventory levels than in the bench-mark simulation (figure 7.29*a*). Also in case of a lower tax rate the level of investment has increased although this increase is smaller than in case of a higher tax rate. Furthermore, the ratio of the actual nominal wage and the expected commodity price has increased because actual nominal wages rise faster than expected commodity prices in a situation of fluctuating unemployment rates and generally increasing prices. This results from the asymmetrical pattern of wage adjustments, on the one hand, and the adaptive nature of the formation of expected commodity prices, on the other hand ([6.42]). As a result, the demand for labour is depressed. Taken together, the developments in the utilization of production factors imply a small increase in production levels. However, since on the one hand, the composition of aggregate demand has changed, as the proportion of consumption expenditures in aggregate demand has increased and on the other hand, consumption expenditures do not affect productive capacity, on average, the level of inventories is lower than in the bench-mark simulation. The rise in aggregate demand due to the increase of aggregate consumption is stronger than the rise in production levels.

Figure 7.31 depicts the developments in the public sector deficit as a result of the different tax policies. A lower tax rate clearly implies an increasing public sector deficit, both as a proportion of the deficit in the bench-mark projection (figure 7.31), as well as absolutely (an increase of almost 500% over the entire simulation period). Although tax revenues increase considerably, both compared with the bench-mark simulation (figure 7.32) and absolutely (+630%), as a result of a higher nominal income, higher nominal government expenditures and increasing interest payments create financial instability in the public sector. The increasing size of the public sector deficit puts upward pressure on the rate of interest. A similar effect has the decreasing supply of bonds by firms which is due to increasing profits. The increasing demand for bonds by households, due to increasing wealth, has a dampening influence on the interest rate. Together these developments imply a small decrease in the rate of interest (figure 7.33). In the opposite situation of a higher proportional tax rate on household income a small deficit remains at the end of the simulation period. Given the sizable increase in the tax rate the economy has experienced, the relatively small difference with the public sector deficit in the bench-mark projection is, however, remarkable. One explanation is offered in figure 7.32, which shows a considerable decrease in tax revenues in comparison with the revenues of the bench-mark case. Since nominal labour income has fallen, tax revenues too have fallen. Furthermore, a lower supply of government bonds, on the one hand, and a lower government demand for short-term loans, on the other hand, have depressed turnover rates in the financial market. Lower turnover rates in the bond market and the market for short-term loans result in lower non-labour income transfers to households, which also imply a fall in tax revenues. As a result, the financial position of the public sector has hardly received any positive impulse from the increase in the household income tax rate. With this conclusion, the discussion of the implications of different tax policies in the model has come to an end. In the next section, we will consider the impact of government expenditures.

figure 7.26a

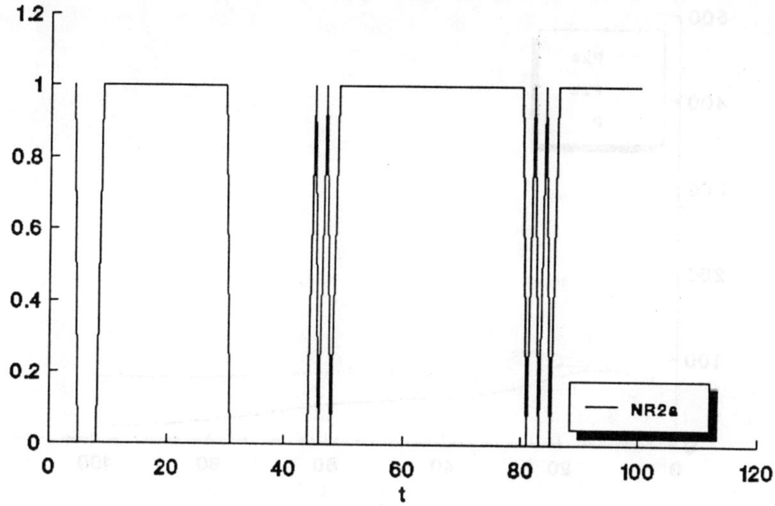

figure 7.26b

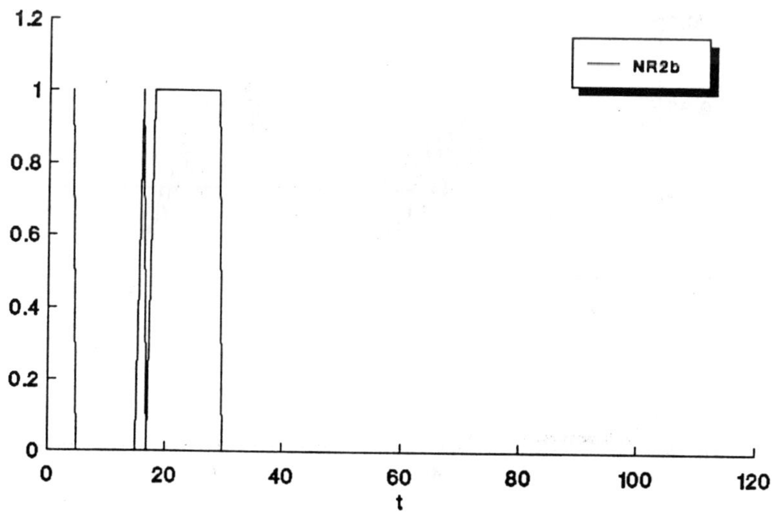

figure 7.27

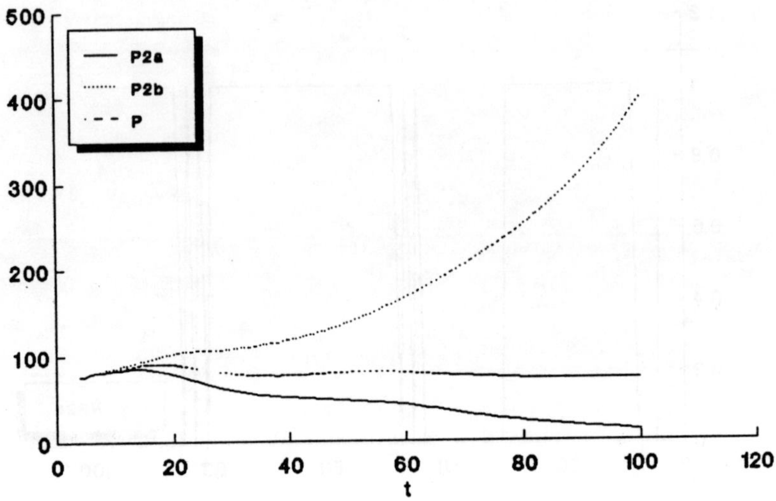

figure 7.28a

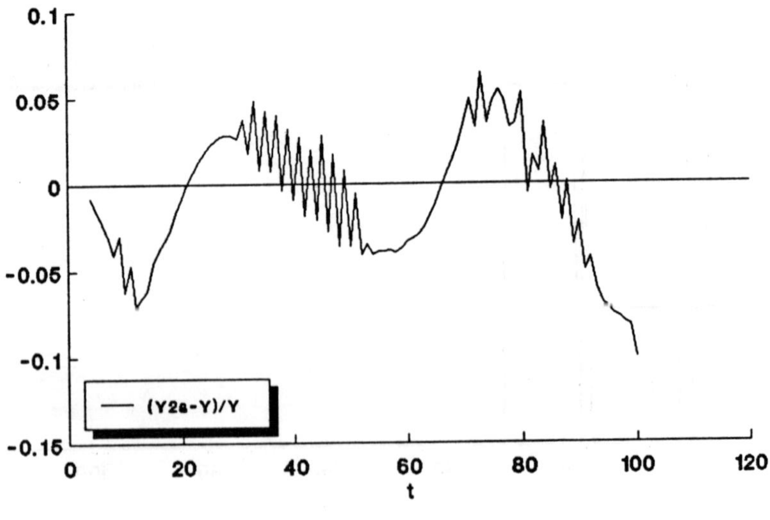

figure 7.28b

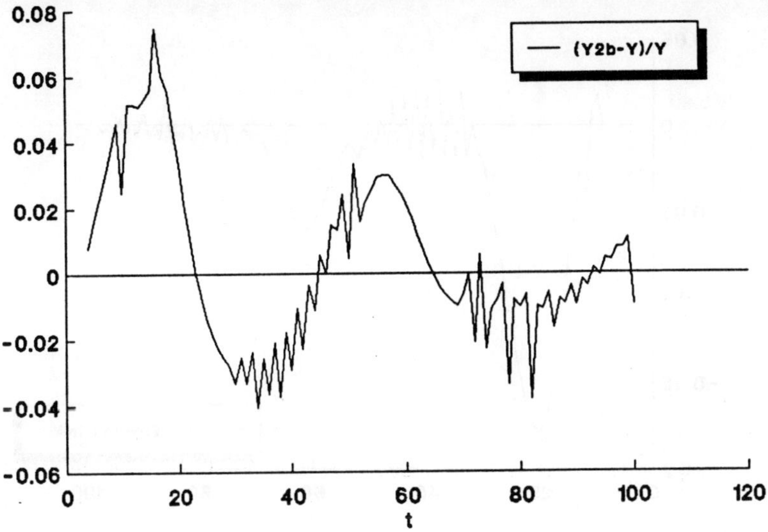

figure 7.29a

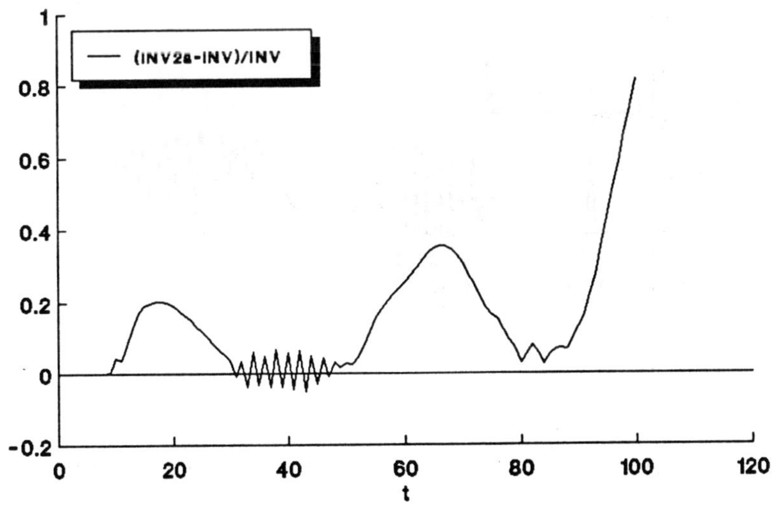

figure 7.29b

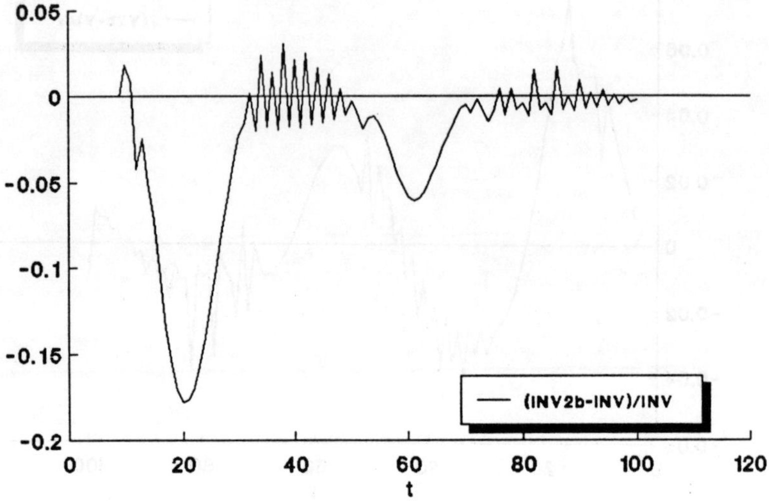

figure 7.30

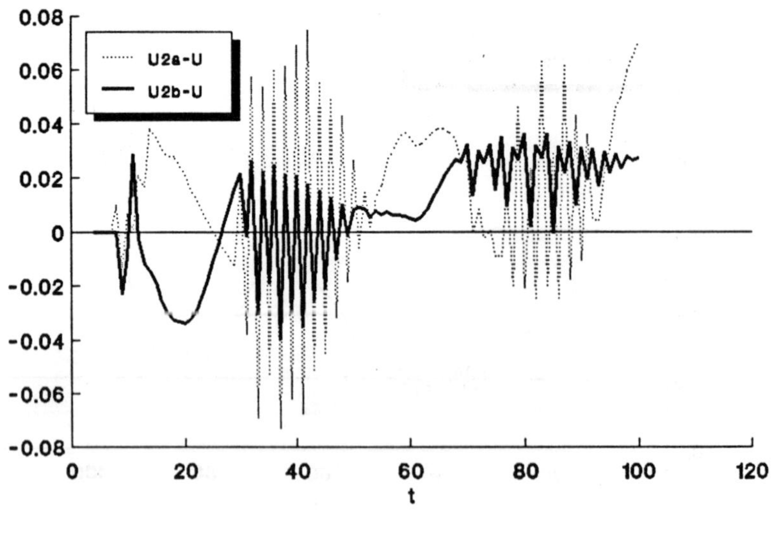

figure 7.31

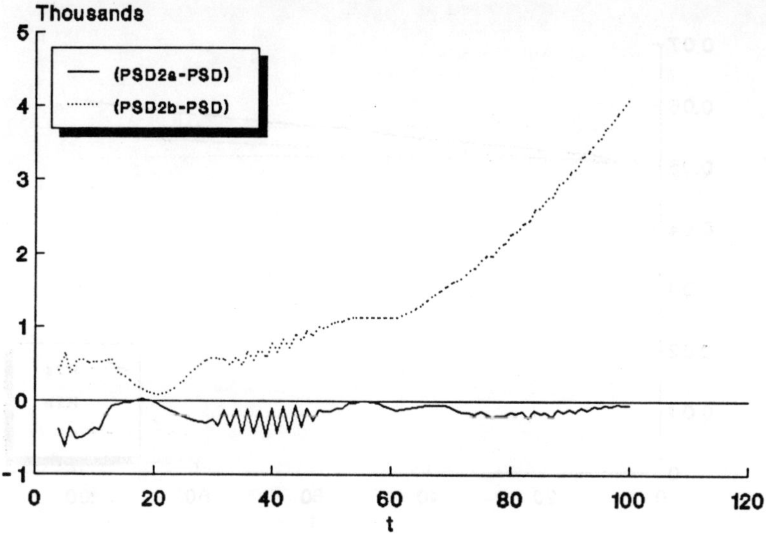

figure 7.32

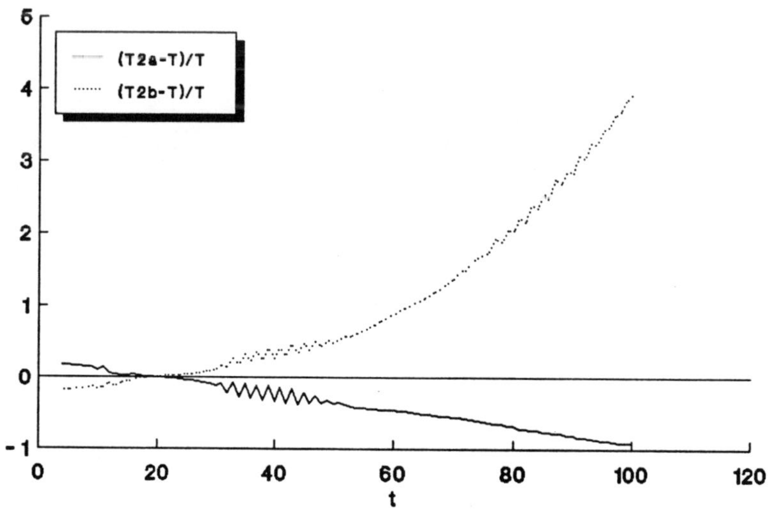

figure 7.33

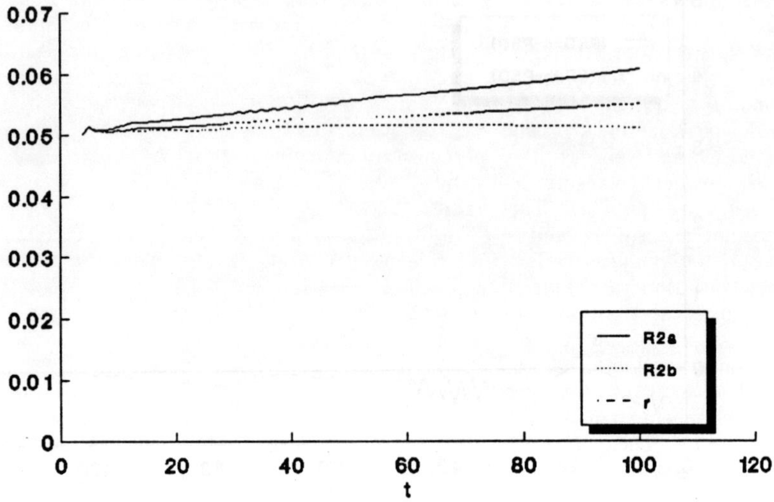

7.3.2 *Expenditure policy*

In the preceding section we have analyzed the implications of different policy regimes with respect to government receipts. In this section we deal with the consequences of alternative expenditure policies. Real government expenditures are determined in the bench-mark projection of the model in line with equation [6.79]. The specification of [6.79] rests upon the assumption that the government sector has a preference for a stable zero-inflation rate, on the one hand, and a stable natural unemployment rate, U_n, on the other hand. Furthermore, with positive values for the policy parameters, γ_2 and γ_3, equation [6.79] reflects a choice for policy activism as well as the perception that deviations from inflation and unemployment targets can be successfully prevented by discretionary expenditure policies. The values that have been chosen for the policy parameters, γ_1, γ_2 and γ_3 are 0.29, 3.00 and 0.3333, respectively. These parameter values reflect a relatively strong preference for a stable zero-inflation rate. Finally, $U_n = 0.03$ (section 7.2.2).

In this section we will consider the implications of a '*Laissez faire*' policy, which we define in this context as an expenditure policy of non-intervention. The government sector does not consider changes in the level of expenditures as a response to changes in the rates of inflation and unemployment. Equation [6.79] has been incorporated into the model with $\gamma_2,\gamma_3 = 0$. The purpose of this alternative simulation experiment is twofold. In the first place, this simulation may illustrate the 'success' of policy activism and at the same time, the extent to which the government sector behaves rationally if it follows a discretionary policy in the context of the model. In the second place, we may consider a more fundamental point of interest, related to the first object of analysis, which concerns the long-run features of private sector behaviour. In particular, we may analyze to what extent the simulation results support the proposition of self-regulating private sector behaviour in the context of the model, where agents decide optimally on the basis of actual quantity constraints observed at the end of every unit-period in the absence of a Walrasian auctioneer.

As in section 7.3.1, the alternative projection consists of two simulation runs. The first simulation is characterized by $\gamma_2 = \gamma_3 = 0$ and $\gamma_1 = 0.29$, which implies that compared to the bench-mark projection the value of γ_1 is not changed. This simulation is denoted by the adjective 3*a* in the symbols in the diagrams. The results of this experiment gave rise to an alternative simulation, which is characterized by $\gamma_2 = \gamma_3 = 0$ and $\gamma_1 = 0.32$. Compared to the bench-mark projection these parameter changes imply that in the absence of stabilization policy, the government sector has a higher structural expenditure level in every unit-period. For that reason this alternative simulation describes a more expansive regime of government policy. A higher value of γ_1 also implies that the results of the simulation cannot be compared straightforwardly with the results of the bench-mark projection. The second simulation is distinguished by the adjective 3*b* in the symbols.

In figure 7.34 the regime switches for both simulation runs are indicated. In the absence of policy a regime of excess commodity demand is established in unit-period 5 in simulation 3*a*. A period of excess commodity supply follows (18 – 43), succeeded again by a period of excess commodity demand (44 – 64). Then after a period of frequent regime switches (9 unit-periods), a period of excess supply is established in the commodity market, which lasts until the end of the simulation period. The regime switches of simulation 3*b* show a similar time pattern as the switches in case of a lower household income tax rate (simulation 2*b*) . A switch to a situation of excess commodity demand in unit-period 5 is followed by a return to a situation of persistent excess commodity supply in unit-period 30. After 17 unit-periods of excess commodity supply the situation of excess commodity demand is re-established in the commodity market. Observe that a higher structural level of government expenditures implies a larger number of unit-periods of excess commodity demand (see also figure 7.1), which illustrates the expansionary impact on the performance of the economy. The results of simulation *3b* are comparable to the results of simulation *2b*, which deals with the impact of a lower proportional households' income tax rate. For that reason, reference is partl made to the arguments developed in the preceding section. In a situation of persistent excess demand, the public sector deficit increases more than proportionally at the end of the simulation period as a result of higher government expenditures and increasing interest payments, which are the natural consequence of the accumulation of government debt. Figure 7.41 illustrates that, in comparison with the level of government expenditures in the bench-mark simulation, the average level of government expenditures is lower in simulation *3a*. Lower government expenditures do not imply a significant decrease in the level of the public sector deficit (figure 7.35), which is the result of the depressing impact of lower government expenditures on nominal income as has been illustrated particularly in simulation *2a*. Also the developments in the interest rate, the commodity price and the rate of unemployment (figures 7.36, 7.37 and 7.38, respectively) resemble for a large part the developments in these variables in projections 2. The downward pressure on interest rates in simulation *3b* (figure 7.36) results from two sources. In the first place, firm profits increase in a situation of excess commodity demand because the real wage rate decreases. Increasing profits have a depressing impact on the supply of bonds by firms since a part of the firms' expenditures can be financed out of profits in that situation. In the second place, wealth accumulation in the household sector increases the demand for bonds.

Commodity prices increase at accelerating rates in simulation *3b*. Despite this development in commodity prices, relatively as well as absolutely, the levels of aggregate demand remain high (figure 7.39), as a result of the growth in household wealth, due to the increasing demand for financial funds by the government. The impact of changes in wealth on the aggregate demand for commodities dominates dominates the growth of production. As a result, the aforementioned developments in the private sector create a situation of persistent excess commodity demand and accelerating rates of inflation. The developments in the rate of unemployment and in production in a situation of a higher structural level of government expenditures show a similarity with the simulation results in case of lower household income tax rate (*2b*). Short-run relative fluctuations in the rate of unemployment can be explained by dovolopmonto in tho otock of capital and in cxpcctcd commodity pricea, as has been described in the preceding section. The stock of capital has increased because a higher rate of inflation implies a decrease in the real user costs of capital in simulation *3b*. As the ratio of nominal wages and the expected future commodity price has increased, the demand for labour is depressed. These developments together have a positive impact on the level of production and a negative impact on the rate of unemployment. To some extent a more capital-intensive technology has been employed in the production process. Finally, it can be observed that a higher level of structural government expenditures has a more sustained expansionary impact on aggregate demand than a decrease of the household income tax rate (figure 7.39 and 7.28*b* respectively). Furthermore, both policies have a small positive impact on the level of production and a negative impact on the level of employment.

The simulation results above illustrate the instability of private sector behaviour within the context of the model. Individual decisions and activities can be regarded as correct, but insufficient responses to market signals observed in the economy. They do not reverse economic developments. Furthermore, the regime in the commodity market is, to a large extent, dominated by the choice of parameter values, which also implies that the choice of policy parameters affects the course of the economy. The behaviour of the government sector has a profound impact on the level of aggregate demand and prices, and a considerably smaller impact on the level of production. The pursuit of an expenditure policy in order to suppress rapid changes in commodity prices, as in the bench-mark simulation, can be considered a successful strategy in the context of the model, as is illustrated in figures 7.40 and 7.41. Relatively low levels of government expenditures (figure 7.41) in periods of inflation exert a downward pressure on inflation rates (figure 7.40, *INF3a* and *INF*). The impact of policy on the unemployment rate is more ambiguous. On the one hand, the parameter values chosen in the bench-mark government expenditure function indicate a relatively low preference for stable unemployment rates. On the other hand, the characteristics of the model do not show a strong impact of aggregate demand conditions on the levels of production and employment. In line with this observation, we may conclude that a well-defined impact of expenditure policy on the unemployment rate cannot be expected as well.

figure 7.34a

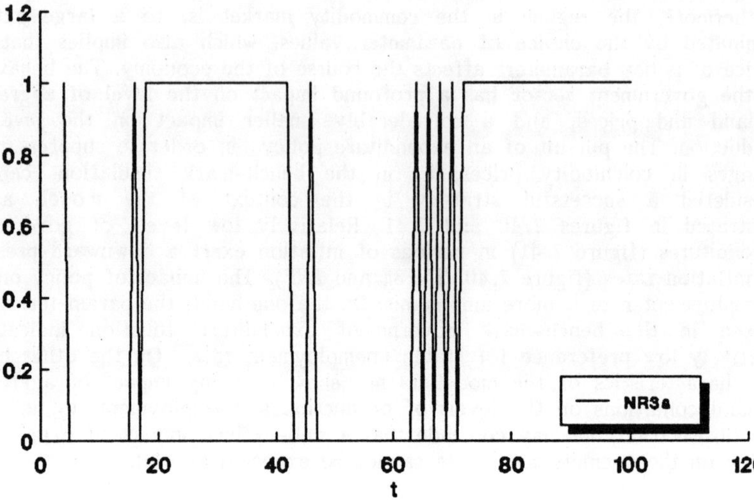

figure 7.34b

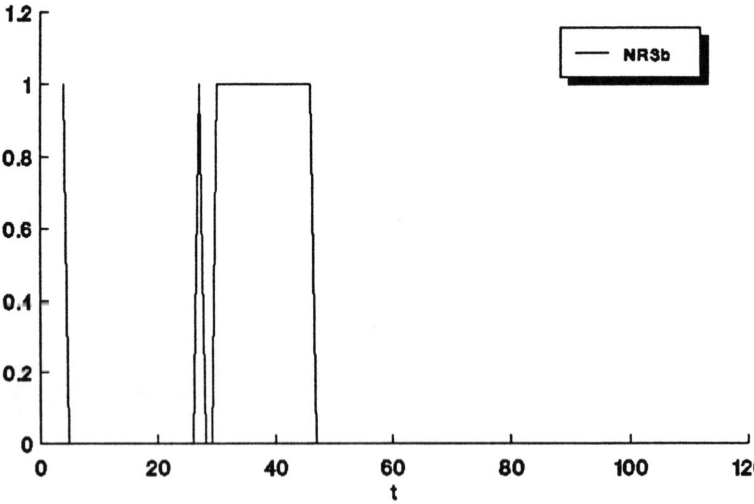

figure 7.35

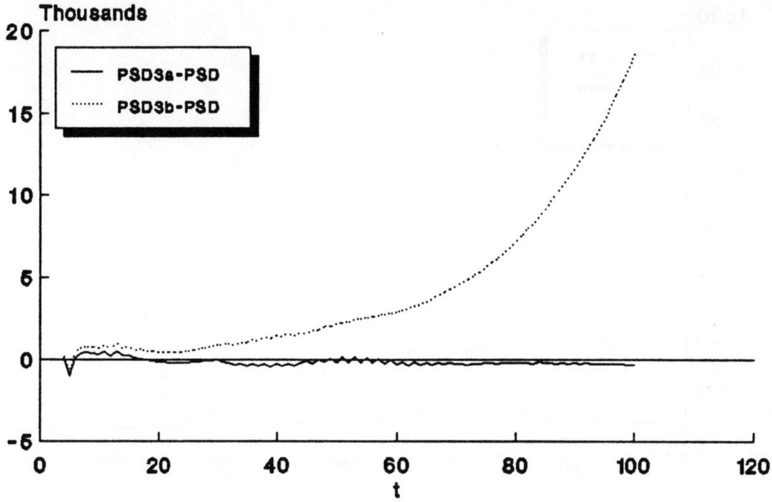

figure 7.36

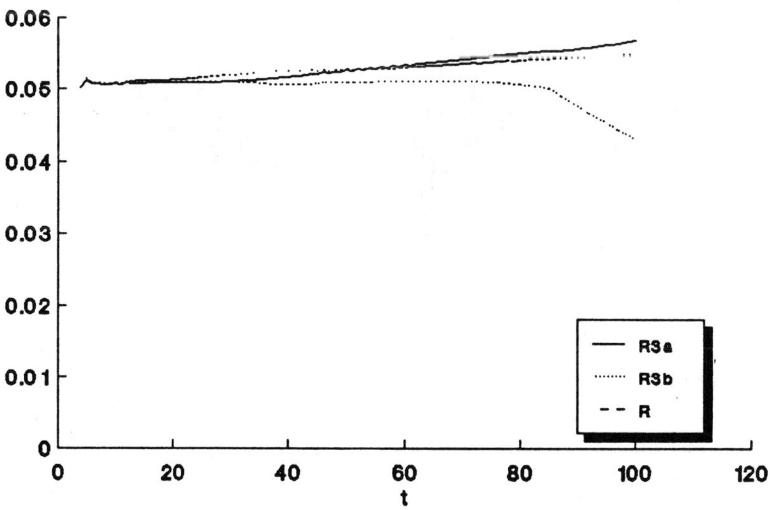

figure 7.37

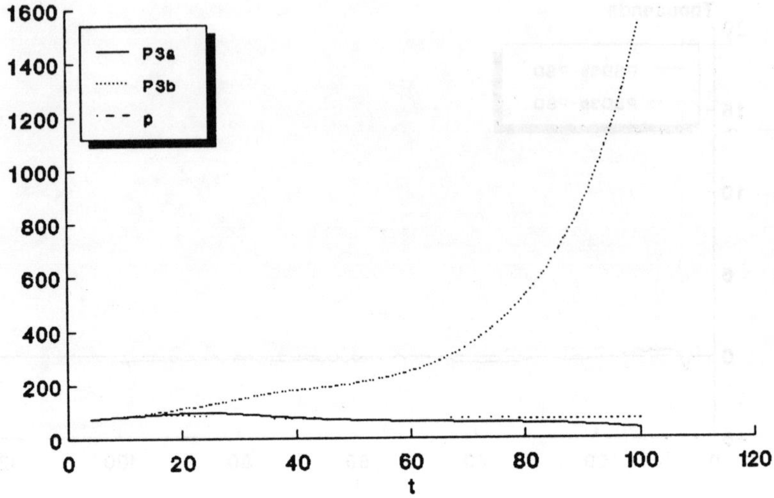

figure 7.38

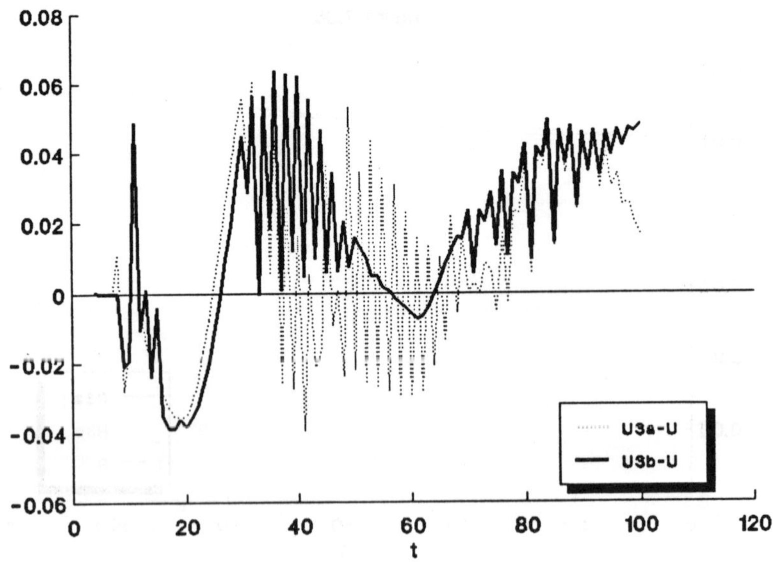

figure 7.39

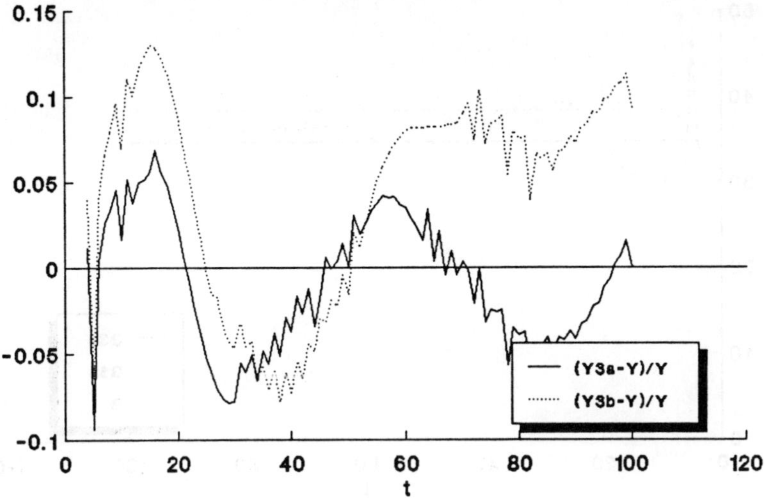

figure 7.40

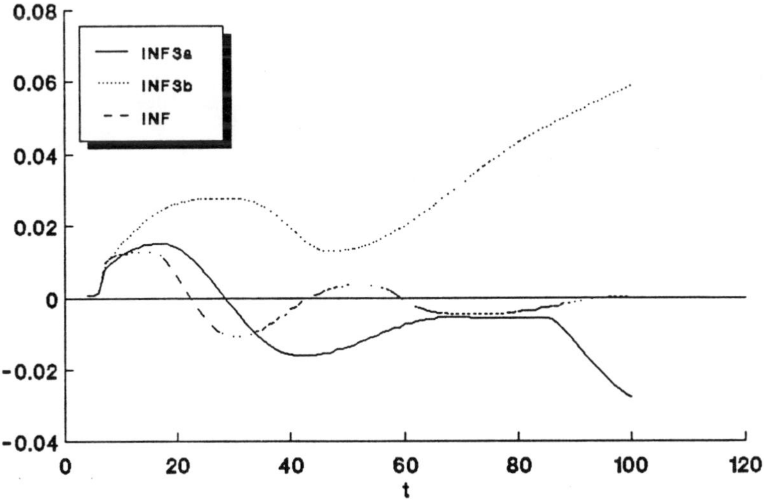

figure 7.41

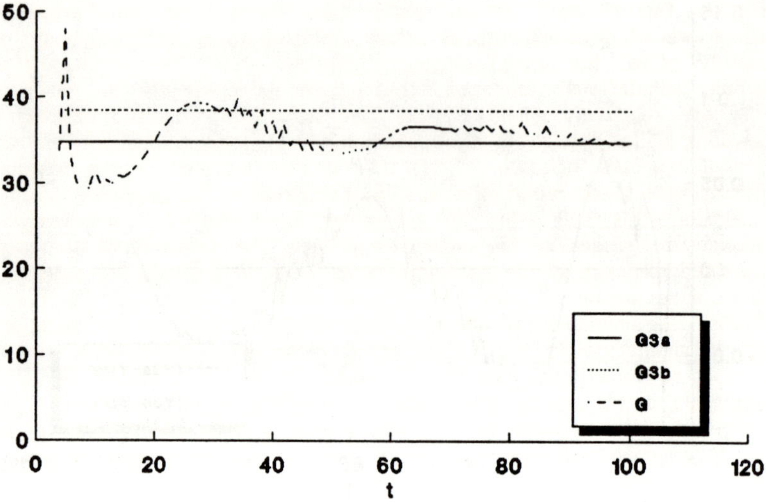

7.4 The impact of expected inflation

The alternative simulations of the two preceding sections describe the implications of changes in demand conditions. Expenditure policies as well as tax rate policies initially affect the level of aggregate demand. Corresponding changes in the levels of production and the utilization of production factors may result, within the context of the model, in situations where developments in prices, interest rates and wages do not completely offset the initial aggregate demand shift. The results of the preceding simulations illustrate that these fluctuations in economic activity are relatively small. In this last simulation we will consider the implications of a change in the parameter (α_8) that determines the time pattern of expected inflation ($\pi^e(t,t)$, *INF* in the diagrams), which may have significant effects on aggregate supply. Furthermore, as will be shown in this section, this simulation in particular illustrates the sensitivity of the model to changes in the parameter values. The features of the model change fundamentally if the parameter value that determines the adjustment speed of expectations to observed forecast errors, changes. In this respect we discuss the simulation results obtained with the following two parameter values. In simulation 4*a* the parameter α_8 is set equal to 0, which implies that expected inflation is completely static: it is not adjusted to actual developments in commodity prices and set equal to 0. In simulation 4*b* the parameter α_8 is set equal to 0.5, which implies that agents believe that actual developments in one unit-period contain a considerable amount of information about the developments in commodity prices in the long run. Hence, it is perceived as rational to adjust expected inflation rather quickly to changes in these prices.

Figure 7.42*a* depicts the situation in the commodity market as can be derived from the time path of the variable $NR4a(t,t)$ in a situation with unchanging expectations. It can be observed that this simulation run is characterized by, respectively, a relatively short period of excess commodity demand, a period of frequent regime switches (16–41) and a prolonged period of excess commodity supply until the end of the simulation period (41–100).

As in the bench-mark simulation, in simulation 4*a* excess commodity demand causes prices as well as expected prices to rise. Since expected inflation is constant and equal to 0, the development in expected future commodity prices is completely determined by the time patterns of inventories and aggregate demand. Furthermore, the distinction between nominal and real rigidity is superfluous. In the discussion of the simulation results of the bench-mark simulation (section 7.2.2) it has been observed that commodity prices may rise at the start of a period of excess commodity supply because of delayed adjustments of expected inflation. In this respect figure 7.5 indicates that in that situation actual commodity prices increase more strongly than expected future commodity prices. Since expected inflation equals 0 in simulation 4*a*, the divergent development in expected and actual commodity prices does no longer arise. The different pattern of expected inflation also explains that actual commodity prices in simulation 4*a* are lower than actual commodity prices in the bench-mark simulation during the first 25 unit-periods (figure 7.46*a*), notwithstanding the existence of excess commodity supply in the bench-mark simulation. Furthermore, the relative level of expected future commodity prices (relative to actual prices) is generally higher in this simulation than in the bench-mark simulation, which implies a larger number of unit-periods with rigid commodity prices in case of excess commodity supply. Commodity prices fall during the last 44 unit–periods of excess commodity supply. During the first phase of the prolonged period of excess commodity supply (41 – 55) only expected future commodity prices are adjusted in a downward direction. Since actual commodity prices do not respond to the situation in the commodity market, aggregate demand does not receive any positive impulse and inventories accumulate (figure 7.45*a*). When eventually commodity prices start to fall in unit–period 56, when expected future prices have fallen sufficiently below actual prices, this will result in a temporary improvement of the situation in the commodity market. In unit–period 67 inventory levels start to increase again because of the underlying development on the supply side, which will be explained below.

As expected inflation equals 0 the level of investment is determined by the developments in real expected wages and the nominal rate of interest. The latter variable is nearly constant; figure 7.50 displays a rather steady increase of 10% over the entire simulation period, which implies that the interest rate effect on the medium–term fluctuations in the level of investment is rather small in simulation 4*a*. As in the bench–mark simulation, the strong decline in the level of investments in the first 4 unit–periods follows from considerable negative adjustments of expected real wages. Around unit–period 20 investments have reached their bottom–level; after unit–period 20 investment are nearly stable (on average, the rate of growth equals 0.2% per unit–period), with the exception of a small increase in the rate of growth in period 45 – 58. It has already been observed that during the first phase of the prolonged period of excess commodity supply expected future commodity prices fall. The expected nominal wage rate still increases (until unit–period 51) because of the delayed adjustment of this variable to changes in actual wages and the deteriorating situation in the labour market. The level of unemployment grows in absolute levels as well as in comparison with the bench–mark unemployment level as can be observed in figure 7.44*a*. After unit–period 60 real expected wages increase only little, which has a persistent positive impact on the level of investments throughout the entire period of excess supply. The increase in the rate of interest has a persistent negative impact. These developments together imply a small positive rate of investment growth, which has a positive effect on the level of production, labour demand and aggregate commodity demand.

From figure 7.46*a* and similar patterns of actual commodity prices and nominal wage in the bench–mark simulation (figure 7.6) it can be observed that aggregate demand for consumption is positively affected during the period of alternating regimes and period 60 – 70; it is negatively affected during the first phase of the period of prolonged excess commodity supply and period 70 – 80, while it is not affected during the last 20 unit–periods. On the other hand, the structural level of unemployment in simulation 4*a* is higher than in the bench–mark simulation (figure 7.44*a*) and increasing very slowly as a result of downward stickiness in nominal wages (the ratio $W(t,t)/P^e_f(t,t+1)$ increases). The fluctuations in the deviations between the two unemployment rates can, to a large extent, be ascribed to developments in the bench–mark unemployment rate as can be derived from an inspection of figures 7.3 and 7.44*a*. The higher level of unemployment puts a downward pressure on the level of production and aggregate consumption demand. The level of government expenditures is affected positively. The depressing impact on consumption demand is reinforced by the structurally lower and negative level of the public sector deficit which has a negative impact on the accumulation of wealth by households (figure 7.49, *PSD*4*a* – *PSD*). These developments together imply that, given the arbitrarily chosen levels of the bench–mark elasticities, the level of production is higher than the level of aggregate demand (figure 7.45*a*) at the end of the simulation period. From figure 7.43 it can be observed that the average level of production is somewhat higher than in the bench-mark simulation $((Q4a-Q)/Q)$. The simulation results permit the opposite conclusion with respect to aggregate demand. Consequently, the situation of excess commodity supply deteriorates. In the absence of a feed-back mechanism as incorporated in the adaptive adjustment in the rate of inflation, which improves the equilibrium response of prices in the commodity market and the stabilizing impact of government expenditures, the simulation results illustrate a situation of persistent excess supply.

It can be observed that the simulation results with a high adjustment speed of expected to actual inflation are radically different. Figure 7.42*b* displays the time pattern of regime switches in case the adjustment parameter of expected to actual inflation is set equal to 0.5. After 1 unit-period of excess commodity demand and a relatively short period where aggregate demand exceeds the level of inventories, simulation 5*b* is characterized by a regularly alternating pattern of regimes. Four periods of excess commodity supply (11 – 23, 36 – 46, 59 – 69 and 83 – 92) are succeeded by 4 periods of excess commodity demand (24 – 35, 47 – 58, 70 – 82 and 93 – 100). Although the average length of the latter periods is somewhat longer, the simulation results do not indicate that the excess demand situation in the commodity market is dominant.

It can be argued that the developments in the variables in simulation 4*b* are, to a large extent, the result of the time patterns of prices. In order to illustrate this statement the time patterns of the actual real wage rate, the expected real wage rate, the ratio of the actual nominal wage and the expected future commodity price and the expected rate of inflation are depicted in figure 7.46*b*. The dots in this graph denote the regime in the commodity market. It can be observed that all variables in the graph display a rather regular pattern. However, there are considerable differences with respect to both the average height and the amplitude of the distinguished time paths. These differences correspond to different developments in real and financial variables. The time pattern of the actual real wage rate ($W(t,t)/P(t,t)$, $W4b/P4b$ in figure 7.46*b*) affects the time pattern of the demand for consumption. The time pattern of the ratio of the actual nominal wage and the expected future commodity price ($W(t,t)/P^e_f(t,t+1)$, $W4b/Pef4b$ in figure 7.46*b*) affects the time patterns of the demand for labour and the unemployment rate. The expected real wage rate ($W^e_f(t,t+1)/P^e_f(t,t+1)$, $Wef4b/Pef4b$ in figure 7.46*b*) affects the time pattern of investment expenditures, whereas the time pattern of the expected rate of inflation ($\pi^e(t,t)$, $INF4b$ in figure 7.46*b*) affects the time patterns of investments, government expenditures, commodity prices and nominal wages. Through the distinguished sector budget constraints the developments in the financial markets follow from the fluctuations in the aforementioned variables. Finally, since the nominal rate of interest is nearly constant (figure 7.50) the abovementioned prices determine, to a large extent, the performance of the economy.

The time pattern of the actual real wage rate can be characterized as a regular succession of relatively long periods of a decreasing and short periods of an increasing real wage. Peak levels are attained in periods of excess commodity supply and correspond to the switch from expected inflation to deflation as can be observed from figure 7.46*b*. Expected deflation has a depressing impact on both variables. However, since nominal wages display downward stickiness, the impact of excess commodity supply on actual prices is stronger than the impact of excess labour supply on actual nominal wages.

Because of the rather rapid improvement of the situation in the commodity market (figure 7.45*b*), the rise in the real wage rate is only of short duration. In a situation of excess commodity demand commodity prices increase faster than nominal wages because the interplay of the unemployment rate and the nominal wage rate prohibits a higher rate of nominal wage inflation. The simulation results reveal a small decrease in the average real wage rate over the entire simulation period. The peak levels are nearly constant whereas a small decrease in the bottom levels can be observed. A similar trend can be discerned in the expected real wage rate ($W^e_f(t,t+1)/P^e_f(t,t+1)$). Moreover, it can be observed that both the trend level and the amplitude are larger for the expected real wage rate than for the actual real wage rate, which indicates that the forecasts of the latter variable are generally too optimistic in our economy. Compared to the fluctuations in the expected real wage rate the time pattern of the ratio of the actual nominal wage and the expected future commodity price ($W(t,t)/P^e_f(t,t+1)$) is more dampened. In general, this ratio rises in periods of excess commodity demand, which implies that the positive impact of the asymmetric wage adjustment in a situation where the labour market is tight dominates the impact of excess commodity demand on expected future commodity prices. As long as inflation is positive and the unemployment rates are relatively small in comparison with the excess of inventories over aggregate demand, the aforementioned development continues. As soon as expected inflation becomes negative the ratio starts to decrease since the situation in the commodity market tends to improve rapidly, whereas the rate of unemployment initially remains high as developments in demand initially (and primarily) affect inventory levels instead of production levels. From figure 7.46*b* it can be observed that to some extent the developments in expected real wages and in the ratio of the actual nominal wage and the expected commodity price are each other's opposite. This asymmetry can be explained from the assumed adaptive adjustment pattern of the expected to the actual nominal wage rate. Because of adaptive adjustments the expected wage rate is still increasing in unit–periods where the actual nominal wage rate and the expected commodity price are already falling under the influence of excess supply in the labour market and the commodity market, respectively. This divergence also explains the relatively large amplitude in the time pattern of the expected real wage rate. From a comparison of the divergent time patterns of the actual real wage rate and the ratio of the actual nominal wage and the expected commodity price, it can be derived that in the model producers prefer to lower prices in periods of excess commodity supply. In particular they do not choose to keep commodity prices rigid (corrected for expected inflation). As we have explained in section 7.2.2 this choice is determined by the difference between the expected and the actual commodity price. It can be derived from figure 7.46*b* that this difference is rather large and increasing in favour of the actual commodity price during the first phase of a period of excess commodity supply, which explains the firms' preference for a decrease in their actual commodity prices. Only at the end of a period of excess commodity supply (in particular the last two unit–periods) rigid commodity prices (corrected for expected inflation) can be observed since actual commodity prices fall more quickly than expected future commodity prices. In periods of excess commodity demand prices increase because of the generally high level of *AU* (beginning–of–period household wealth plus current–period income). Finally, the correspondence between regime switches and the time pattern of expected inflation resembles that in the bench–mark simulation. Because of the adaptive adjustment of the expected rate of inflation to the actual developments in the commodity price, expected inflation is still negative at the beginning of a period of excess commodity demand and positive at the beginning of a period of excess commodity supply. As a result, the developments in expected inflation initially fortify the scarcity pattern in the commodity market. It can be concluded that the divergent time patterns of the relative prices, which have been discussed above, are mainly the result of the arbitrary assumptions about the adjustment parameters and the adjustment patterns. In this respect it has to be emphasized once more that the purpose of these simulations is only to illustrate some possible features of the model of chapter 6. On the other hand, the observed pervasive role of expectations formation on the performance of the economy can be considered a more general observation of our analysis.

It has already been argued that the developments in the variables depicted in figure 7.46*b*, to a large extent, determine the developments in the real and financial sectors of the economy, given the observed invariance of the nominal interest rate. Despite the fact that agents incorporate the implications of observed real quantity constraints in their plans in the long run the economy is mainly driven by fluctuations in relative prices. The time pattern of demand for labour is inversely related to the time pattern of the ratio of the actual nominal wage and the expected commodity price. Since labour supply is constant and equal to the size of the working population, a peak level of this ratio corresponds to a peak in the unemployment rate. From figures 7.44*b* (remember that the unemployment rate in the bench-mark simulation is relatively stable (figure 7.3)) and 7.46*b* it can be derived that these peaks fall in a regime of excess commodity supply. Hence, these periods can be characterized as periods of general excess supply, where unemployment is partly classical and partly Keynesian in nature. In periods of excess commodity demand unemployment is generally low. Under these circumstances the existence of unemployment can be explained from the pattern of wage adjustment in response to fluctuations in the rate of unemployment in an on average tight labour market. Hence, unemployment may characterized as classical unemployment. The sharp short-term fluctuations in the unemployment rate can be ascribed to asymmetric wage adjustments as well. Because of the upward moving trend in the ratio of the actual nominal wage and the expected commodity price (figure 7.46*b*), on the one hand, and the decline in the trend of investments (figure 7.48), on the other hand, the average level of the unemployment rate is moving upward as well.

Figures 7.42*b*, 7.45*b*, 7.46*b* and 7.48 illustrate that regime switches in the commodity market correspond to fluctuations in investment levels. Every period of excess demand experiences a peak in the level of investment demand at the beginning of this period. From equations [6.72] and [6.73] it can be derived that the demand for investment goods is affected by the expected level of the real wage rate, real user costs of capital and the size of the working population. The last variable is constant since $g = 0$. Real user costs of capital are affected by the rate of interest and the rate of inflation. The rate of interest is nearly stable as can be derived from figure 7.50. The simulation results (and, for instance, figures 7.47 and 7.50) indicate that fluctuations in investments are, to a considerable extent, driven by fluctuations in expected prices and nominal wages. In the first place, every peak in investment demand corresponds to a peak in the expected real wage rate. It can be derived from figures 7.46*b* and 7.48 that the negative impact of expected deflation is more than compensated by the developments in the expected real wage rate. In the second place, the average level of the expected real wage rate falls slightly over the entire simulation period. As a result, the average level of investments is declining slowly over the entire simulation period, notwithstanding the negative impact of expected inflation on the real user costs of capital.

The developments in actual production follow from the developments in the production factors and can thus be derived from the time patterns of investment and the unemployment rate. The level of actual production in simulation 4*b* in periods of excess commodity demand can be derived from figure 7.45*b*, since the level of inventories equals the level of production in these situations. The simulation results reveal a very small decline in average production levels at the end of the entire simulation period, which corresponds to developments in the input of production factors and real factor prices. Furthermore, from the development in these last variables it can be derived that production levels in situations of excess commodity demand are higher than in situations of excess commodity supply, since both the level of employment and the level of the capital stock are higher (figures 7.44, 7.46*b* and 7.48). This observation and the differences between the pattern of regime switches in simulation 4*b* and the bench-mark simulation also explain the relatively large short-term fluctuations in figure 7.43. However, the average levels of the proportional differences depicted in figure 7.43 are close to zero, which illustrates the relative insensitivity of the level of production to developments in the scarcity pattern in the commodity market as well as the buffer function of the stock of commodities (see also figure 7.45*b*).

The developments in aggregate consumption demand are related to the interdependent patterns of commodity prices and the variable *AU* (beginning-of-period household wealth plus current-period income). The level of *AU* initially decreases in periods of excess commodity supply, because of declining real wages, a rising level of unemployment and generally a public sector budget surplus (positive rates of inflation depress government expenditures). Since the negative impact of a decrease in *AU* is initially reinforced by an increasing commodity price (expected inflation is still positive), consumption expenditures fall sharply in the beginning of a situation of excess commodity supply. The improvement of consumer demand starts as soon as the commodity price decreases in response to the quickly deteriorating situation in the commodity market. Because of the adaptive nature of adjustments, expected inflation turns into deflation two unit-periods after the start of the decrease in actual commodity prices, which implies an acceleration of the rate of decrease in commodity prices and an additional stimulus to aggregate consumption. The level of *AU* is positively affected by the rise of the real wage rate, on the one hand, and the increased demand for financial funds by the government as a result of higher government expenditures. In this respect it can be observed from figures 7.42*b* and 7.49 that, as is the case in the bench-mark simulation, periods of excess commodity supply are characterized by increasing levels of the public sector deficit (*PSD*), whereas periods of excess commodity demand are characterized by increasing levels of the public sector budget surplus. Furthermore, the employment situation improves at the end of a period of excess commodity supply. These developments together have a rather strong positive impact on the level of consumer demand at the end of a period of excess commodity supply. It can be observed that the recovery of aggregate demand in a situation of excess commodity supply starts with an increase of consumer demand in response to the developments in actual commodity prices. Since government expenditures are related to expected inflation and since the latter variable adjusts with some delay to actual inflation, a subsequent increase in government expenditures reinforces the initial improvement in aggregate demand. A similar observation can be made with respect to the level of investments. All these developments imply a rather rapid recovery of aggregate demand. At the same time, commodity prices still fall sharply as a result of expected deflation. As a result, the commodity market enters the regime of excess commodity demand. In a situation of excess commodity demand the level of *AU* increases mainly because of a forced accumulation of money balances, which has a positive impact on aggregate consumer demand. As has been explained in section 7.2.2, the fact that households behave as if they are monopsonists in the commodity market depresses the demand for consumer goods, a development which is reinforced by the increasing level of prices (corrected for expected inflation). The rise of *AU* slows down by the decline in the public sector deficit, which also has a depressing impact on consumer demand. Furthermore, government expenditures decrease at the end of a period of excess demand because of the developments in expected inflation and unemployment. Investments attain a peak level in the beginning and then start to fall towards the end of a period of excess commodity demand. Given the arbitrary levels of the parameters in equation [6.81] it can be observed that the expenditure behaviour of the government enforces the probability of a switch from a situation of excess commodity demand to a situation of excess commodity supply.

We may conclude from the results of the last two simulations that the assumed structure of expectations formation has a profound impact on the level of the most important economic variables of the model. An unambiguous impact can be established on the time patterns of investments, employment, production, aggregate demand, commodity prices and nominal wages. In this respect, relatively small shifts in the adjustment parameter of expected inflation changes the performance of the economy completely, although some fundamental features of the model as the shock-absorbing function of inventories, the relative insensitivity of production and employment levels to demand shifts, the implications of wage adjustment on the basis of a non-linear Phillips curve and the conditions under which commodity prices are sticky, are relatively immune to these alterations.

figure 7.42a

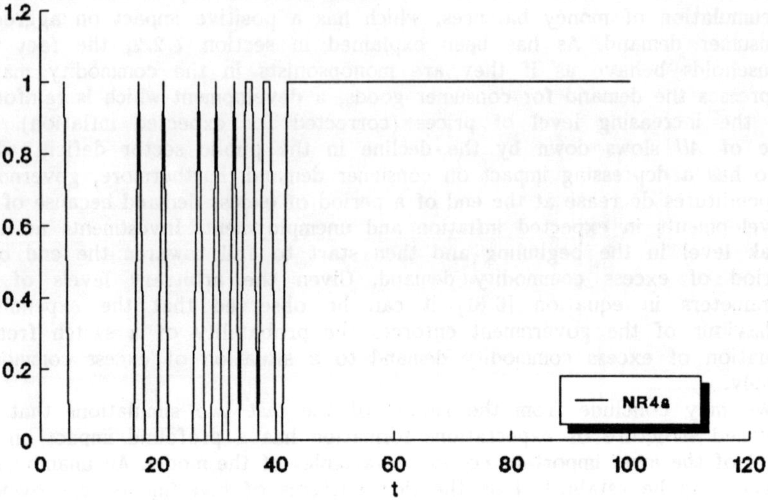

figure 7.42b

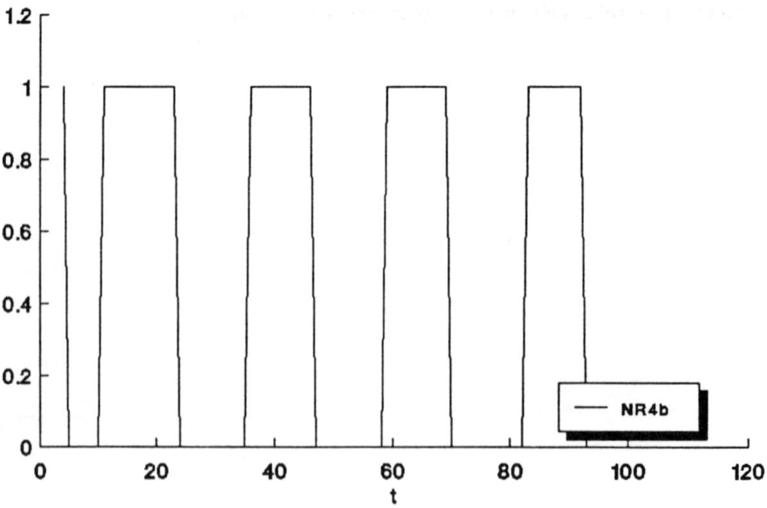

figure 7.43

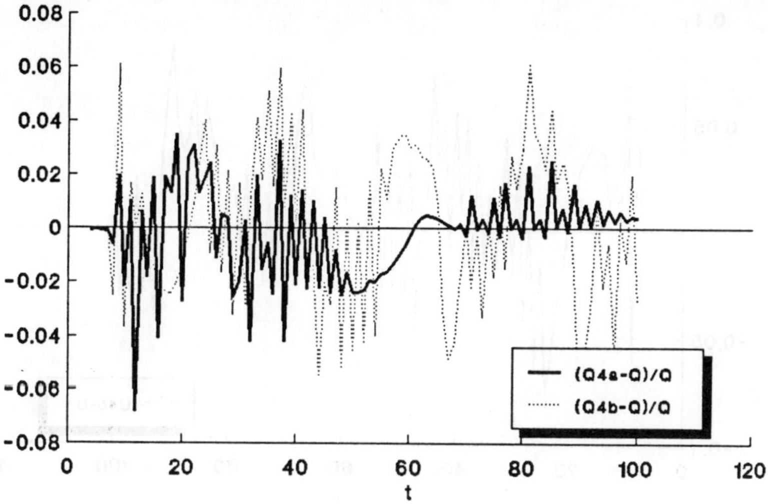

figure 7.44a

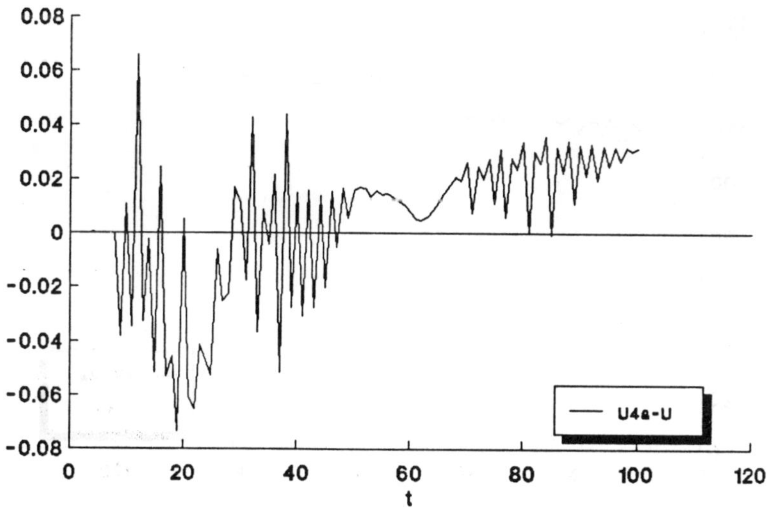

figure 7.44b

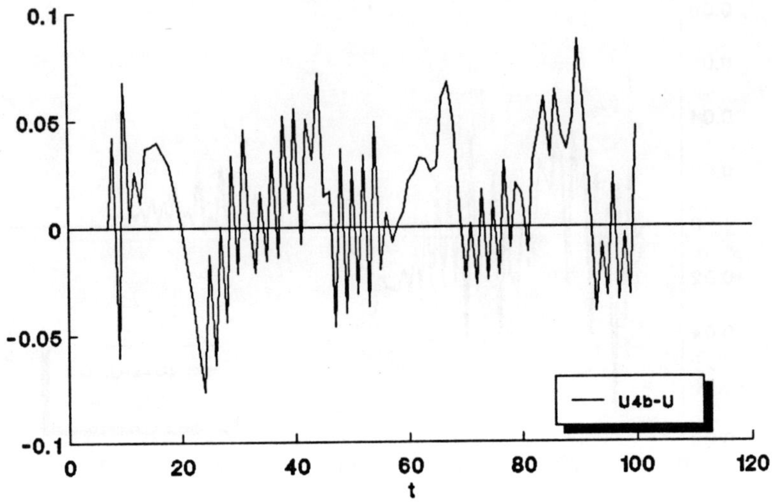

figure 7.45a

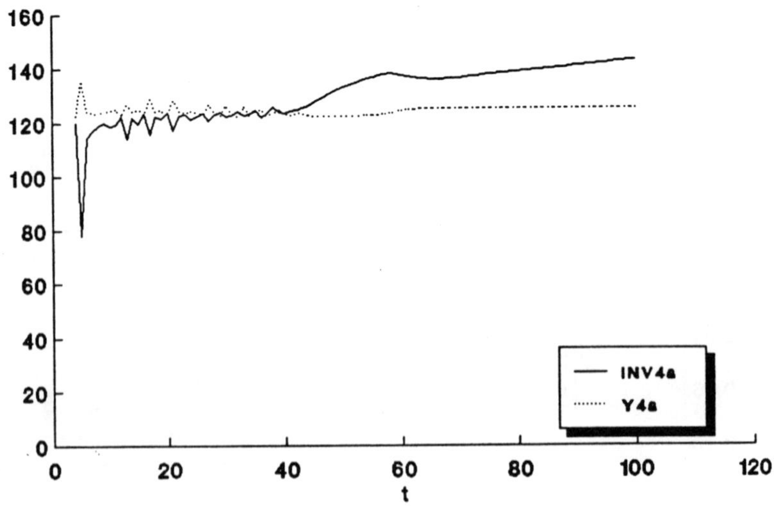

figure 7.45b

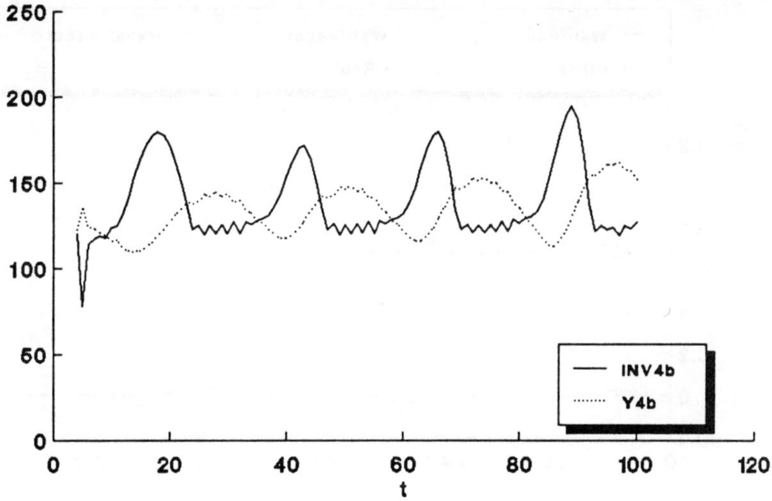

figure 7.46a

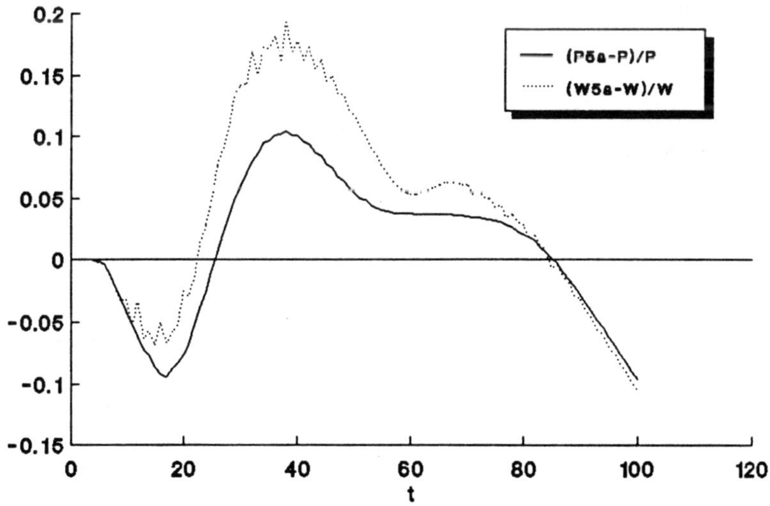

figure 7.46b

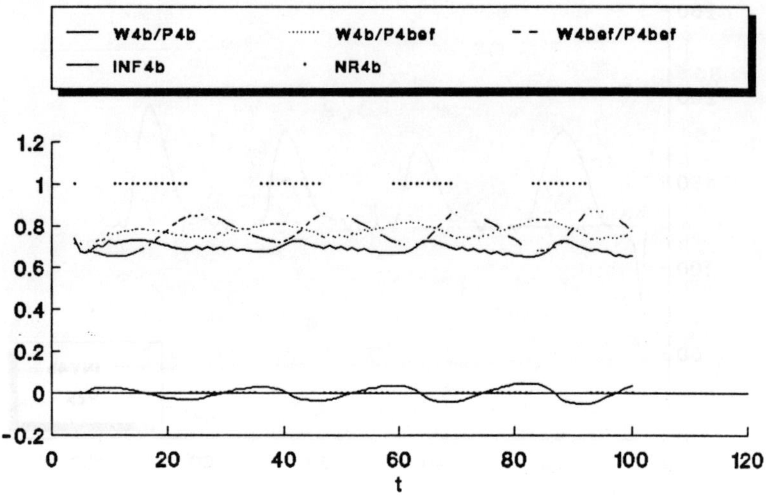

figure 7.47

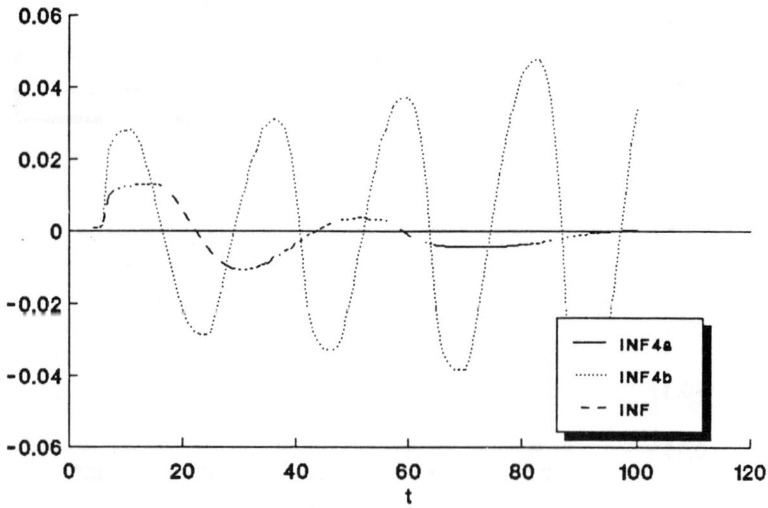

figure 7.48

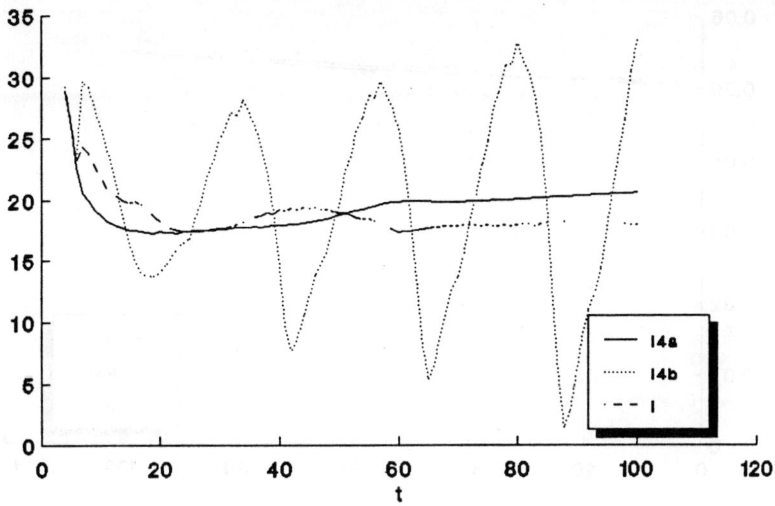

figure 7.49

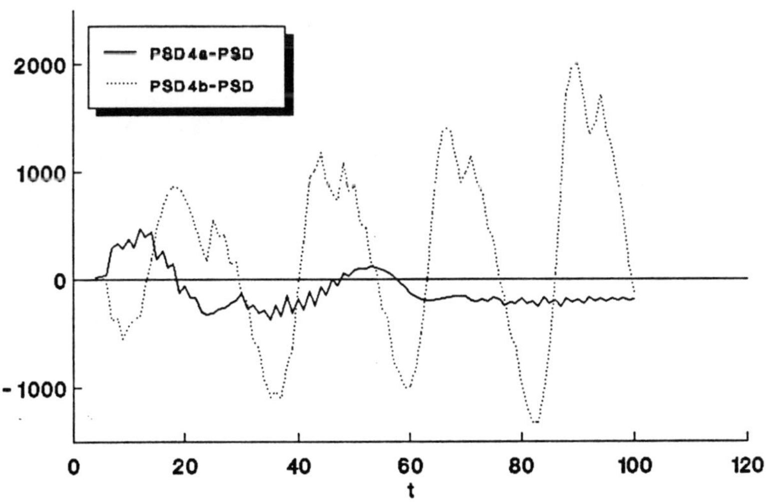

figure 7.50

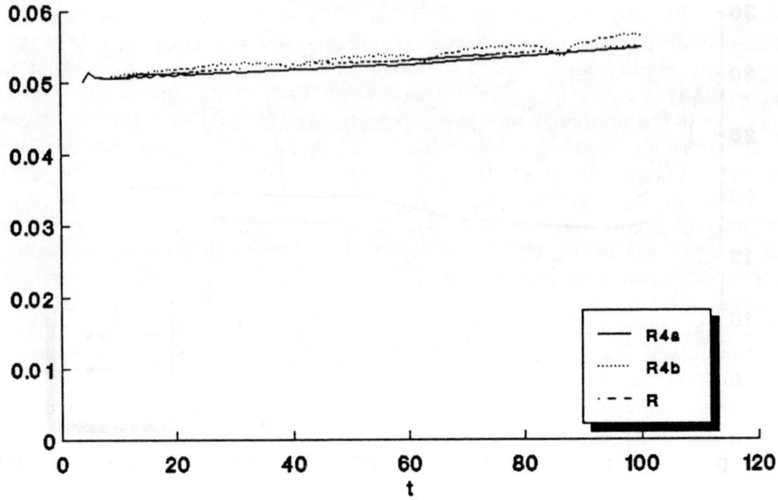

7.5 Some final observations

In order to analyze the characteristics of the model developed in chapter 6, several simulation experiments have been carried out in this chapter. The analysis of the simulation results has been performed with the following aims in mind. In the first place, the simulations are an attempt to provide some insight into the features of economic processes in a setting where the existence of perfect coordination is not assumed beforehand. In the second place, the implications of heterogeneity among agents are considered in as far as they may affect the formation of commodity prices. In the third place, we have analyzed to what extent storage possibilities may be regarded as an additional source of price rigidity, on the one hand, and as a buffer between demand and production, on the other hand. In general, the analysis has been concentrated on developments in the real sector in the economy and particularly on developments in the commodity market. In the absence of a full–fledged model of portfolio behaviour, this model does not have the appropriate characteristics for a detailed analysis of the behaviour in financial markets.

From the simulation experiments the following conclusions may be drawn In the first place, we may observe that the influence of inventory formation on price behaviour in the model is in line with the conclusions of the relevant literature. Commodity prices display downward rigidity, while inventories absorb fluctuations in aggregate demand. In the second place, price–setting behaviour of firms is, to a considerable extent, dominated by expectations about future price developments. This implies that prices may rise in periods of excess commodity supply in case this situation is short and preceded by a relatively long period of excess commodity demand. In somewhat more prolonged periods of excess supply prices are rigid (corrected for expected inflation), whereas they eventually decline in a period of sustained excess supply as a result of a downward shift of expected future commodity prices. In situations of excess demand commodity prices rise. Furthermore, households consider the implications of excess demand in advance, since already at the beginning of this regime they *a priori* decide to reduce intended consumption given the level of wealth. In the third place, it can be observed that policy changes have a considerable impact on the level of aggregate demand. The effect on the supply side of the economy is smaller, because of the offsetting developments in commodity prices. In the fourth place, it can be concluded that the simulation results do not indicate a tendency toward a situation of rest. In particular the behaviour of the private sector does not show a tendency to a situation of equilibrium growth.

Finally, it should be emphasized that the observations above have only some significance within the context of the theoretical model developed in chapter 6. Although some parameter changes may illustrate some remote correspondence with actual changes in policy regimes, the model does not allow a straightforward generalization of the observations made. Given the parameterization we have chosen, the simulation results illustrate a number of implications of optimizing behaviour of representative agents in the context of a highly aggregated system of markets where fictitious equilibrium devices have been banned from the commodity market. Although no tendency towards a situation of rest could be discovered, this does not prove that there does not exist such a situation. In this respect, the sequential–analytical method has a clear disadvantage in comparison with the (temporary) equilibrium method. An object of subsequent research would be to investigate, to what extent, more analytical rigour could be applied fruitfully in the context of a sequential–analytical approach, in order to offer more general conclusions about the characteristics of economic processes. In this respect, recent applications of chaos and catastrophe theory in economics may offer opportunities that allow for a more analytical treatment of seemingly chaotic time patterns. A combination of these insights with the sequential–analytical method perhaps represents a promising area of subsequent research. For the moment, our simulation exercises illustrate that there may be limits to the equilibrium tendencies in a model, which, on any view of the case, incorporates quite a number of features of standard equilibrium models with a Walrasian auctioneer.

Notes

1. In order to avoid the frequent use of lengthy and somewhat artificial verbiage we will refer to the macroeconomic model developed in chapter 6 as 'the model' in the remaining part of this book.

2. Unless defined otherwise all variables refer to unit–period values in this chapter. For instance, the expected next–period commodity price refers to the expected commodity price in the immediately following unit–period and beginning–of–period wealth only refers to the level of wealth at the start of the unit–period under consideration.

8 Summary and conclusions

8.1 Summary

This study is an attempt to provide some insight into the characteristics of economic processes. In our view, an analysis of economic processes has to consider the following propositions. In the first place, adjustment processes themselves, which lead to the establishment of different equilibria need further consideration. In the second place and related to the first observation, the heterogeneity of agents has to be considered more explicitly. With respect to the first proposition it can be argued that the assumption of perfect coordination is very restrictive, since it neglects the implications of trade as a fundamental manifestation of the workings of a market economy. However, both new classical as well as a large number of new Keynesian theories take the establishment of equilibrium outcomes of the coordination process for granted. Primarily the characteristics of terminal states are analyzed, whereas the question how these states come about is not considered. In this monograph a similar approach is followed in chapter 5. In
our opinion this approach is allowed in case adjustment processes do not take much time or are of no interest to the problem at hand. Also as a first orientation of a particular problem this method may be appropriate. In other cases an explicit analysis of adjustment processes is required, for instance, along the lines of a sequential–analytical approach as in chapters 6 and 7. With respect to the second proposition it can be observed that heterogeneity of agents has important implications for the determination of market prices and for the assumed interdependence between agents or sectors in the economy. For the sake of simplicity we confine our analysis to the impact of heterogeneity among agents on the determination of commodity prices. To that purpose kinked perceived demand and supply curves are introduced in the commodity market (Stiglitz, 1987). In the literature (see

chapters 4 and 5), kinked demand curves have served as an analytical device that enabled the explanation of commodity price rigidity. In chapters 6 and 7 we analyze the implications of kinked demand and supply curves in a more dynamic environment.

The first four chapters of the monograph deal with the abovementioned problems by means of a discussion of the relevant literature. In chapter 2 we consider flexprice models of economic fluctuations. A major characteristic of this approach is the assumption of perfect coordination. Deviations from the natural levels of output and employment are explained by the introduction of imperfect information. However, the explanation of persistent fluctuations in monetary business cycle models is not very convincing. Alternatively, in the context of real business cycle models persistent fluctuations in economic activity arise as an equilibrium response to stochastic fluctuations in technology and preference orderings. The real business cycle approach can be criticized on theoretical and empirical grounds. Representative agent models do not leave scope for the presence of externalities. On the other hand, the successful coordination of individual activities is assumed rather than explained. Furthermore, if the process of obtaining knowledge is monotonic or if technology shocks are not economy-wide, the rationale for fluctuations disappears altogether. Hence, the claim that fluctuations in output and employment can be analyzed in the context of a perfectly competitive system cannot be confirmed.

In chapters 3 and 4 analytical approaches that abandon the assumption of perfect coordination are discussed. In chapter 3 we concluded from an analysis of fixprice models that they do not provide a convincing explanation of fluctuations in output and employment. The following arguments apply. In the first place, it is not explained why agents refrain from price adjustments to relieve perceived constraints (Arrow, 1959). In the second place, it can be argued that Pareto improving trades are prohibited because agents only consider the impact of a perceived constraint in a particular market on their own behaviour in other markets. However, in a situation of general excess supply, the activities of one agent may have a non-negligible impact on the behaviour of other agents. Yet, strategic behaviour is not considered in fixprice models. The Walrasian auctioneer who guarantees the successful coordination (and cooperation) of individual activities (perfect information) is (implicitly) reintroduced into fixprice theory. As a result, quantity-constrained equilibria can only follow from *ad hoc* restrictions imposed on the process of trade and information dispersion.

In chapter 4 new Keynesian explanations of price and wage rigidities and theories of coordination failures and indeterminacies are discussed. New Keynesian models are characterized by absence of the Walrasian auctioneer, which implies the introduction of incomplete and asymmetric information in the economy. As a result, individual activities may not be socially efficient and the economy may get *stuck* in an equilibrium with a low level of economic activity. Prices do not reveal all available information about relative scarcities and may signal additional information beside scarcity relationships at the same time, as in the theory of implicit contracts and efficiency wages. However, prices are only one element in the theory of coordination failures. Coordination failures may arise in the context of a number of different models as is illustrated in chapter 4. It can be observed that the new Keynesian literature does not take for granted that the exchange process coordinates economic activities in the best possible way. On the other hand, the exchange process itself is not really analyzed.

Only the characteristics of socially inefficient equilibrium outcomes of the exchange process are emphasized. The question how a (non-cooperative Nash) equilibrium may come about is left unanswered. Obviously, this question calls for a dynamic approach. In this respect, the analysis in chapters 6 and 7 can be considered as an illustration of the latter.

Preceding the dynamic analysis of the last two chapters a new Keynesian static macroeconomic model is developed in chapter 5 , which may explain both real and nominal rigidities and inefficiently low equilibrium levels of economic activity. Rigidity in real wages is explained by the efficiency wage theory. Rigidity in real commodity prices may originate from the existence of positive search costs, which give rise to a kinked demand curve. In case the economy is characterized by real (relative) wage stickiness, flexible (relative) prices and flexible nominal wages, it is concluded that real aggregate demand cannot be affected by demand management. In particular a change in the level of money supply does not influence the level of economic activity. An increase in the level of money supply will only result in an increase in the general price level. On the other hand, if the economy is characterized by real price and real wage rigidity as an optimal response to a change in demand conditions a different picture emerges. Aggregate demand shocks directly influence the level of economic activity. Real economic activity can be stimulated by an increase in real government expenditure. Monetary policy and money-financed fiscal policy can be effective in a situation where firms are Nash-competitors and commodity markets are characterized by imperfect information and small positive search costs.

The approach followed in chapter 5 provides a straightforward suggestion for subsequent research. Since the model is static, the characteristics of adjustment processes cannot be analyzed. To that purpose, a dynamic model is developed in chapter 6. Time is divided in arbitrary small discrete periods. In this way and since *current-period* expectations precede and are independent of actual events in the current period, the irreversibility of economic processes is incorporated in the model. At the same time a more explicit framework for the analysis of activities that move economic processes is developed. The model has the following additional characteristics. Agents' real and financial decisions are intertwined and taken at the beginning of every unit-period. Financial markets clear. Production takes one period and all commodities are stored. Sales are only made out of stock. The determination of commodity prices is analogous to Hahn (1978) and incorporates the implications of asymmetric information (Stiglitz, 1987). The adjustment of wages in between periods rests upon the Phillips curve, whereas expectations are adaptive.

Despite the introduction of the last two simplifications, the model cannot be solved analytically. The characteristics of the model have been studied by means of a number of simulation experiments, which are reported in chapter 7. The analysis of the simulation results is performed with the following aims in mind. In the first place, the simulations are an attempt to provide some insight into the features of economic processes in a setting where the existence of perfect coordination is not assumed beforehand. In the second place, the implications of heterogeneity among agents are considered in as far as they may affect the formation of commodity prices. In the third place, it is analyzed to what extent storage possibilities may be regarded as an additional source of price rigidity, on the one hand, and as a buffer between demand and production, on the other hand. The analysis is concentrated on the developments in the real sector in the economy and particularly on the developments in the commodity market, since the model does not permit a detailed analysis of financial behaviour.

From the simulation experiments the following conclusions may be drawn. In the first place, the influence of inventory formation on price behaviour is in line with observations in the relevant literature. Commodity prices display downward rigidity, while inventories absorb fluctuations in aggregate demand. In the second place, price-setting behaviour of firms is dominated by future price expectations. This implies that prices may rise in periods of excess commodity supply in case this situation is short and preceded by a relatively long period of excess commodity demand. In somewhat more prolonged periods of excess supply prices are rigid (corrected for expected inflation), whereas they eventually decline in period of sustained excess supply as a result of a downward shift of expected future commodity prices. In situations of excess demand commodity prices rise. Furthermore, households consider the implications of excess demand in advance, since already at the beginning of this regime they *a priori* decide to reduce intended consumption given the level of wealth. In the third place, it can be observed that policy changes have a considerable impact on the level of aggregate demand. The effect on the supply side of the economy is smaller, because of offsetting developments in commodity prices. In the fourth place, it can be concluded that the simulation results do not indicate a tendency toward a situation of rest. In particular the behaviour of the private sector does not show a tendency to a situation of equilibrium growth.

It should be emphasized that the sequential–analytical procedure we have followed has some drawbacks. The most important argument against our approach is that it does not permit any observations about the establishment or the characteristics of some terminal (steady) state in the context of the model. The implication of our rejection of the temporary equilibrium method is that we cannot determine an equilibrium position or time path at all. The observations are always conditional on the set of parameter values used. Simulation experiments only illustrate possible time patterns that can be generated within the context of the model. We will not attempt to generalize the results. On the other hand, we do not regard the temporary equilibrium assumption as a useful starting device for the analysis of dynamic processes, since it assumes what it has to explain, the establishment of an equilibrium position. Seen from that perspective, the approach followed here has to be preferred.

8.2 Conclusion

In our opinion, the last lines of the previous section reveal a fundamental problem of macroeconomic theory. On the one hand, mainstream macroeconomic literature can be criticized for the neglect of an essential feature of macroeconomics, the coordination issue. On the other hand, the analysis of chapters 6 and 7 illustrates the inability to generalize results that are obtained from an approach that focused more explicitly on this issue. The question arises what direction subsequent research should take.

In our view macroeconomic theory has to deal with problems of coordination. The mere assumption that coordination is perfect, implies a denial of this essential feature of macroeconomics. For that reason it can be argued that the development of (microfoundations for) macroeconomics should not start from the proposition that coordination is perfect. Macroeconomics should start from the interdependence of supply and demand and therefore from the recognition that variables that may be taken as given in microeconomic problems do not have to be exogenous in macroeconomics. In this respect, it can be argued that the search for microfoundations is quite often not only an attempt to provide macroeconomics with an individualistic foundation but also an attempt to legitimize the assumed exogeneity of certain variables in a macroeconomic analysis and in the relationship between aggregates. This approach is only legitimate in situations where the coordination of individual activities has already been achieved or is of no interest to the problem at hand. For a large part, however, these situations do not reveal interesting problems from a macroeconomic point of view. The difference between micro and macroeconomics, among others, concerns the legitimacy of the *ceteris paribus* clause of given resources in macroeconomics. To put it differently, it concerns the recognition of the fact that demand and supply are not one-sided transactions. We do not however, consider *ceteris paribus* clauses as a permit for 'anything goes.' *Ceteris paribus* clauses can be fruitfully applied in order to reduce the complexity of economic problems. However, it is important to judge the value and applicability of the analytical results obtained, against the losses due to a reduced complexity of the problem at hand. For instance, in our view, macroeconomics as a method of abstraction within a general equilibrium framework requires the introduction of heterogeneity among agents and of incomplete markets in order to be meaningful at all. Nonetheless, more explicit analyses of coordination processes remain necessary. Although it may be hard to derive general results from these studies, at least they may supplement the former and illuminate the restrictions on the general applicability of its results. However abstract and imperfect, macroeconomic theory should not evade the issue of coordination.

List of symbols

$a_f^e(0,0)$ = firms' beginning-of-period 0 estimation of the period 0 value of parameter a, above the kink in the perceived demand curve

$a_f^{1e}(0,0)$ = firms' beginning-of-period 0 estimation of the period 0 value of parameter a, below the kink in the perceived demand curve

$a_h^e(0,0)$ = households' beginning-of-period 0 estimation of the period 0 value of parameter a, below the kink in the perceived supply curve

$a_h^{1e}(0,0)$ = households' beginning-of-period 0 estimation of the period 0 value of parameter a, above the kink in the perceived supply curve

A = total factor productivity

b = discount factor

$BDB(0)$ = banks' beginning-of-period 0 demand for an end-of-period 0 number of bonds

$BDH(0)$ = households' beginning-of-period 0 demand for an end-of-period 0 number of bonds

$BSG(0)$ = the number of bonds issued by the government in period 0

$BSF(0)$ = the number of bonds issued by firms in period 0

c = agent's actual current period consumption

$c(e)$ = (dis)utility of effort ($c', c'' > 0$)

C = aggregate consumption

C_{de} = (households) effective demand for consumer goods

C_d = notional demand for consumer goods

C_i = consumption of variety i of a composite consumer good C

$C^e(0,0)$ = households' current-period consumption plans at the beginning of period 0

$C(0,0)$	= realized consumption in period 0
$CRDF(0)$	= end–of–period 0 stock of credit demanded by firms
$CRDG(0)$	= end–of–period 0 stock of credit demanded by the government sector
$CRSB(0)$	= end–of–period 0 stock of credit supplied by banks
d	= real unemployment benefit
d_{hi}	= the perceived upper bound on agent h's purchases inmarket i
$DIV(-1)$	= corporate earnings in period −1 transferred to households in period 0
e	= effort supply
f	= total number of firms
F_L	= the physical marginal productivity of labour
F_K	= the physical marginal productivity of capital
g	= rate of population growth
g_i	= real government expenditure of commodities of variety i
G	= aggregate real government expenditure
$G(0,0)$	= realized (=intended) government expenditures in period 0
h	= index of agents (consumers, firms, customers)
H	= total number of agents
i	= index of markets
inv_{0*}	= firm's beginning – of – period commodity stock
inv^*	= the optimal notional level of the firms' beginning–of–period commodity stock
inv	= end – of – period commodity stock
$inv(0,0)$	= part of the beginning–of–current–period stock, that firms plan to transfer to the next period.
INV_{0*}	= aggregate beginning – of – period commodity stock
INV^*	= the optimal notional level of the aggregate beginning–of–period commodity stock
$I(0,0)$	= gross investments in period 0
$INV(-1)$	= the beginning–of–period 0 stock of commodities
j	= index of time
k	= total average production costs
K	= the capital stock
$K(-1)$	= the fixed beginning–of–period stock of capital, which is equal to the capital stock at the end of the preceding period
l_*	= employment
l	= labour in efficiency units
l_s	= notional supply of labour
l_{se}	= effective supply of labour
l_d	= notional demand for labour
l_{de}	= effective demand of labour
L	= aggregate employment
L_{se}	= effective aggregate supply of labour
L_{de}	= effective aggregate demand of labour
$L(0,0)$	= the level of employment in period 0
m	= agent's real money balances
$\bar{m}$	= agent's beginning–of–period real money balances
m_d	= notional demand for real money balances
M	= aggregate money supply
M_d	= aggregate demand for money balances,
$\bar{M}$	= beginning–of–period aggregate stock of money balances
$\bar{M}_r$	= beginning–of–period aggregate stock of real money balances

$MDF(0)$ = firms' end-of-period 0 stock of money balances
$MDH^e(0)$ = households' beginning-of-period 0 desire of the end-of-period t stock of money balances
$MDH(-1)$ = households' beginning-of-period 0 stock of money balances
n = number of markets
N = working population
p = the real relative commodity price (in terms of a numeraire)
P = the aggregate price level
P_i = local market price
P_{ih} = the commodity price of variety i set by firm h
P_n = commodity price set by a non-maximizing firm
P_m = commodity price set by a profit maximizing firm
prf = real firm profits
PRF = nominal firm profits
$P(0,0)$ = period 0 level of commodity price
$P^e_f(0,1)$ = firms' beginning-of-period 0 expectation of period 1 commodity price.
$P^e_h(0,1)$ = households' beginning-of-period 0 expectation of the level of commodity prices in period 1
$PRLG(0)$ = private sector loans to the government in period 0
$PSD(0,0)$ = the current-period government budget deficit
q = firm production
$\underline{q}_{ih}$ = production of commodities of variety i by firm h
$\underline{q}$ = equilibrium demand of commodities by firm h
Q = aggregate production
$Q(0,0)$ = planned production in period 0
$R(0,0)$ = period 0 level of the rate of interest on bonds
s_{hi} = perceived upper bound on h's sales in market i
sa = real firm sales
sa_s = real notional firm sales
sa_{se} = real effective firm sales
st = a particular state drawnfrom a given distribution of possible states
$s(P_i)$ = search costs
S = aggregate nominal savings
S_r = aggregate real savings
SA = real aggregate current-period sales
SA_{se} = real aggregate effective sales
SA_s = real aggregate notional sales
$SB(0,0)$ = period 0 flow of savings of banks
$SF(0,0)$ = period 0 flow of savings of firms
$SG(0,0)$ = period 0 flow of savings of the government
$SH(0,0)$ = period 0 flow of savings of households,
t = time
t_{hi} = net transaction of agent h in market i
t_{ih} = net demand (demand supply) of agent h in market i
$T(0,0)$ = total current-period tax payments.
u = the unemployment rate
U = utility
$\overline{U}$ = reservation level of utility
$U(t,t)$ = the actual rate of unemployment in period t.
U_n = the "natural" rate of unemployment
v = number of customers attached to a particular firm

vf	= real discounted firm profits
V	= indirect utility
w	= real wage rate
w_n	= real wage rate of non–maximizing firms
w_m	= real wage rate of maximizing firms
w	= efficiency wage
w_{ih}	= the real wage offered by firm h in commodity market i
W	= the nominal wage rate
W_{ih}	= the nominal wage offered by firm h ($h = 1,..,f$)
$W(0,0)$	= period 0 level of the nominal wage rate
$WB(0)$	= end–of–period 0 level of bank wealth
$WF(0)$	= end–of–period 0 level of firm wealth
$WG(0)$	= end–of–period 0 level of government wealth
$WH(0)$	= end–of–period 0 level of household wealth
x	= actual (observed) demand shift
x^e	= expected demand shift
X	= real aggregate disposable income
Y	= real aggregate demand
Y_i	= quantity supplied (= demand) market i
Y_t	= aggregate supply (= demand)
Y_{nt}	= natural aggregate output
Y_{ct}	= cyclical component in aggregate output
$Y_f^e(0,0)$	= producers' beginning–of–period perception of current–period commodity demand
$Y(0,0)$	= period t level of aggregate demand
$Y_f^e(0,1)$	= the expected level of commodity demand in period 1 at the beginning of 0
$Y(0,2)$	= the beginning–of–period 0 expectation of sales in period 2
A_1, A_2	= auxiliary variables in the perceived demand curve
A_3	= auxiliary variable in the production function chapter 6
$A^e(0,0)$	= auxiliary variable in the perceived supply curve of period 0
$\mathbf{A}$	= competitive allocation of goods
AU	= auxiliary variable denoting beginning–of–period household wealth and current–period household income
$b_f(0,0)$	= auxiliary variable in the perceived demand curve
$b_f^1(0,0)$	= auxiliary variable in the perceived demand curve
$B(0,0)$	= auxiliary variable in the perceived supply curve of period 0
$\mathbf{d}_h$	= vector of perceived upper bounds on agent h's purchases in all markets
E	= expectation operator
$det\ H$	= determinant of the Hessian matrix
He_1, He_2	= principal minors of $det\ H$
L	= lag operator
$\mathbf{p}$	= commodity price vector
$\mathbf{s}_h$	= vector of perceived upper bounds on agent h's sales in all markets
$\mathbf{t}_h$	= vector of net transactions of agent h in all markets
$\mathbf{t}_h$	= vector of net demands of agent h in all markets
$\mathbf{t}_{-h}$	= set of vectors of net demands of all agents except h
Z	= auxiliary symbol to denote a variable in general

CU = regime of classical unemployment
KU = regime of general excess supply (Keynesian unemployment)
RI = regime of repressed inflation
UC = regime of underconsumption
WA = regime of general market clearing (Walrasian regime)

$\alpha,\alpha_1,..,\alpha_3$ = parameters utility function
α_4 = the share of bank earnings on bonds transferred to households
α_5 = the share of bank earnings on credit transferred to households
α_6 = fixed mark-up rate on the bond interest rate, which determines the interest rate on credit
α_7 = income tax rate
α_8 = parameter of adjustment of expected to actual inflation
β = parameter effort supply function chapter 5
$\beta_1,..,\beta_3$ = dummy variables
β_4,β_5 = adjustment parameters with respect to expected commodity prices
β_6 = parameter in Cobb–Douglas production function chapter 6
β_7 = parameter that determines the maximum transfer of commodities out of the beginning-of-period stock to the next period
β_8 = rate of depreciation
$\delta_1,..,\delta_5$ = parameters chapter 1
ε_1, ε_2 = stochastic processes, i.e. unanticipated sequences of random preference and productivity shocks, respectively
$\gamma_1,\gamma_2,\gamma_3$ = policy parameters determining government expenditures
γ_4,γ_5 = corporate tax rate with respect to bank earnings
γ_6 = proportion of the government budget deficit financed by long-term loans
γ_7,γ_8 = parameters with respect to the demand for bonds by banks
γ_9,γ_{10} = adjustment parameters in the wage equation determining the Phillips curve effect
γ_{11},γ_{12} = adjustment parameters of the long-run wage rate
$\Psi(t)$ = information set in period t
$\kappa_1,..,\kappa_8$ = parameters chapter 2
Λ = constant chapter 2
λ = Lagrange parameter
θ = price elasticity of firm demand
$\pi^e(0,0)$ = beginning-of-period 0 estimation of the current-period rate of inflation.
$\pi(-1,-1)$ = rate of inflation in period -1
ρ_1^2 = variance of general price level
ρ_2^2 = variance of local prices
ρ_3 = variance of local prices as a proportion of total variance in commodity prices.
$\Theta(.)$ = employment risk passed on to workers
σ_1 = parameter chapter 5
τ = parameter Cobb–Douglas production function chapter 5
τ_1 = labour time per worker
$\tau_1,..,\tau_6$ = parameters chapter 4
ν,ν_1,ν_2 = roots difference equation

References

Akerlof, G.A. (1982), 'Labour Contracts as Partial Gift Exchange,' *Quarterly Journal of Economics*, pp. 543–569.

Akerlof, G.A. and J. Yellen (1985a), 'Can Small Deviations from Rationality Make Significant Differences to Economic Equilibria?,' *American Economic Review*, 75, pp. 708–721.

Akerlof, G.A. and J. Yellen (1985b), 'A Near-Rational Model of the Business Cycle with Wage and Price Inertia,' *Quarterly Journal of Economics*, 100, Supplement, pp. 823–838.

Akerlof, G.A. and J. Yellen (1986), *Efficiency Wage Models of the Labour Market*, Cambridge University Press, Cambridge.

Amihud, U. and H. Mendelson (1983), 'Price Smoothing and Inventory Behaviour,' *Review of Economic Studies*, pp. 87–98.

Arrow, K.J. (1959), 'Toward a Theory of Price Adjustment,' in A. Abramovitz (ed.): *The Allocation of Economic Resources*, Stanford University Press, Stanford, pp. 41–51.

Arrow K.J. (1970), *Essays in the Theory of Risk-Bearing*, North-Holland Publishing Company, Amsterdam.

Arrow K.J. and G. Debreu (1954), 'Existence of Equilibrium for a Competitive Economy,' *Econometrica*, 22, pp. 265–296.

Arrow K.J. and F.H. Hahn (1971), *General Competitive Analysis*, Holdenday, San Francisco.

Azariadis, C.(1975), 'Implicit Contracts and Unemployment Equilibria,' *Journal of Political Economy*, 83, 6, pp. 1183–1202.

Azariadis, C. (1979), 'Implicit Contracts and Related Topics,' in Hornstein (ed.): *The Economics of the Labour Market*, Her Majesty's Stationery Office, London.

Azariadis, C. (1983), 'Employment with Asymmetric Information,' *Quarterly Journal of Economics*, 98, Supplement, pp. 157–173.

Azariadis, C. and J.E. Stiglitz (1983), 'Implicit Contracts and Fixed-Price Equilibria,' *Quarterly Journal of Economics*, 98, Supplement, pp. 1–22.

Bailey, M.N. (1974), 'Wages and Employment Under Uncertain Demand,' *Review of Economic Studies*, 41, 1, pp. 37–50.

Ball, R. and D. Romer (1987a), 'Are Prices Too Sticky?,' *NBER Working Paper*, No. 2171.

Ball,R. and D. Romer (1987b), 'Sticky Prices as Coordination Failure,' *NBER Working Paper*, No. 2327.

Ball, R. and D. Romer (1987c), 'Real Rigidities and the Non-Neutrality of Money,' *NBER Working Paper*, No. 2476.

Barro, R.J. (1974), 'Are Government Bonds Net Wealth?,' *Journal of Political Economy*, 81, 6, pp. 1095–1117.

Barro, R.J. (1976), 'Rational Expectations and The Role of Monetary Policy,' *Journal of Monetary Economics*, pp. 1–32.

Barro, R.J. (1977), 'Long-term Contracting, Sticky Prices and Monetary Policy,' *Journal of Monetary Economics*, 3, pp.305–316.

Barro, R.J. (1980), 'A Capital Market in an Equilibrium Business Cycle Model,' *Econometrica*, 48, pp. 1393–1417, reprinted in R.J. Barro: *Money, Expectations and Business Cycles*, Academic Press, New York.

Barro, R.J. (1981), 'The Equilibrium Approach to Business Cycles,' in R.J. Barro: *Money, Expectations and Business Cycles*, Academic Press, New York.

Barro, R.J. and H.I. Grossman (1971), 'A General Disequilibrium Model of Income and Employment,' reprinted in P.G. Korliras and R.S. Thorn: *Modern Macroeconomics: Major Contributions to Contemporary Thought*, 1979, Harper & Row, New York, pp. 327–338.

Barro, R.J. and H.I. Grossman (1976), *Money, Employment and Inflation*, Cambridge University Press, Cambridge.

Baumol, W.J. (1952), 'The Transactions Demand for Cash: An Inventory Theoretic Approach,' *Quarterly Journal of Economics*, 66, pp. 545–556.

Benassy, J.P. (1975), 'Neo-Keynesian Disequilibrium Theory in a Monetary Economy,' *Review of Economic Studies*, 42, pp. 502–523.

Benassy, J.P. (1977), 'A Neo-Keynesian Model of Price and Quantity Determination,' in G. Schwödiauer(ed.): *Equilibrium and Disequilibrium in Economic Theory*, D. Reidel Publishing Company, Boston, pp. 511–544.

Benassy, J.P. (1982), *The Economics of Market Disequilibrium*, Academic Press, New York.

Benassy, J.P. (1987), 'Non-Walrasian Equilibria: Money and Macroeconomics,' *CEPREMAP*, No. 8725.

Bernheim, D. (1984), 'Rationalizable Strategies,' *Econometrica*, 52, pp. 1007–1028

Blanchard, O.J. (1987), 'Why does Money affect Output? A Survey,' *NBER Working Paper*, No. 2285.

Blanchard, O.J. and N. Kiyotaki (1987), 'Monopolistic Competition and the Effects of Aggregate Demand,' *American Economic Review*, 77, 4, pp. 647–666.

Blanchard, O.J. and L.H. Summers (1986), 'Hysteresis and the European Unemployment Problem,' *NBER Macroeconomics Annual*, 1, MIT Press.

Blinder, A.S. (1982), 'Inventories and Sticky Prices: More on the Microfoundations of Macroeconomics,' *American Economic Review*, 72, pp. 334–348.

Blinder, A.S. (1985), 'Credit Rationing and Effective Supply Failures,' *NBER Working Paper*, No. 1257.

Blinder, A.S. and S. Fischer (1981), 'Inventories, Rational Expectations and the Business Cycle,' *Journal of Monetary Economics*, 8, pp. 277–304.
Böhm, V. (1978), 'Disequilibrium Dynamics in a Simple Macroeconomic Model,' *Journal of Economic Theory*, 17, pp. 179–199.
Böhm, V. (1987), 'Dynamics of Prices and Wages in an Overlapping Generations Model with Quantity Rationing,' Paper Presented at the European Meeting of the Econometric Society, Copenhagen 1987.
Braverman, A. (1980), 'Consumer Search and Alternative Market Equilibria,' *Review of Economic Studies*, 48, pp. 487–502.
Buiter, W.H. (1980), 'Walras' Law and All That: Budget Constraints and Balance Sheet Constraints in Period Models and Continuous Time Models,' *International Economic Review*, 21, pp.1–16.
Buiter, W.H. (1987), 'The Right Combination of Demand and Supply Policies: The Case for a Two–Handed Approach,' *NBER Working Paper*, No. 2333.
Buiter, W.H. (1989), *Macroeconomic Theory and Stabilization Policy*, Manchester.
Bulow, J.I., J. Geneakoplos and P. Klemperer (1985), 'Multimarket Oligopoly: Strategic Substitutes and Complements,' *Journal of Political Economy*, 93, pp. 488–511.
Bulow, J.I. and L.H. Summers (1986), 'A Theory of Dual Labour Markets With Application to Industrial Policy Discrimination and Keynesian Unemployment,' *Journal of Labour Economics*, 4, pp. 376–414.
Chatterjee, S. and R. Cooper (1989) 'Multiplicity of Equilibria and Fluctuations in Dynamic Imperfectly Competitive Economies,' *American Economic Review*, p. 353–358.
Clower, R. (1965), 'The Keynesian Counter–Revolution: A Theoretical Appraisal,' in F. Brechling and F.H. Hahn (eds.): *The Theory of Interest Rates*, Mac Millan, London, pp. 103–125.
Cooper, R. (1986), 'Optimal Labor Contracts, Imperfect Competition, and Underemployment Equilibria,' *NBER Working Paper*, No. 2060.
Cooper, R. (1987), *Wage and Employment Patterns in Labour Contracts: Microfoundations and Macroeconomic Implications*, Harwood Academic Publishers, Chur.
Cooper, R. (1987a), 'Dynamic Behavior of Imperfectly Competitive Economies with Multiple Equilibria,' *NBER Working Paper no.* 2388.
Cooper, R. and A. John (1988), 'Coordinating Coordination Failures,' *Quarterly Journal of Economics*, 103, pp. 441–465.
Cukierman, A. (1984), *Inflation, Stagflation, Relative Prices, and Imperfect Information*, Cambridge University Press, Cambridge.
Davidson, P., (1978), *Money and the Real World*, London, 2nd. edition.
Diamond, P. (1965), 'National Debt in a Neoclassical Growth Model,' *American Economic Review*, 55, pp. 1126–1150.
Diamond, P. (1971), 'A Model of Price Adjustments,' *Journal of Economic Theory*, 3, pp. 156–168.
Diamond, P. (1982), 'Aggregate Demand Management in Search Equilibrium,' *Journal of Political Economy*, 51, pp. 881–894.
Dixit, A. and J.E. Stiglitz (1977), 'Monopolistic Competition and Optimum Product Diversity,' *American Economic Review*, pp. 961–963.
Drabicki, J.Z. and A. Takayama (1979), 'The General Equilibrium Framework of Economic Analysis: Stocks and Flows – with Special Application to Macroeconomic Models,' in J.R. Green and J.A. Scheinkman (eds.): *General Equilibrium Growth and Trade, Essays in Honor of Lionel McKenzie*, Academic Press, New York, pp. 357–398.

Drazen, J.H. (1980), 'Recent Developments in Macroeconomic Disequilibrium Theory,' *Econometrica*, 48, pp. 283–305.

Drèze, J.H. (1975), 'Existence of Exchange Equilibrium under Price Rigidities,' *International Economic Review*, 16, pp. 301–320.

Eaton, B.C. and W. White (1982), 'Agent Compensation and the limits of bonding,' *Economic Inquiry*, 20, pp. 330–343.

Ees, H. van (1989), 'An Explanation of Unemployment through an Integration of the Efficiency Wage Theory and the Kinked Demand Curve Approach,' *Jahrbuch für Sozialwissenschaft*, 40, pp.82–94.

Fisher, F.M. (1972), 'On Price Adjustment Without an Auctioneer,' *Review of Economic Studies*, 39, pp. 1–15.

Fischer, S. (1977), 'Long-term Contracts, Rational Expectations and the Optimal Money Supply Rule,' *Journal of Political Economy*, 85, pp. 191–206.

Fischer, S. (1979), 'Capital Accumulation on the Transition Path in a Monetary Optimizing Model,' *Econometrica*, 47, pp. 1433– 1439.

Fischer, S. (1988), 'Recent Developments in Macroeconomics,' *Economic Journal*, pp. 293 – 340.

Frank, J. (1986), *The New Keynesian Economics*, Wheatsheaf Books, Brighton.

Friedman, B.M. (1978), 'The Theoretical Non Debate about Monetarism,' in: T Mayer (ed.), *The Structure of Monetarism*, New York.

Gale, D. (1979), 'Large Economies with Trading Uncertainty,' *Review of Economic Studies*, 46, pp. 319–338.

Gale, D. (1983), 'Competitive Models with Keynesian Features,' *Economic Journal*, 93, Supplement, pp. 17–33.

Garretsen, H and M.C.W. Janssen, (1989), 'Two Fallacies of Composition in a Keynesian OLG Model,' *IER Research memorandum no.* 317, Groningen.

Geanakoplos, J.D. and H.M. Polemarchakis, (1986), 'Walrasian Indeterminacy and Keynesian Macroeconomics,' *Review of Economic Studies*, 53, p. 755–779.

Gordon, R.J. (1981), 'Output Fluctuations and Gradual Price Adjustment,' *Journal of Economic Literature*, 19, pp. 493–530.

Grandmont, J.M. and G. Laroque (1977), 'On Temporary Keynesian Equilibria,' in G.C. Harcourt (ed.): *The Microeconomic Foundations of Macroeconomics*, MacMillan, London, pp. 41–61.

Grandmont, J.M. and Y. Younes (1973), 'On the Role of Money and the Existence of a Monetary Equilibrium,' *Review of Economic Studies*, 39, pp. 355–372.

Gray, J.A. (1976), 'Wage Indexation: A Macroeconomic Approach,' *Journal of Monetary Economics*, 2, pp. 221–235.

Gray, J.A. (1978), 'On Indexation and Contract Length,' *Journal of Political Economy*, 86, pp. 1–18.

Green, J. (1980), 'On the Theory of Effective Demand,' *Economic Journal*, 99, pp. 341–353.

Greenwald, B. and J.E. Stiglitz (1987), 'Keynesian, New Keynesian and New Classical Economics', *Oxford Economic Papers*, 39 pp. 119–133.

Groenveld, K. (1982), *Onevenwichtige markten: een sequentie-analytische benadering van aanpassingsprocessen*, Unpublished PhD thesis, Groningen.

Grossman, S. (1976), 'On the Efficiency of Competitive Stock Markets Where Traders Have Diverse Information,' *Journal of Finance*, 31, pp. 573–585.

Grossman, S. (1978), 'Further Results on the Informational Efficiency of Competitive Stock Markets,' *Journal of Economic Theory*, 18, pp. 81–101.

Grossman, S. (1983), 'Implicit contracts under Asymmetric Information,'

Quarterly Journal of Economics, 71, pp. 123–157.

Grossman, S. and O. Hart (1983), 'Implicit Contracts under Asymmetric Information,' *Quarterly Journal of Economics*, 98, pp. 123–156.

Hahn, F.H. (1965), 'On Some Problems of Proving the Existence of an Equilibrium in a Monetary Economy,' in F.P.R. Brechling and F.H Hahn (eds.): *Theory of Interest Rates*, Mac Millan, London.

Hahn, F.H. (1977), 'Exercises in Conjectural Equilibria,' *Scandinavian Journal of Economics*, 79, pp. 210–226.

Hahn, F.H. (1978), 'On Non-Walrasian Equilibria,' *Review of Economic Studies*, 45, pp. 1–17.

Hahn, F.H. (1983), 'Comment' in: D. Worswick and J. Trevithick (eds.), *Keynes and the Modern World*, Cambridge, p. 72–75.

Hahn, F.H. (1984), *Equilibrium and Macroeconomics*, Blackwell, Oxford.

Hall, R. and E. Lazear (1984), 'The Excess Sensitivity of Layoffs and Quits to Demands,' *Journal of Labor Economics*, 2, pp. 233–258.

Hart, O. (1982), 'A Model of Imperfect Competition with Keynesian Features,' *Quarterly Journal of Economics*, 97, pp. 109–138.

Hart, O. (1983), 'Optimal Labour Contracts Under Asymmetric Information: An Introduction,' *Review of Economic Studies*, 50, pp. 3–35.

Heller, W.P. (1986), 'Coordination Failure under Complete Markets with Applications to Effective Demand' in: W.P. Heller, R.M. Starr and D.A. Starrett (eds.), *Equilibrium Analysis. Essays in Honour of Kenneth J. Arrow*, Volume ii, Cambridge, pp.155–175.

Henin, P.Y and P. Michel (1982), 'Croissance et Accumulation en Deséquilibre,' *Economica*, Paris.

Heuvel, P. van den (1983), *The Stability of a Macroeconomic System with Quantity Constraints*, Springer Verlag, Berlin/ Heidelberg/ New York.

Hey, J.D. (1974), 'Price Adjustment in an Atomistic Market,' *Journal of Economic Theory*, 8, pp. 483–499.

Hey, J.D. (1981), *Economics in Disequilibrium*, Martin Robertson and Company Ltd., Oxford.

Hicks, J.R. (1937), 'Mr. Keynes and the Classics,' *Econometrica*

Hicks, J.R. (1939), *Value and Capital*, Clarendon Press, Oxford.

Hicks, J.R. (1965), *Capital and Growth*, Oxford University Press, Oxford.

Hicks, J.R. (1985), *Methods of Dynamic Economics*, Oxford University Press, Oxford.

Holstrom, B. (1983), 'Equilibrium Long Term Contracts,' *Quarterly Journal of Economics (Supplement)*, 98, pp. 23–54.

Honkapohja, S. (1979), 'On the Dynamics of Disequilibrium in a Macro Model with Flexible Wages and Prices,' in M. Aoki and A. Marzello (eds.): *New Trends in Dynamic System Theory and Economics*, Academic Press, New York.

Honkapohja, S. (1980), 'The Employment Multiplier after Disequilibrium Dynamics,' *Scandinavian Journal of Economics*, pp.1–14.

Honkapohja, S. and T. Ito (1980), 'Inventory Dynamics in a Simple Disequilibrium Macro Model,' *Scandinavian Journal of Economics*, 82, pp. 184–198.

Honkapohja, S. and T. Ito (1983), 'Stability with Regime Switching,' *Journal of Economic Theory*, 29, pp. 22–48.

Hoogduin L.H. and J. Snippe (1987), 'Uncertainty in/of Macroeconomics: An Essay on Adequate Abstraction' *De Economist*, 135, pp. 429–442.

Ioannides, Y. and C. Pissaridis (1983), 'Wages and Employment with Firm Specific Seniority,' *The Bell Journal of Economics*, 14, pp. 573–581.

Ito, T. (1980), 'Disequilibrium Growth Theory,' *Journal of Economic Theory*, 23, pp. 380–404.

Ito, T. and S. Honkapohja (1985), 'On Macroeconomic Equilibrium with Stochastic Rationing,' *Scandinavian Journal of Economics*, 87, pp. 66–88.

Janssen, M.C.W., (1989), 'On the Necessity of Microfoundations,' University of Groningen, *mimeo*.

John, A., (1988), 'Imperfect Competition, Keynesian Dynamics and the Paradox of Thrift,' Michigan State University, *mimeo*.

Kaldor, N. (1983), 'Keynesian Economics after Fifty Years,' in: D. Worswick and J. Trevithick (eds.): *Keynes and the Modern World*, Cambridge, pp. 1–28.

Katz, L. (1986), 'Efficiency Wage Theories: A Partial Evaluation,' *NBER Macroeconomics Annual*, 1, pp. 235–290.

Keesing, F.A.G. (1939), *Het evenwichtsbegrip in de economische literatuur*, PhD thesis, Amsterdam

Keynes, J.M. (1936), *The General Theory of Employment, Interest and Money*, Collected Writings vol. vii, MacMilllan, London, 1973.

King, R. (1981), 'Monetary Information and Monetary Neutrality,' *Journal of Monetary Economics*, 7, pp. 195–206.

King, R., C. Plosser and S.T. Rebelo (1988), 'Production, Growth and Business Cycles: I The Basic Neoclassical Model,' *Journal of Monetary Economics*, 21, pp. 195–232.

Klundert, Th. van de (1987), 'Coordination Failure in an Industrial Society,' *De Economist*, 135, pp. 467–487.

Klundert, Th. van de and P. Peters (1988), 'Price Inertia in a Macroeconomic Model of Monopolistic Competition,' *Economica*, 55, pp. 203–218.

Klundert, Th. van de and A. van Schaik (1989), 'Unemployment Persistence and Loss of Productive Capacity: A Keynesian Approach,' *CentER Discussion Paper no.* 8905.

Knoester, A. (1979a), 'Theoretical Principles of the Buffer Mechanism, Monetary Quasi Equilibrium and its Spillover Effects,' *Discussion Paper* 7908*I G/M*, Institute for Economic Research, Erasmus University, Rotterdam. Also published in *Kredit und Kapital*, 17 (1984), pp. 243–260.

Knoester, A. (1984), 'Pigou and Buffer Effects in Monetary Economics,' *Discussion Paper*, No. 8406 G/M, Rotterdam.

Korliras, P.G. and R.S. Thorn (1984), *Modern Macroeconomics*, Harper & Row Publishers, Inc., New York.

Kregel, J.A. (1987). 'Rational Spirits and the Post Keynesian Macrotheory of Microeconomics,' *De Economist*, 135, pp. 520–533.

Krueger, A.B. and L.H. Summers (1988), 'Efficiency Wages and the Inter–Industry Wage Structure,' *Econometrica*, 56, pp. 259–294.

Kuipers, S.K. (1981), 'Keynesian and Neo–Classical Growth Models: a Sequential Analytical Approach,' *De Economist*, pp. 58–104.

Kuipers, S.K. (1988), 'The Trade Cycle under Capital Shortage and Labour Shortage,' in W. Eizenga, E.F. Limburg and J.J. Polak (eds.): *The Quest for National and Global Economic Stability*, Kluwer, Dordrecht/ London/ Boston, pp. 79–117.

Kydland, F.E. and E.C. Presscott (1982), 'Time to Build and Aggregate Fluctuations,' *Econometrica*, 50, pp. 1345–1370.

Laidler, D. (1982), *Monetarist Perspectives*, Oxford.

Laroque, G. (1978), 'On the Dynamics of Disequilibrium: A Simple Remark,'

Review of Economic Studies, 45, pp. 273–278.
Leibenstein, H. (1957), 'The Theory of Underemployment in Densely Populated Backward Areas,' in H. Leibenstein: *Economic Backwardness and Economic Growth: Studies in the Theory of Economic Development*, Wiley, New York.
Leijonhufvud, A. (1968), *On Keynesian Economics and the Economics of Keynes*, Oxford University Press, New York.
Leijonhufvud, A. (1981), *Information and Coordination*, Oxford University Press, New York.
Lindahl, E. (1930), 'Penningspolitikens Model,' reprinted in *Studies in the Theory of Money and Capital*, 1939, Kelley, New York.
Lindbeck, A. and D.J. Snower (1986), 'Efficiency Wages versus Insiders and Outsiders,' *European Economic Review*, pp. 405–413.
Long, J.B. and I. Plosser (1983), 'Real Business Cycles,' *Journal of Political Economy*, 91, 1, pp. 39–69.
Lorie, H.R. (1978), 'Price–Quantity Adjustments in a Macro–disequilibrium Model,' *Economic Inquiry*, 16, pp. 265–287.
Lucas, R.E. Jr. (1972), 'Expectations and the Neutrality of Money,' *Journal of Economic Theory*, 4, pp. 103–124.
Lucas, R.E. Jr. (1973), 'Some International Evidence on Output–Inflation Tradeoffs,' *American Economic Review*, 63, pp. 326–334, reprinted in R.E., Jr. Lucas (1983): *Studies on Business Cycle Theory*, Basil Blackwell, Oxford.
Lucas, R.E. Jr. (1975), 'An Equilibrium Model of Business Cycles,'*Journal of Political Economy*,83, 6, pp.1113–1144.
Lucas, R.E. Jr. and L. Rapping (1969), 'Real Wages, Employment and Inflation,' *Journal of Political Economy*, 77, pp. 721–754.
Malinvaud, E. (1977), *The Theory of Unemployment Reconsidered*, Basil Blackwell, Oxford.
Malinvaud, E. (1980), '*Profitability and Unemployment*, Cambridge University Press, Cambridge.
Mankiw, N.G. (1985), 'Small Menu Costs and Large Business Cycles: A Macroeconomic Model of Monopoly,' *Quarterly Journal of Economics*, pp. 529–537.
Markowitz, H. (1959), *Portfolio Selection*, New York.
McCallum, B.T. (1979), 'The Current State of the Policy Ineffectiveness Debate,' *American Economic Review*, 69, pp.
McCallum, B.T. (1984), 'On Low–Frequency Estimates of Long–Run Relationships in Macroeconomics,' *Journal of Monetary Economics*, 14, pp. 3–14.
McCallum, B.T. (1987), 'Inflation: Theory and Evidence,' *NBER Working Paper*, No. 2312.
McCallum, B.T. (1988), 'The Role of Demand Management in the Maintenance of Full Employment,' *NBER Working Paper*, No. 2520.
McKenzie, L.W. (1959), 'On the Existence of General Equilibrium for a Competitive Market,' *Econometrica*, 27, pp. 54–71.
Miller, M.H. (1982), 'Credit Rationing in a Disequilibrium Macroeconomic Model,' *Journal of Macroeconomics*, 4, pp. 129–154.
Muellbauer, J. and R. Portes (1978), 'Macroeconomic Models with Quantity Rationing,' *Economic Journal*, 88, pp. 788–821.
Nagatani, K. (1981), '*Macroeconomic Dynamics*,' Cambridge University Press, Cambridge.
Neary, J.P. and K.W.S. Roberts (1980), 'The Theory of Household Behaviour under Rationing,' *European Economic Review*, 13, pp. 25–42.
Neary, J.P. and J.E. Stiglitz (1983), 'Toward a Reconstruction of Keynesian

Economics: Expectations and Constrained Equilibria,' *Quarterly Journal of Economics*, 98, Supplement, pp. 199–228.
Negishi, T. (1974), 'Unemployment, Inflation and the Microfoundations of Macroeconomics,' in M.J. Artis and A.R. Nobay (eds.): *Essays in Economic Analysis: The Proceedings of the Association of University Teachers of Economics Sheffield* 1975, Cambridge University Press, Cambridge, pp. 33–42.
Negishi, T. (1979), *Microeconomic Foundations of Keynesian Macroeconomics*, North-Holland Publishing Company, Amsterdam.
Nelson, C.R. and C.I. Plosser (1982), 'Trends and Random Walks in Macroeconomic Time Series: Some Evidence and Implications,' *Journal of Monetary Economics*, 10, pp. 139–167.
Ohlin, B. (1937), 'Some Notes of the Stockholm Theory of Savings and Investment I and II,' *Economic Journal*, 47, pp. 53–69, 221–252.
Patinkin, D. (1956), *Money, Interest and Prices, An Integration of Monetary and Value Theory*, 2nd edition, Harper and Row, New York, 1965.
Peeters, M. (1987), 'A Dismal Science; An Essay on New Classical Economics,' *De Economist*, 135, pp. 442–467.
Persson, T. and L.E.O. Svensson (1983), 'Is Optimism Good in a Keynesian Economy,' *Economica*, 50, pp. 291–300.
Phelps, E.S. (1968), 'Money Wage Dynamics and Labor Market Equilibrium,' *Journal of Political Economy*, 76, pp. 687–711.
Phelps, E.S. and G. Winter (1970), 'Optimal Price Policy under Atomistic Competition,' in E.S Phelps, A.A. Alchian and C.C. Holt (eds.): *Microeconomic Foundations of Employment and Inflation Theory*, Mac Millan, London.
Ploeg, F. van der (1987), 'Rationing in Open Economy and Dynamic Macroeconomics,' *De Economist*, 135, pp. 488–519.
Price, S. (1988), 'Unemployment and Worker Quality,' in R. Cross (ed.): *Unemployment, Hysteresis & and the Natural Rate Hypothesis*, Basil Blackwell, pp. 158–180.
Radner, R. (1968), 'Competitive Equilibrium under Uncertainty,' *Econometrica*, 36, pp. 31–58.
Reagan, P.B. (1982), 'Inventory and Price Behaviour,' *Review of Economic Studies*, 49, 137–142.
Reagan, P.B. and M.L. Weitzman (1982), 'Asymmetries in Price and Quantity Adjustment by the Competitive Firm,' *Journal of Economic Theory*, 27, pp. 410–420.
Roberts, J. (1987), 'An Equilibrium Model with Unvoluntary Unemployment at Flexible Competitive Prices and Wages,' *American Economic Review*, pp. 856–874.
Rosen, S. (1985), 'Implicit Contracts: A Survey,' *Journal of Economic Literature*, 23, pp. 1144–1175.
Rotemberg, J.J. (1987), 'The New Keynesian Microfoundations,' *NBER Macroeconomic Annual* 1987, Cambridge, Massachusetts, pp. 69–104.
Rothschild, M. (1973), 'Models of Market Organization with Imperfect Information: A Survey,' *Journal of Political Economy*, 81, pp. 1283–1308.
Salop, S. (1979), 'A Model of the Natural Rate of Unemployment,' *American Economic Review*, 69, pp. 117–125.
Samuelson, P.A. (1947), *Foundations of Economic Analysis*, Harvard University Press, Cambridge.
Samuelson, P.A. (1958), 'An Exact Consumption Loan Model of Interest with or

without the Social Contrivance of Money,' *Journal of Political Economy*, 66, pp. 467–482.

Sargent, T.J. (1987), *Macroeconomic Theory*, 2nd edition, Academic Press, New York.

Sargent, T.J. and N. Wallace (1975), 'Rational Expectations, The Optimal Monetary Instrument and the Optimal Money Supply Rule,' *Journal of Political Economy*, 83, pp. 241–254.

Scitovsky, T. (1950), *Welfare and Competition, Economics in a Fully Employed Economy*, Richard D. Erwin, Inc., Chicago.

Scitovsky, T. (1978), 'Asymmetries in Economics,' *Scottish Journal of Political Economy*, 25, pp. 227–237.

Shaked, A. and J. Sutton (1984), 'Involuntary Unemployment as a Perfect Equilibrium in a Bargaining Model, *Econometrica*, 52, pp. 1351–1364.

Shapiro, C. and J.E. Stiglitz (1984), 'Equilibrium Unemployment as a Worker Discipline Device,' *American Economic Review*, 74, pp. 433–444.

Sheffrin, S.M. (1983), *Rational Expectations*, Cambridge Surveys on Economic Literature, Cambridge University Press, Cambridge.

Sims, C.A. (1980a), 'Macroeconomics and Reality,' *Econometrica*, 48, pp. 1–48.

Sims, C.A. (1980b), 'Comparison of Interwar and Postwar Business Cycles: Monetarism Reconsidered,' *American Economic Review*, 70, pp. 250–257.

Solow, R.M (1956), 'A Contribution to the Theory of Economic Growth,' *Quarterly Journal of Economics*.

Solow, R.M. (1979), 'An other Possible Source of Wage Stickiness,' *Journal of Macroeconomics*, 1, pp. 79–82.

Snippe, J. (1985), *Macroeconomic Adjustment Processes: A Sequential Analytical Approach*, Unpublished PhD thesis, Groningen.

Sterken, E. (1988), 'A Model of Real and Financial Household Behaviour,' *De Economist*, 136, pp. 317–338.

Stigler (1961), 'The Economics of Information,' *Journal of Political Economy*, 69, pp. 213–225.

Stiglitz, J.E. (1979), 'Equilibrium in Product Markets with Imperfect Information,' *American Economic Review*, 69, pp. 339–345.

Stiglitz, J.E. (1986), 'Theories of Wage Rigidity,' in J. Butkiewicz *et al* (eds.): *Keynes' Economic Legacy: Contemporary Economic Theories*, Praeger Publishers, New York.

Stiglitz, J.E. (1987), 'Competition and the Number of Firms in a Market: Are Duopolies More Competitive than Atomistic Markets?,' *Journal of Political Economy*, 95, pp. 1041–1061.

Stiglitz, J.E. (1987a), 'The Causes and Consequences of the Dependence of Quality on Price,' *Journal of Economic Literature*, 25, pp. 1–48.

Summers, L.H. (1988), 'Relative Wages, Efficiency Wages, and Keynesian Unemployment,' *NBER Working Paper*, No. 2590.

Svensson, L.E.O. (1980), 'Effective Demand and Stochastic Rationing,' *Review of Economic Studies*, 47, pp. 339–355.

Svensson, L.E.O. (1981), 'Effective Demand in a Sequence of Markets,' *Scandinavian Journal of Economics*, 83, pp. 1–21.

Sweezy, P.M. (1939), 'Demand under Condition of Oligopoly,' *Journal of Political Economy*, 47, pp. 568–573.

Taylor, J.B. (1980), 'Aggregate Dynamics and Staggered Contracts,'*Journal of Political Economy*, 88, pp. 1–23.

Tobin, J. (1956), 'The Interest Elasticity of the Transactions Demand for Cash,' *Review of Economics and Statistics*, 38, pp.241–247.

Tobin, J. (1958), 'Liquidity Preference as Behaviour towards Risk,' *Review of Economic Studies*, XXV, pp.65–86.
Tobin, J. (1965), 'Money and Economic Growth,' *Econometrica*, 33, pp. 671–684.
Tobin, J. (1978), *Asset Accumulation and Economic Activity*, Chicago.
Tobin, J. (1982), 'Money and Finance in the Macroeconomic Process,' *Journal of Money Credit and Banking*, 14, pp. 171–204.
Tobin, J. and H.S. Houthakker (1951), 'The Effects of Rationing on Demand Elasticities,' *Review of Economic Studies*, 18, pp. 140–153.
Ulph, A.M. and D.T. Ulph (1975), 'Transaction Costs in GeneralEquilibrium Theory: A Survey,' *Economica*, 42, pp. 355–372.
Varian, H. (1984), *Microeconomic Analysis*, (2nd ed.), Norton, New York.
Wald, A. (1936), 'Über einige Gleichungssysteme der Mathematischen Ökonomie,' *Zeitschrift für National-Ökonomie*, pp. 637–670.
Walras, L. (1954), *Elements of Pure Economics; Or: The Theory of Social Wealth*, Translated by W. Jaffé, Irwin, Homewood, Ill./ Allen & Urwin, London, first published in French as *Éléments d'Economie Politique Pure* in 1874.
Weintraub, E.R. (1977), 'The Microfoundations of Macroeconomics: a Critical Survey,' *Journal of Economic Literature*, 15, pp. 1–23.
Weintraub, E.R. (1979), *Microfoundations*, Cambridge U.P., 1979.
Weiss, L. (1980), 'Job Queues and Layoffs in Labor Markets with Flexible Wages,' *Journal of Political Economy*, 88, pp. 526–538.
Weitzman, M.L. (1982), 'Increasing Returns and the Foundations of Unemployment Theory,' *Economic Journal*, 92, 4, pp. 787–804.
Witteveen, H.J. (1956), 'Structuur en conjunctuur,' Erven, F. Bohn, Haarlem.
Woglom, G. (1982), 'Underemployment Equilibria with Rational Expectations,' *Quarterly Journal of Economics*, 97, pp. 89–108.
Yellen, J. (1984), 'Efficiency Wage Models of Unemployment,' *American Economic Review*, Papers and Proceedings, 74, pp. 200–205.